The Wages of Guilt
Memories of War in Germany and Japan

The Wages of Guilt
Memories of War in Germany and Japan

Ian Buruma

NEW YORK REVIEW BOOKS

New York

FOR MY FATHER

THIS IS A NEW YORK REVIEW BOOK
PUBLISHED BY THE NEW YORK REVIEW OF BOOKS

Copyright © 1994 by Ian Buruma
Preface copyright © 2015 by Ian Buruma

Published by The New York Review of Books, 435 Hudson Street, Suite 300, New York NY 10014
www.nyrb.com

Library of Congress Cataloging-in-Publication Data

Buruma, Ian.
  The wages of guilt : memories of war in Germany and Japan / by Ian Buruma.
    pages cm. — (New York review books collections)
  Includes bibliographical references and index.
  ISBN 978-1-59017-858-4 (alk. paper)
  1. World War, 1939-1945—Moral and ethical aspects. 2. World War, 1939-1945—Influence. 3. Germa-
ny—Moral conditions. 4. Japan—Moral conditions. 5. Guilt. 6. Shame. 7. Ethnopsychology. I. Title.
  D744.4.B87 2015
  940.53'1—dc23
                                    2014041582

ISBN 978-1-59017-858-4

Available as an electronic book; 978-1-59017-859-1

Printed in the United States of America on acid-free paper

1 3 5 7 9 10 8 6 4 2

Contents

PREFACE TO THE 2015 EDITION | *vii*

INTRODUCTION TO THE 1995 EDITION: *THE ENEMIES* | 3

PART ONE

War Against the West | *13*

Romance of the Ruins | 47

PART TWO

Auschwitz | 69

Hiroshima | 92

Nanking | *112*

PART THREE

History on Trial | *137*

Textbook Resistance | *177*

Memorials, Museums, and Monuments | 202

PART FOUR

A Normal Country | *239*

Two Normal Towns | 262

Clearing Up the Ruins | 292

NOTES | *311*

ACKNOWLEDGMENTS | 319

INDEX | *321*

Preface to the 2015 Edition

SOCCER, ESPECIALLY IN Europe, can be a useful way to gauge the state of nations. In 2006, the World Cup was staged in Germany. Apart from Zinedine Zidane's head-butt in the final, the occasion was remarkable for the unselfconscious, festive outpouring of German patriotism. Germans, for good reasons, had been hesitant before to wave their national symbols in the face of the world. This time they did so in such a friendly spirit that no one could mistake it for anything sinister. In 2006, even though their team failed to reach the final, people seemed happy to be German.

It used to be, if you were Dutch, French, Czech, or Polish, that losing to Germany was like being invaded all over again. And the rare victories over Germany were celebrated as sweet revenge. More than half a century after the end of World War II, this feeling seems at last to have evaporated. When Germany won the World Cup in 2014, most Europeans even rejoiced. But then the country visibly was no longer what it once was. The team included two players born in Poland, as well as men of Tunisian, Turkish, Ghanaian, and Albanian descent.

Changing attitudes come with fading memories, even though some historical memories can be lethally tenacious. But I believe there was more to it in this case. When I wrote *The Wages of Guilt* in 1994, there was still a good deal of fear and distrust of Germany— the economic powerhouse of Europe—whose recent reunification was celebrated in the streets of Dresden, Leipzig, and Berlin with raucous cries of "We are one people!" This sounded ominous to people whose memories had not yet faded, not least to some Germans themselves. But by 2006, Günter Grass's famous remark that the memory of Auschwitz should have kept Germany divided forever sounded even more absurdly self-flagellating than it had in 1989. Germany had been such a good European, safely embedded for many decades in European institutions and NATO, that it seemed churlish to distrust a generation of Germans who were not yet alive when their country was at war. But the main reason why Germans were more trusted by their neighbors was that they were learning, slowly and painfully, and not always fully, to trust themselves.

In the western half of Germany, at any rate, novelists, historians, journalists, teachers, politicians, and filmmakers had already considered the monstrosities of recent Germany history, sometimes obsessively, but often with remarkable openness and honesty. Few German schoolchildren were unaware of their country's horrors. If anything, some had begun to resent the relentless fashion in which they were sometimes pushed down their throats. There were still, in the twenty-first century, instances of public figures making dubious or tactless statements about the war, but they would be very swiftly taken to task by other Germans. Demonstrations against immigrants, especially Muslim immigrants, were swiftly countered by demonstrations against racism or xenophobia.

The war was never a laughing matter to Germans, nor should it have been. But the fact that a comedy film, entitled *Mein Führer*, made by a Swiss-Jewish director, was a hit in 2008 was probably a healthy sign too. Laughter at their own country's expense is surely preferable to self-flagellation. To the extent that the darkest chapters in history can be "coped" with, the Germans, on the whole, had coped.

———

Why can't the same thing be said with equal confidence about Japan? The Japanese also hosted a World Cup, together with Korea, in 2002. And young Japanese celebrated the unexpected victories of their team of hip young players with the same carnival spirit as the Germans did four years later. Yet the distrust of Japan, in Korea and other neighboring countries, did not go away. For while the flag-waving young looked innocent of bellicose thoughts (or any thoughts about history at all, which was part of the problem), some of their elders, in government and the mass media, still voice opinions about the Japanese war that are unsettling, to say the least. Conservative politicians still pay their annual respects at a shrine where war criminals are officially remembered. Justifications and denials of war crimes are still heard. Too many Japanese in conspicuous places, including the prime minister's office itself, have clearly not "coped" with the war.

It should have been easier for the Japanese. The war in Asia was savage, to be sure. The sackings of Nanking and Manila, the slaves worked to death on the Thai–Burma railroad, the brutal POW camps from Manchuria to Sumatra, the millions of dead in China: these have left permanent scars on the history of Asia. But unlike Nazi Germany, Japan had no systematic program to destroy the life of every man, woman, and child of a people that, for ideological reasons, was deemed to have no right to exist.

Perversely, this may actually have made it harder for the Japanese to come to terms with their history. After the fall of the Third Reich, few Germans outside a deranged fringe could condone, let alone be proud of the Holocaust. "We never knew," a common reaction in the 1950s, had worn shamefully thin in the eyes of a younger generation by the 1960s. The extraordinary criminality of a deliberate genocide was so obvious that it left no room for argument.

The Japanese never reached the same kind of consensus. Right-wing nationalists like to cite the absence of a Japanese Holocaust as proof that Japanese have no reason to feel remorse about their war at all. It was, in their eyes, a war like any other; brutal, yes, just as wars fought by all great nations in history have been brutal. In fact, since the Pacific War was fought against Western imperialists, it was a justified—even noble—war of Asian liberation.

Few Japanese would have taken this view in the late 1940s or 1950s, a time when most Germans were still trying hard not to remember. It is in fact extraordinary how honestly Japanese novelists and filmmakers dealt with the horrors of militarism in those early postwar years. Such honesty is much less evident now. Popular comic books, aimed at the young, extol the heroics of Japanese soldiers and kamikaze pilots, while the Chinese and their Western allies are depicted as treacherous and belligerent. In 2008, the chief of staff of the Japanese Air Self-Defense Force stated that Japan had been "tricked" into the war by China and the US. In 2013, Prime Minister Abe Shinzo publicly doubted whether Japan's military aggression in China could even be called an invasion.

Why? It has often been assumed that there must be a cultural explanation. Shame, to the Oriental mind, has to be covered in silence, or denial, and so forth. I rather dismissed this claim when I wrote *The Wages of Guilt*, and I still do. The Germans are not a morally superior people, with a keener sense of guilt, or shame, than the Japanese. Evasions, there too, were once the order of the day.

The fact is that Japan is still haunted by historical issues that should have been settled decades ago. The reasons are political rather than cultural, and have to do with the pacifist constitution—written by American jurists in 1946—and with the imperial institution, absolved of war guilt by General Douglas MacArthur after the war for the sake of expediency.

The end of the Third Reich in Germany was a complete break in history. Japan, even under Allied occupation, continued to be governed by much the same bureaucratic and political elite, albeit under a new, more democratic constitution, after the emperor was made to renounce his divine status. Since there had been no equivalent of the Nazi Party in Japan, and thus no *Führer*, Japanese militarism was blamed on "feudal" culture and the samurai spirit. Like a reformed alcoholic who cannot be trusted with another sip of the hard stuff, Japan was constitutionally banned from using military force, or indeed from maintaining its own armed forces. Henceforth, the US would be responsible for Japanese security.

Even though most Japanese were more than glad to be relieved of martial duties, and the constitution was soon fudged to allow for a Self-Defense Force, a number of conservatives felt humiliated by what they rightly saw as an infringement of their national sovereignty. Henceforth, to them, everything from the Allied Tokyo War Crimes Tribunal to the denunciations of Japan's war record by left-wing teachers and intellectuals would be seen in this light. The more "progressive" Japanese used the history of wartime atrocities as a warning against turning away from pacifism, the more defensive right-wing politicians and commentators became about the Japanese war.

Views of history, in other words, were politicized—and polarized—from the beginning. To take the sting out of this confrontation between constitutional pacifists and revisionists, which had led to much political turmoil in the 1950s, mainstream conservatives made a deliberate attempt to distract people's attention from war and politics by concentrating on economic growth.

It largely worked. Japan became increasingly wealthy, and a rather oppressive stability was found under the continuous rule of one large conservative party, the Liberal Democrats (LDP). And yet history refused to go away. Resentment over the postwar deal continues to fester in the nationalist right wing of the LDP. At a cruder level, it is voiced, or rather shouted, by thuggish young men in quasi-military uniforms blaring wartime military marches from flag-bearing sound trucks—not at all in the festive spirit of the football fans in 2002.

For several decades, the chauvinistic right wing, with its reactionary views on everything from high school education to the emperor's status, was kept in check by the sometimes equally dogmatic Japanese left. Marxism was the prevailing ideology of the teachers union and academics. Like everywhere else in the world, however, the influence of Marxism waned after the collapse of the Soviet empire in the early 1990s, and the brutal records of Chairman Mao and Pol Pot became widely known.

This collapse resulted in the ascent of neoconservatism in the US. In Japan, the consequences have been graver. Marginalized in the de facto one-party LDP state and discredited by its own dogmatism, the Japanese left did not just wane, it collapsed. This gave a great boost to the war-justifying right-wing nationalists, who even gained strength in such bastions of progressive learning as Tokyo University. Committees sprang up to "reform" history curriculums by purging textbooks of all facts that might stand in the way of healthy patriotic pride.

The Japanese young, perhaps out of boredom with nothing but materialistic goals, perhaps out of frustration with being made to feel guilty, perhaps out of sheer ignorance, or most probably out of a combination of all three, are not unreceptive to these patriotic blandishments. Anxiety about the rise of China, whose rulers have a habit of using Japan's historical crimes as a form of political blackmail, has boosted a prickly national pride, even at the expense of facing the truth about the past.

Briefly, just after *The Wages of Guilt* was first published, I thought that things were moving in a more positive direction. For the first time since 1955, the LDP had been replaced in government by a coalition of liberal-left parties led by the socialist prime minister Murayama Tomiichi. One of the first things this very decent man did was apologize unequivocally for Japan's military atrocities on the fiftieth anniversary of the Pacific War.

Many Japanese were in sympathy with Murayama. His clear repudiation of Japan's wartime behavior would surely make it easier to talk about Japanese security and revising the constitution in a rational manner. Alas, expectations of a break with the postwar order proved to be premature. Murayama was not able to change anything in the political landscape. By 1996, the LDP was back in power, the constitutional issue had not been resolved, and historical debates continue to be loaded with political ideology. In fact, they are not really debates at all, but exercises in propaganda, tilted toward the reactionary side.

Given these differences between Germany and Japan, one might have expected *The Wages of Guilt* to have been better received in the former country. In fact, the opposite was true. Not only did the book sell more copies in Japan, but it got a more positive reception. I can only speculate about the reasons. The Japanese quite like their country to be compared to Germany—efficient, clean, industrious, disciplined, and so on. Postwar Germans, bent on being model members of the liberal, progressive Western community, are less keen to be compared to Japan. It smacks too much of pre-war admiration for the warrior spirit of "the Germans of the East."

If I am right, however, and the differences between the two nations, in terms of historical memory, are less cultural than political, then such German sensitivity is misplaced. It would be naive—and it has proved to be dangerous in the past—to assume that culture doesn't matter, that all human beings can be cast in the same universal mold. To assume, however, that cultural differences are absolute—what academic theorists like to call "essentializing"—is equally wrong, and indeed dangerous.

It was partly to test these grounds, to find out how comparable traumas have affected two very different nations, that I wrote this book. My instinct—call it a prejudice, if you prefer—before embarking on this venture was that people from distinct cultures still react quite similarly to similar circumstances. The Japanese and the Germans, on the whole, did not behave in the same ways—but then the circumstances, both wartime and postwar, were quite different in the two Germanies and Japan. They still are.

THE
WAGES
OF GUILT

Introduction

THE ENEMIES

THERE WAS NEVER any doubt, where I grew up, who our enemies were. There was the Soviet Union, of course, but that, from a Dutch schoolboy's perspective in the 1950s, was rather remote. No, the enemies were the Germans. They were the comic-book villains of my childhood in The Hague. When I say Germans, I mean just that—not Nazis, but Germans. The occupation between 1940 and 1945 and the animosity that followed were seen in national, not political terms. The Germans had conquered our country. They had forced my father to work in their factories. And they had left behind the bunkers along our coast, like great stone toads, squat relics of a recent occupation, dark and damp and smelling of urine. We were not allowed to go inside them. Stories were told of boys who defied this order and were blown up by rusty German hand grenades.

Our teachers told us stories of German wickedness and their own acts of bravery. Every member of the older generation, it appeared, had been in the resistance. That is to say, everybody except for the butcher on the corner of the high street, who had been a collaborator; one didn't go shopping there. And then there was the woman at the tobacconist; she had had a German lover. One didn't go there either.

Each year, on the afternoon of May 4, we would gather in the assembly hall to hear the headmaster commemorate the war dead. May 4 was Commemoration Day; May 5 was Liberation Day. On the evening of May 4 there would be a slow procession through the sand dunes to the former German execution ground. I watched it on television in black and white. All you heard was the sound of slowly shuffling feet, a church bell ringing in the distance, and wind brushing the microphone. May 4 was also the occasion for youths to smash the windows of German cars or insult German tourists from a safe distance.

The headmaster, normally a humorous man, would get tearful on May 4. In his long leather coat, he was invariably at the head of the procession through the dunes, with an oddly defiant expression on his face, as though he were facing the enemy once again. He lectured me once after I had been caught drawing swastikas. I was never to draw swastikas, he said, for they were wicked and the sight of them still distressed people. I continued drawing them, of course, but as a secret vice, with the added thrill of breaking a mysterious, adult taboo.

Comic-book Germans (were there any others?) roughly fell into two categories: the fat, slow-witted, ludicrous type, played to perfection in Hollywood movies by Gert Fröbe, and the thin, sinister type, the torturer with a monocle, the one who always said: "Ve have vays of making you talk." Conrad Veidt in *Casablanca*. The enemy was both frightening and ridiculous. Too many Gert Fröbe films and Hitler imitations had made a mockery of the German language itself, which, as a result, we refused to learn properly. The German teacher sounded defensive in his effort to inspire enthusiasm for the language of Goethe and Rilke. Fröbe and Hitler had ruined it for us.

As we grew up, we heard more stories. Our sense of history was shaped as local stories of German sweethearts and collaborators made way for larger stories, stories about the concentration camps and the destruction of the Jews. My mother was saved from deportation and almost certain death only by the good fortune of having been born in England. Our comic-book prejudices turned into an attitude of moral outrage. This made life easier in a way. It was comforting to know that a border divided us from a nation that personified evil. They were bad, so we must be good. To grow up after the war in a country that had suffered German occupation was to know that one was on the side of the angels.

We did not spend our holidays in Germany. We had no German friends. And we hardly heard, let alone spoke the language. When I say we, I am generalizing of course, but even in 1989, when I began, for the first time, to travel extensively in Germany, this was considered among my Dutch friends an interesting but slightly eccentric thing to do. To them, London, Paris, even New York felt nearer than Berlin. They felt this way despite the obvious similarities between Holland and Germany, in culture, in language, in food and drink.

Perhaps that was part of the problem: the Dutch had not suffered as much as the Poles or the Russians; they were classified as a "Nordic race," after all, so long as they were not Jews. Before the war there had been more sympathy in Holland for National Socialist discipline and the idea of the *Herrenvolk*, the master race, standing up to Bolshevism than my teachers cared to remember. The German invasion was more than an act of war; it was a betrayal. And it brought to pass the worst fears of a small nation always in danger of being swallowed by its neighbor. Which is why the Dutch turned their backs on Germany after the war. The cultural similarities were embarrassing, even threatening. The borders had to be clearly drawn, geographically and mentally; Germany had to be beyond the pale.

Christopher Isherwood once described what it was like to grow up after World War I, as the younger brother or son of men who had died in battle. Those who had been too young to fight or die, he said, felt as though they had yet to face a test of manhood, a test which had to be passed again and again, for one could never make up for having missed the slaughter. It was not quite like that for us, the first generation to be born after 1945. But the war cast its shadow nonetheless, to the point that some of us grew obsessed by it. For we too faced an imaginary test. The question that obsessed us was not how we would have acquitted ourselves in uniform, going over the top, running into machine-gun fire or mustard gas, but whether we would have joined the resistance, whether we would have cracked under torture, whether we would have hidden Jews and risked deportation ourselves. Our particular shadow was not war, but occupation.

Occupation is always a humiliating business—not just because of the loss of sovereignty and political rights but because it dramatically shows up human weakness. Heroes are very few in such times, and only a fool would put himself or herself among the imaginary heroes. It is easier to understand the ugly little compromises people make to save their own skins, the furtive services rendered to the uniformed masters, the looking away when the Gestapo kicks in the neighbor's door. When I grew up, everything was done to forget the humiliation and to identify with the heroes. I read piles of books about Dutch Maquis and silk-scarfed RAF pilots. And yet the frightened man who betrayed to save his life, who looked the other way, who grasped the wrong horn of a hideous moral dilemma, interested me more than the hero. This is no doubt partly because I fear I would be much like that frightened man myself. And partly because, to me, failure is more typical of the human condition than heroism. It is why I wanted to know more about the memories of our former enemies, for theirs was a past of the most terrible failure: moral, political, and, in the end, military too. Which is not to say that the Nazis were more human than their victims, but it would be equally wrong—though no doubt comforting—to assume that they were less so.

The other enemies of World War II, the Japanese, were too far away to have had much of an impact on our imagination. The Dutch East Indies meant nothing to me, even though some of my friends had been born there. Nonetheless, the Japanese too were comic-book villains: short yellow people with buckteeth and spectacles, who shouted *"Banzai!"* as their Zero fighters attacked the brave American pilots, led in a popular comic book by a dashing blond hero named Buck Danny and his doughty crew. (Buck Danny was definitely "Nordic.") The Japs, I was told, could not be trusted. They had no regard for human life. They had attacked Pearl Harbor without warning. They pulled out people's fingernails. They made white women bow to their emperor. One of my high school teachers had worked as a slave on the Burma railroad. My aunt was in a "Jap camp." Alec Guinness was made to crawl into a hot steel cage.

Much of the 1970s and 1980s I spent in or around Japan, for reasons that had nothing to do with the war. But I was curious to learn how Japanese saw the war, how *they* remembered it, what *they* imagined it to have been like, how *they* saw themselves in view of their past. What I heard and read was often surprising to a European: the treatment of Western POWs was hardly remembered at all, even though *The Bridge on the River Kwai* had been a popular success in Japan. (I often wondered who the Japanese identified with, the Japanese commandant or Alec Guinness? Neither, said a Japanese friend: "We liked the American hero, William Holden.") Bataan, the sacking of Manila, the massacres in Singapore, these were barely mentioned. But the suffering of the Japanese, in China, Manchuria, the Philippines, and especially in Hiroshima and Nagasaki, was remembered vividly, as was the imprisonment of Japanese soldiers in Siberia after the war. The Japanese have two days of remembrance: August 6, when Hiroshima was bombed, and August 15, the date of the Japanese surrender.

I wanted to write about Japanese memories of the war, and this led me to the related subject of modern Japanese nationalism. I became fascinated by the writings of various emperor worshippers, historical revisionists, and romantic seekers after the unique essence of Japaneseness. The abstruseness of their ideas didn't stop them from being widely published in popular Japanese magazines and newspapers or from appearing as guests on television talk shows. I began to notice how the same German names cropped up in their often oblique and florid prose: Spengler, Herder, Fichte, even Wagner. The more Japanese romantics went on about the essence of Japaneseness, the more they sounded like German metaphysicians. This is perhaps true of romantic nationalists everywhere but the nineteenth-century German influence is still particularly striking in Japan. The more I studied Japanese nationalism, the more I wished to turn to the well, so to speak, from which so many modern Japanese ideas had been drawn. Since the late nineteenth century, Japan had often looked to Germany as a model. The curious thing was that much of what attracted Japanese to Germany before the war—Prussian authoritarianism, romantic nationalism, pseudo-scientific racialism—had lingered in Japan while becoming distinctly unfashionable in Germany. Why? It was with this question in mind that I decided to expand my original idea, and write about the memories of war in Germany as well as Japan.

In the summer of 1991, a year after the two Germanys had become one, I was in Berlin to write a magazine article. I noticed an announcement in a local newspaper of a lecture at the Jewish Community Center, to be given by the psychologist Margarethe Mitscherlich. The title of her lecture was "The Labor of Remembrance: About the Psychoanalysis of the Inability to Mourn" ("Erinnerungsarbeit: Zur Psychoanalyse der Unfähigkeit zu trauern"). The mourning concerned the Nazi period. I expected a half-empty hall. But I found a huge crowd of mostly young people, casually dressed, rather like a rock concert audience, queuing up to the end of the street. I should not have been surprised. The German war was not only remembered on television, on the radio, in community halls, schools, and museums; it was actively worked on, labored, rehearsed. One sometimes got the impression, especially in Berlin, that German memory was like a massive tongue seeking out, over and over, a sore tooth.

Some Japanese are puzzled by this. An elderly German diplomat recalled to me, rather sorrowfully, how a Japanese colleague told him that Germany's preoccupation with its past sins, and its willingness to apologize to its former victims, had surely led to a loss of German identity. Another, much younger man told me of his visit to Tokyo, where he was shocked to hear Japanese sing German military marches in a beer hall. I do not wish to exaggerate the contrast. Not every Japanese suffers from historical amnesia, and there are many Germans who would like to forget, just as there are Germans who are only too pleased to hear the old songs echo around the beer hall. It is nonetheless impossible to imagine a Japanese Mitscherlich drawing huge crowds in the center of Tokyo by lecturing on the inability to mourn. Nor has a Japanese politician ever gone down on his knees, as Willy Brandt did in the former Warsaw ghetto, to apologize for historical crimes.

Even during the war the Axis partnership was not an easy one. Hitler could not but feel ambivalent about a yellow *Herrenvolk*, and the Japanese, after all, wanted to push "the white race" out of Asia. Yet the two peoples saw their own purported virtues reflected in each other: the warrior spirit, racial purity, self-sacrifice, discipline, and so on. After the war, West Germans tried hard to discard this image of themselves. This was less true of the Japanese. Which meant that any residual feelings of nostalgia for the old partnership in Japan were likely to be met with embarrassment in Germany.

The story of the former Japanese embassy in Berlin is a case in point. Built in 1936, the old embassy is a neoclassicist monument of the Nazi style, conceived as part of Hitler's new capital, Germania. The embassy was one of the few buildings in Hitler's and Speer's grand plan that actually got built. After the war it was abandoned, a ruined hulk, left to *Autonomen*, the black-clad bands of young people seeking an anarchistic lifestyle, who squatted among piles of useless diplomatic mail. But in 1984 the Japanese Prime Minister, Nakasone Yasuhiro, and the German Chancellor, Helmut Kohl, decided to rebuild the embassy as a Japanese-German center for scholars. The Germans, wary of the Japanese weakness for nationalist nostalgia, wanted the center to reflect how times had changed since the days of the Axis. It was opened officially in 1987. To celebrate the occasion, the Japanese had proposed a seminar examining the parallels between Shintoist emperor worship and the myths of the German Volk. No criticism or irony was intended: the idea had come from the priests of a Shinto shrine in Tokyo. The Germans politely declined.

All this points to a gap between Japanese views of the war and German ones, leaving aside, for now, the differences between the Federal Republic and the GDR. The question is why this should be so, why the collective German memory should appear to be so different from the Japanese. Is it cultural? Is it political? Is the explanation to be found in postwar history, or in the history of the war itself? Do Germans perhaps have more reason to mourn? Is it because Japan has an Asian "shame culture," to quote Ruth Benedict's phrase, and Germany a Christian "guilt culture"?

These questions effectively narrowed my scope. Since I was interested in those aspects of the past that continue to excite the greatest controversy in Germany and Japan, I have left out many historic events. The battle of Nomonhan, between the Japanese Imperial Army and General Zhukov's tank brigades, was of enormous military importance. And so were the Imphal campaign and the Normandy landing. But I have not mentioned any of these. Instead, in the case of Japan, I have emphasized the war in China and the bombing of Hiroshima, for these episodes, more than others, have lodged themselves, often in highly symbolic ways, in Japanese public life. Likewise, I have concentrated on the war against the Jews in the case of Germany, since it was that parallel war, rather than, say, the U-boat battles in the Atlantic, or even the battle of Stalingrad, that left the most sensitive scar on the collective memory of (West) Germany.

I could not have known when I started on the book how much current news events would form an increasingly dramatic backdrop to my story. First came the end of the Cold War, then German unification, then the Gulf War, and finally, in 1993, the first election in Japan to break the political monopoly of the conservative Liberal Democratic Party. I decided to begin my book with the Gulf War, as I experienced it in Germany and Japan. For those few weeks dramatized the traumas and memories of the last world war more vividly than any other event since 1945, more so even than the war in Vietnam, in which neither country was asked to take part. Both Japan and Germany were constitutionally unable to play a military role in the war, which resulted in a great deal of argument: could they or could they not be trusted, or indeed trust themselves, to take part in future conflicts? Now, as I write, German airmen are patrolling the skies above the former Yugoslavia, and Japanese troops are trying to keep the peace in Cambodia, though still without the legal right to use force.

One of the clichés of our time is that two of the old Axis powers lost the war but won the peace. Many people fear Japanese and German power. Europeans are afraid of German domination. Some Americans have already described their economic difficulties with Japan in terms of war. But if other people are disturbed by German and Japanese power, so are many Germans and Japanese. If the two peoples still have anything in common after the war, it is a residual distrust of themselves.

The official unification of Germany came without much fuss or celebration in the week of the Frankfurt Book Fair of 1990. Every year, the Book Fair pays special attention to the literature of a particular country. The focus that year was on Japan. As part of the festivities, a public discussion took place between Günter Grass and Oe Kenzaburo, the Japanese novelist. Both men grew up during the war—that is, both were indoctrinated at school with militarist propaganda—and both became literary advocates of the antifascist cause, even though Oe, unlike Grass, had not said much about politics of late. Both, in any event, were committed liberals. (I use the word throughout this book in the American sense.)

It was a remarkable event. Grass began by lamenting German unification. Auschwitz, he said, should have made reunification impossible. A unified Germany was a danger to itself and to the world. Oe nodded gravely and added that Japan was a great danger too. The Japanese, he said, had never faced up to their crimes. Japan was a racist country. Yes, but so was Germany, said Grass, not to be outdone, so was Germany; in fact, Germany was worse: what about the hatred of Poles, Turks, and foreigners in general? Ah, said Oe, but what about Japanese discrimination against Koreans and Ainu? No, the Japanese must surely be worse.

These litanies of German and Japanese flaws went on for some time. Then there was a lull in the conversation. Both men tried to think of something else to say. The lull became an uncomfortable silence. People began to shift in their seats, waiting to disperse. But then, as a fitting conclusion to the meeting of minds, common ground was found. I forget whether it was Grass or Oe who brought it up, but Mitsubishi and Daimler-Benz had announced a new "cooperative relationship." Journalists had dubbed it the Daimler-Mitsubishi Axis. Grass and Oe looked solemn and agreed that this was just the beginning of a dangerous friendship. Then Grass rose from his chair and wrapped Oe in a bear hug, which Oe, a small man not much used to this kind of thing, tried to reciprocate as best he could.

PART ONE

WAR AGAINST THE WEST

BONN

IT WAS NIGHT, and still some years before the war, when Konrad Adenauer crossed the river Elbe. He was on his way to Berlin, dozing in his wagon-lit. As the train moved into the east, Adenauer opened one eye and muttered to himself: "Asien, Asien" ("Asia, Asia").

The story may, of course, be untrue. But as chairman of the Christian Democratic Party in the British zone, Adenauer *did* write in 1946 to a friend in the United States: "The danger is grave. Asia stands at the river Elbe. Only an economically and politically healthy Europe under the guidance of England and France, a Western Europe to which as an essential part the free part of Germany belongs, can stop further advancement of Asian ideology and power."

Adenauer meant the advancement of Soviet Communism. His use of the word Asia was interesting, however. To the politician from Cologne, the old Roman city on the western border of Germany, barbarism lay in the east, where neither the civilized Romans nor the empire of Charlemagne had penetrated. Freedom and democracy defined the civilized Roman, Christian, Enlightened West; Asia meant orthodoxy, tyranny, and war. The Third Reich was Asia. Adenauer's mission was to bring his

Germany, western Germany, to the West, to cut out, as though it were a cancerous growth, the vestiges of Asia.

I arrived in Adenauer's chosen, western capital, Bonn, during the second week of the Gulf War—that is to say, the last week of January 1991. It was snowing heavily. Bonn was an interesting place to be for the conflict constantly released memories of the last world war. At times the old wounds looked so fresh, it was as though Germany were still in ruins.

I had spent the previous week, like most people in the world, watching the war on television. British television, in my case. The mood on British TV was almost cheerful. Retired air marshals and naval commodores in double-breasted blazers appeared every day and night to point out battle lines on maps. They spoke with a sense of professional as well as patriotic pride. Behind the technical talk and the speculation of journalists was the feeling that Britain was reliving, in a small but heartening way, a little bit of her finest hour. It was as though decades of economic humiliation, the loss of empire, and general decline had been but a bad dream. It was war: finally the men would be sorted from the boys.

Foreigners might be better at making cars or computers, wrote a British newspaper columnist, famous for his provocative jingoism, but when there is fighting to be done, when the defense of the West, our way of life, freedom, and so forth, was at stake, the British could be counted on to stand shoulder to shoulder with the Yanks. Could the same be said of the Germans? When the German government hesitated about lending its full support to the war, doubts were cast on its reliability as a Western ally. Once again the timid continentals would look up to England as their savior. At this time of peril (such words were back in fashion: peril, valor, honor), Common Market policies were but trifling affairs, the bickering of merchants: at this time of peril, British was best again.

There was something both touching and pathetic about England then. Less than a year before Saddam Hussein's war broke out, a fleet of Spitfires, Hurricanes, and a Lancaster bomber had flown over London to commemorate the Battle of Britain. It was a sunny day and the planes glinted as they dipped their wings over Buckingham Palace. I watched from the top of a hill in North London. The hill was blanketed with people, young people, old people, children, peering at the vintage machines in the sky. There was no shouting or cheering or laughter. There was, rather, an atmosphere of quiet pride and sadness, a sadness that was almost painful, the way nostalgia always is.

The spirit in Bonn was quite different. The first thing I noticed as the airport bus drove into town were bedsheets hanging from the windows of old town houses, with slogans painted in red and black: "No blood for oil!" "We are too young to die." "There can be no just war." "Our hope crashes with every bomb." There had been a massive antiwar demonstration in Bonn the week before. Posters saying "We are frightened!" or "Never another war!" or "Bush is a war criminal!" were still pasted to windows and walls. There was a barely contained hysteria in the air, an atmosphere of impending apocalypse, of *Weltuntergang*, of a world brought down by military as well as ecological disaster.

The simple eighteenth-century architecture of Bonn reflects the classicism of the Enlightenment. Bonn lacks the pompous grandeur of Wilhelmine Berlin. On the central market square, covered with a grubby blanket of snow, stood a bronze statue of Beethoven. In his icy hand was a white flag with the ban-the-bomb sign. In front of the statue were several tents, decorated with banners, and outside the tents boards had been set up to display various images and texts. The banners were the same ones I had seen before: "No blood for oil!" and so on. One of the boards said: "Remember these images." Underneath was a series of photographs, newspaper clippings, and drawings: of soldiers in the trenches during World War I, of cities being bombed in World War II, of Nazi soldiers marching through the Ukraine, of the naked Vietnamese girl running from a napalm attack, of Israeli troops in Lebanon, and of U.S. bombers taking off for Baghdad. "There can be no just war," it said.

A bearded man in his early forties, wearing an anorak, handed out pamphlets. I took one and he began to explain his views: "This war is fought for purely materialistic reasons. When Iraq gassed the Kurds, we didn't do anything. Now we are starting a war. We must stop it at once." He did not speak in a hectoring manner; more like a prophet who was used to being misunderstood, a man who had seen the truth to which others were still blind.

I then did what foreigners in Germany are so often tempted to do, with varying degrees of self-righteousness. I reminded him of the Nazis: "We did nothing after the *Kristallnacht* in 1938. Was that a reason not to fight in 1939?" "Well," he said, "I wasn't born then, so I wouldn't know about that. But I do know that Israel massacred Palestinians in 1948. And now our own Foreign Minister, Genscher, goes to Israel to give them money and weapons—all because of our guilt complex. Do you think that's right?"

This reference to a German "guilt complex" was unexpected. For he was a peace activist, a member of the Green Party, by age a "68er," a child of the radical sixties. The rhetoric about Israel and the German guilt complex is something one expects to see in extreme right-wing publications such as the *Deutsche National-Zeitung*, published in Munich by Gerhard Frey, a veteran of the far right fringe, an enemy of Adenauer's West. In the latest edition of that paper German politicians were ridiculed for going to Israel to offer help and consolation. The war was condemned as an example of American genocide: "Genocide in the Gulf," it said, "a typical crime against humanity." Other articles in the paper included "the Holocaust of American Indians" and "Israel's war of terror." Not that the *National-Zeitung* is a pacifist paper. The virtues of the German Wehrmacht and even the Waffen SS are proudly saluted. Calendars with pictures of German soldiers in uniform are on offer to readers at discount prices. Videotapes of the Blitzkrieg are advertised.

Yet these advertisements hardly reflected the same air of pride that made those retired air marshals glow on British television.

They were defensive, as though something had to be covered up. It was as though German guilt was eased, even negated, by writing about Israeli terror or American Holocausts. It is here —perhaps only here—that the two extremes of German politics meet. On one side the *National-Zeitung*, on the other a spokesman for the peace movement in Berlin, who called the air attacks on Iraq "the greatest war crime since Hitler."

Echoes of the last world war were everywhere, but they were loudest at the political extremes. The fear that American materialism would bring down the world had long been part of the rhetoric of both right and left. In the Gulf War, these fears appeared to be coming true. But there was an older resentment, which one would expect of the right, but which emerged on the left as well. In November 1991, an unofficial war crimes tribunal was staged in Stuttgart, where "ecological war crimes" committed by the Americans as well as their "genocide" in Iraq were judged. Alfred Mechtersheimer, a prominent peace activist, reminded his audience that the Nuremberg war crimes trials were a case of victors' justice. And a socialist politician criticized West German slavishness toward the United States. But if the shared animosity of right and left toward the United States was relatively straightforward, attitudes toward Israel could never be simple. America evoked memories of bombers destroying German cities, of battles fought in Normandy or the Ardennes, of black markets and of black GIs seducing German girls with chocolate and silk stockings. Israel could not be dissociated from the Holocaust.

I had been introduced to an Israeli living in Bonn. I shall call him Michael, since he did not want to be mentioned by his real name. Michael was an embittered expert on German guilt. I met him at the Israeli embassy, a well-defended villa in a suburb of Bonn. We talked in a room without windows, with a bare desk and posters of Israeli landscapes on the wall. He was a stocky man with curly hair, in his early thirties, a post-68er. He was born in Russia, but had come to West Germany as a child. He grew up near Cologne, the only Jewish boy in his school. It had been an unhappy experience. For he was singled out as a special case. Teachers would ask him to talk to the class about Auschwitz. He got away with mischief for which the other boys were punished.

I was reminded of Michael when, a few months later, I read a novel by Peter Schneider, entitled *Vati* (*Daddy*), about the son of a Nazi war criminal, based on the Auschwitz doctor Josef Mengele. The son complains about the way he was treated at school: "It was their consideration which oppressed me. My biology teacher actually apologized for giving me a bad mark: I was by no means to regard this as punishment for what some relative of mine had done. When I neglected my homework, I was not called lazy. It was, they said, because of 'difficult family circumstances.' "

Germany, said Michael, was sick. "I believe that if you were to do a heart test on a German, any German, young or old, you would see the adrenaline surge at the mention of the word Jew."

Which is why, he said, the Gulf War had caused such panic in Germany. People had been calling the Israeli embassy in tears, at all hours. Some asked whether they might help Israeli children if something terrible happened, and whether they could return the children once the war was over. These Germans had to be calmed down, he said. Then he shrugged. "Ach," he said, with the hint of a smile, "it is hard to be a German."

Michael despised young pacifists as much as he did the older generation, the fathers, the guilty ones (*Täter* in German). The older generation, he said, were almost all philosemitic after the war. Pastors, mayors, teachers, priests, all would go to Israel at the first opportunity. An odd reversal of roles had taken place. Before the war, Michael said, Jews were seen as gentle, bookish pacifists. The Germans, on the other hand, had Prussian discipline. They were "hard as Krupp steel," and so on. But now the Israelis had become the disciplined, hardworking warriors. Many older Germans admired them for this, as much as they despised the Arabs for being lazy and dirty. Now it was the

Germans who had become the pacifists. "We Israelis laugh at German soldiers now," said Michael.

In the late sixties, particularly after the Six-Day War in 1967, attitudes began to change. Many young Germans rejected everything their parents stood for. They sat in judgment over their past, hated them for their silence, and despised their philosemitism too. The student radicals claimed to be on the side of the victims, especially the Palestinians. They would never associate with the guilty, the *Täter*, not in Germany, not in Vietnam, not in Israel. They would make up for their parents' cowardice. They would resist. They were idealists. They would fight to save the world from ecological disaster. They would resist American consumerism and Israeli militarism. Michael said: "They believed that being on the left was a vaccination against being antisemitic." So when Michael sees thousands of German peace demonstrators, he does not see thousands of gentle people who have learned their lesson from the past; he sees "100 percent German Protestant rigorism, aggressive, intolerant, hard."

In February 1991, the Israeli writer Amos Oz was interviewed about the Gulf War in the *Frankfurter Allgemeine Zeitung*. Oz is a liberal. The *FAZ* is a conservative newspaper, with little sympathy for peace movements, Greens, leftists, or 68ers. The editors were in favor of German participation in the Gulf War, or at the very least a firm German commitment to support the allied cause. The *FAZ* is anti-Communist, pro-NATO, and liberal (more in the nineteenth-century European than in the twentieth-century American sense). One of the editors is Joachim Fest, who wrote a famous biography of Hitler. A film was made of the book, which made Fest a wealthy man. The Hitler period, especially in the film, is shown as a form of collective madness, a murderous opéra bouffe, a demented aberration in the history of a great nation.

Fest was agitated that week, for, in his view, Germany had shown itself to be a prisoner of its past once again, by its display of nervous pacifism instead of political and military resolve. Germany, Fest often argued, should be a normal, responsible power again. By which he meant what Adenauer meant: a normal Western power. This aim was blocked by what he saw as an instinctive guilty cringe, which resulted, perversely, in a feeling of moral superiority: we who committed terrible sins will now heal the ills of the world. This prevented Germany from doing its duty as a Western ally. As a German patriot, Fest was embarrassed, even humiliated that Britain, France, and the United States should be fighting a war without active German support. When I mentioned the antiwar demonstrations, he sighed and said: "All because of Hitler."

Amos Oz was not really an *FAZ* type, for his liberalism is left of center, but in his interview he spoke critically of romanticism about the Third World in leftist European and especially German circles. He saw traces of Rousseau's worship of the noble savage—an almost theological celebration of those who are doomed to suffer. "Perhaps," he said, "this is the result of a highly simplified and sentimental image of Christianity, according to which the victim is purified by his suffering."

The Jews, then, were "purified" by the Holocaust, "as though the showers in the gas chambers had sprayed the victims with a moral detergent." They have to be purer and better than other people. But how did this purity rub off on the children and grandchildren of the *Täter?* Could it be that they had a secret wish to be among the suffering too?

Moral purity was cruelly tested during the Gulf War by the news that poison gas sold by German firms was about to be unleashed on Israel by Iraqi Scud missiles. There can be no just war, yet Jews were threatened by German gas. It was not a pretty dilemma. It split the ranks of the peace movement. The poet and songwriter Wolf Biermann, who had demonstrated in the past against American missile bases in Germany and whose politics were far to the left of the *FAZ,* outraged many former comrades by voicing his support for the war. "No blood for oil," he wrote in the weekly *Die Zeit,* "that's the latest anti-American slogan. Dear me! Of course the Americans are also concerned about oil . . . And thank God for that, I say . . . Yes, I am happy that there are such lousy interests. Otherwise Israel would stand alone." Biermann's father died at Auschwitz.

There is a German word which is hard to translate into English but which sums up the mood of many Germans during the Gulf War: *betroffen*. Dictionaries offer the following translations: "stricken (with), affected (by) . . . shock, dismay, consternation, bewilderment." None of these quite hits the right tone. Perhaps the French word *bouleversé* comes closest. *Betroffen* is much used by pacifists, liberals, and socialists, as often as the term "normal nation" is heard from German conservatives. To be *betroffen* implies a sense of guilt, a sense of shame, or even embarrassment. To be *betroffen* is to be speechless. But it also implies an idea of moral purity. To be *betroffen* is one way to "master the past," to show contriteness, to confess, and to be absolved and purified.

The frequent admonishments in West Germany to "mourn" the past, to do "the labor of mourning" (*Trauerarbeit*), are part of this act of purification. In their famous book, written in the sixties, entitled *The Inability to Mourn*, Alexander and Margarethe Mitscherlich analyzed the moral anesthesia that afflicted postwar Germans who would not face their past. They were numbed by defeat; their memories appeared to be blocked. They would or could not do their labor, and confess. They appeared to have completely forgotten that they had glorified a leader who caused the death of millions. Many Germans had reveled in the operatic self-glorification staged by the Nazi movement. By denying this after the Reich's collapse, the Mitscherlichs argued, Germans wished to shield themselves not only from punishment or guilt but also from the sense of utter impotence that followed their defeat. Only those who have suffered a loss can mourn. But what exactly had the Germans lost? The Jews, of course, but that was hardly felt to be a German loss. Many Germans had lost their homes, their sons, their absurd ideals, and their Leader. But mourning these was not what the Mitscherlichs meant by *Trauerarbeit*: mourning Hitler, after 1945, was impossible. Thirty years later, Margarethe Mitscherlich would say that the inability to mourn no longer applied to the younger generations. She was right: the Jews are mourned in Germany, and so, in certain extreme circles, is the loss of Hitler.

There is something religious about the act of being *betroffen*, something close to Pietism, which has a long and rich tradition in Germany. It began in the seventeenth century with the works of Philipp Jakob Spener. He wanted to reform the Church and bring the Gospel into daily life, as it were, by stressing good works and individual spiritual labor. Gordon Craig wrote: "The heart of Pietism was the moral renovation of the individual, achieved by passing through the anguish of contrition into the overwhelming realization of the assurance of God's grace." Pietism served as an antidote to the secular and rational ideas of the French Enlightenment. It inspired the nineteenth-century German middle class as well as Prussian officers and the men around Bismarck. It is this spirit, I think, that Michael, the Israeli in Bonn, was referring to when he spoke about the Protestant rigor of German pacifists.

During the Gulf War, Bonn was *betroffen*. It was supposed to have been very different, for it was carnival season, time for fancy-dress parties, beer, women, and songs. But this seemed inappropriate at a time of war and impending doom, so carnival committees became crisis committees. The regional government of Rheinland-Pfalz awarded money to all organizations willing to abandon the carnival feast. It proved an effective measure. Only in Cologne did an unofficial street celebration take place, under the motto "We stick to life."

In Berlin a group of music school students organized an antiwar day, because, so their spokesman said, "all the students feel so sad and *betroffen* that we felt the need to get together to talk about our fears." They built an altar and lit candles. And a local radio station broadcast their peace song, with a refrain that went: "We are *betroffen* and deeply shocked."

The square outside my hotel was cold and mostly empty. There was one small beer stand where a few young men drank, danced around a bit, and shouted in what was meant to be a festive manner. I could hear their beery songs waft in through the window of my room. The heavy, foot-stamping rhythms brought to mind countless war movies in which German hilarity is meant to serve as an ironic counterpoint to some act of brutality. It is better to learn to resist such associations in Germany, for it is all too easy to become self-righteous and obsessed, even if one's memories can only be of films.

I watched television and once again marveled at the contrast with Britain. German television is rich in earnest discussion programs where people sit at round tables and debate the issues of the day. The audience sits at smaller tables, sipping drinks as the featured guests hold forth. The tone is generally serious, but sometimes the arguments get heated. It is easy to laugh at the solemnity of these programs, but there is much to admire about them. It is partly through these talk shows that a large number of Germans have become accustomed to political debate.

During the Gulf War, it was hard for a television viewer to avoid the roundtable discussions. There were so many, you could switch channels and follow several debates at once. Pastors were frequent guests. Some wore suits, some wore jeans. Their presence was fitting, for at the center of the debate was the question of conscience. Could one fight in a war with a good conscience? A German fighter pilot said that he found it hard to accept the idea of killing people. He didn't know whether his conscience would allow it. A young doctor working in a hospital near an American air force base said his conscience was troubled by the idea of treating American pilots wounded in the Gulf War, for this would make him an accomplice.

In one typical show, the discussion group consisted of a man who had resisted the Nazis, an army conscript, an elderly housewife, a working mother, and some high school students. The twenty-seven-year-old mother, Angelika, said that Germany had to help Israel, because of "what we did during the war," but surely nothing would be gained by fighting this war in the Gulf.

"What about the British and the French?" said the former resistance man. "Should we leave it up to them to do the dirty work while we stay at home?" (There was no mention of the Americans.)

"Well," said Angelika, "we can't go against our own convictions. How can we ignore our education, which taught us never to fight another war again. In other countries, we were ashamed to be German. People were always afraid of us, and now they blame us for not being more aggressive . . ."

Andrea, an eighteen-year-old high school student, said: "We unleashed two wars on the world. How can we forget that? I can't say I'm proud to be German."

But when the elderly housewife talked about her suffering in World War II—the bombings, the lack of food, the fathers and sons who failed to return—and said that we should oppose all wars, a young student said: "I understand that terrible things happen in war, but terrible things can also happen if we don't fight when we have to."

There were cries of disbelief from the audience, but the student was supported by the old resistance fighter. He compared Saddam Hussein to Hitler and said he had to be stopped for the same reason Hitler had to be stopped: "Saddam has already killed hundreds of thousands. Do we let him go on just because we cannot morally allow ourselves to shoot?"

Finally, the young soldier, dressed in jeans and a flowered shirt, spoke up. Asked how he felt about killing people, he said: "If Germany or NATO were attacked, I would have to. But if I didn't agree with the war, I would refuse."

He was sticking to the orthodox interpretation of the postwar constitution of the Federal Republic of Germany. A German conscript can refuse to fight on grounds of conscience. Never again can "*Befehl ist Befehl*" ("Orders are orders") count as an excuse for atrocities. And German military forces can only act in defense of German or allied territory. Since Germany is part of NATO, allied territory is commonly interpreted as NATO territory. The right wanted to broaden this interpretation; the left, so far, had resisted.

But the soldier was not engaging in a legal discussion. He was trying to answer a moral question, a question of conscience. And he gave an honest answer, one that reflected better, perhaps, the feelings of young Germans today than the complete rejection of war, any war, by many pacifists. The 68ers had one overriding moral aim: to be utterly different from their parents, to crack their guilty silence, to spread the word of peace, or simply to make sure Germans would never be tempted again. The leader of the Social Democrats, Oskar Lafontaine, said during the Gulf War that asking Germans to participate in military activities was "like offering brandy chocolates to a reformed alcoholic." You could almost hear the anxious shriek.

Fest may have been right. It probably was because of Hitler. But the Gulf War showed that German pacifism could not be dismissed simply as anti-Americanism or a rebellion against Adenauer's West. There was a real dilemma: at least two generations had been educated to renounce war and never again to send German soldiers to the front, educated, in other words, to want Germany to be a larger version of Switzerland. But they had also been taught to feel responsible for the fate of Israel, and to be citizens of a Western nation, firmly embedded in a family of allied Western nations. The question was whether they really could be both. What if Saddam really was another Hitler, and Germany failed to help the Jews?

This is why Hitler analogies were painful. And this is where Hans Magnus Enzensberger decided to plunge his sharpened knife. He compared Saddam to Hitler in *Der Spiegel*. Enzensberger is a fine poet and essayist. He also knows precisely how to hit his fellow Germans where it hurts. He can be an exquisite provocateur. His article was acclaimed by some, but made many others furious, especially intellectuals of the left. I heard one critic in Berlin say that Enzensberger was a traitor. A traitor to what? I asked. To the spirit, he said, the *Geist*. For many years,

Enzensberger was himself an intellectual of the left. He is a member of the generation that went to school under the Nazis, joined the Hitler Youth, and was drafted into antiaircraft units at the end of the war. With other writers, such as Günter Grass and Heinrich Böll, Enzensberger formed a kind of leftist Maquis after the war against the vestiges of German authoritarianism. Chasing the ghosts of Nazism was for many years a more or less full-time occupation.

In his *Spiegel* article Enzensberger argued that Saddam, like Hitler, was not just another dictator; he was an enemy of mankind, a self-destructive monster in love with death. If he had the means, he would be capable of destroying the world, including, of course, his own people, for whom, like Hitler, he felt contempt. The question, then, was what produced such monsters? Enzensberger's answer was that humiliated peoples produced them, masses of permanent losers who have been demoralized for too long, by intellectual failure, by poverty, by a sense of impotence to affect their own lives. The Germans, Enzensberger wrote, should be able to recognize themselves in the Arab masses.

Yet nothing could have been further from German minds. For such an insight, said Enzensberger, "would destroy the basis for any racial interpretation of the present conflict. Besides, it would bring to light hidden continuities, remnants of fascism which no one wants to remember. German industry never had occasion to regret the good services it rendered Hitler. That it rushes out to help his successor with equal zeal can only be called consistent. And ignorance alone cannot explain why a considerable proportion of German youth identifies more with the Palestinians than the Israelis, or would rather protest against George Bush than Saddam Hussein."

This is the voice of the postwar Maquis, the scourge of hidden continuities, but with a new twist. He may have been unfair to the Iraqis, who hardly supported Saddam with the same zeal that Germans accorded Hitler, but he was finding continuities among the very people who thought they had shaken them off, by doing their labor of mourning, by holding the candle for peace a little too zealously.

Enzensberger's generation learned to distrust Germans. The continuities in the forties and fifties were still too visible, the experiences of the Hitler Youth and the flak battalion too raw. Enzensberger's Maquis distrusted the complacent rush of the West Germans toward material prosperity, which covered the past like a blanket of snow, hiding all traces, muffling all sound. Enzensberger wrote a famous poem which began:

> What have I lost, here
> in this land, to which my parents
> brought me in all innocence?
> Native-born, but unconsoled,
> I am here without being here,
> resident in cozy squalor,
> in this nice, contented grave.

The distrust of Germans was especially acute during the Gulf War because of what had happened the year before. The unification of Germany was watched with dismay in neighboring countries. This was understandable; they had been occupied and knew very well what Germans had been capable of. But it also showed, once again, the distrust of Enzensberger's generation, or at least the members of the Maquis. When Günter Grass protested against unification, because a unified Germany had produced Auschwitz, he used the word "Auschwitz" almost in a religious sense, like a negative talisman. He brandished it like an evil eye to ward off evil. "Auschwitz" had been for a long time the main amulet against hidden continuities.

On a less abstract, and hackneyed, level, there was the West German mistrust of East Germans—the East Germans whose soldiers still marched in goose step, whose petit bourgeois style smacked of the thirties, whose system of government, though built on a pedestal of antifascism, contained so many disturbing remnants of the Nazi past; the East Germans, in short, who had been living in "Asia." Michael, the Israeli, compared the encounter of Westerners ("Wessies") with Easterners ("Ossies") with the unveiling of the portrait of Dorian Gray: the Wessies saw their own image and they didn't like what they saw.

One famous West German writer rolled his eyes when I mentioned the Ossies. He told me how bored he was with the prospect of seeing history repeated. "Purification, reeducation, I have seen it all. I don't like those people in the East. I feel I know them. I want nothing to do with them." I was surprised to hear this, and repeated what he had said to the literary critic Roland Wiegenstein, at his handsome flat in Berlin. The furniture was made of steel and black leather; on the walls were large abstract paintings.

Wiegenstein dressed fashionably and with care. He is demonstratively *après guerre* in his tastes. "I understand him very well," he said. "I'm only a few years older than he is. It is a miracle, really, how quickly the Germans in the Federal Republic became civilized. We are truly part of the West now. We have internalized democracy. But the Germans of the former GDR, they are still stuck in a premodern age. They are the ugly Germans, very much like the West Germans after the war, the people I grew up with. They are not yet civilized."

This cultural distaste for the ugly Ossies in their badly cut suits, their stonewashed denims, and their plastic shoes, was more than simple snobbery. The unspoken message was that Wessies had only barely escaped from being crypto-Nazi, goosestepping Germans themselves, by becoming something else, modern Europeans perhaps. Just before the unification of Germany, a novelist of the '68 generation, Patrick Süskind, wrote that Tuscany felt nearer to him (and by implication to his friends and fellow Wessies) than Dresden.

Distrust is part of the political language in Germany. Norbert Gansel, a Social Democrat member of the Bundestag and a specialist on foreign affairs, was fifty during the Gulf War. He, too, dressed fashionably, in a plum-colored suit. He poured us both a cup of Japanese rice wine. "Goes down like oil," he said.

I suppose the irony was intended. He chose his words with care: "My personal political philosophy and maybe even my political ambition has to do with an element of distrust for the people I represent, people whose parents and grandparents made Hitler and the persecution of the Jews possible." Above his desk was a picture of Kiel, the northern German port city, where Gansel was born. The picture was of Kiel in 1945, a city in ruins. He saw me looking at it and said: "It's true that whoever is being bombed is entitled to some sympathy from us."

Gansel had spent much time on the Nazi legacy. His university thesis was on the SS. And in the seventies he had tried to nullify verdicts given in Nazi courts—without success until well into the eighties. One of the problems was that the Nazi judiciary itself was never purged. This continuity was broken only by time. The failures of justice in the fifties and sixties, Gansel said, were no longer possible. A new political generation had come of age. The grandchildren of the *Täter* were asking questions about the past with less self-righteousness than the generation of '68. The Germans had become realistic, said Gansel, much more so than the Japanese. The Gulf War had come like a bracing cold bath.

It is hard to say which was more bracing: the Gulf War or the coming of the Ossies. That the two events more or less coincided caused an extra strain. There had been a tradition in the Social Democratic Party of nationalist neutralism. Many politicians on the left thought the Western alliance had prevented German unification. In the fifties the Social Democrats had been more nationalistic in this respect than the conservative Christian Democrats. For years the left had attacked Adenauer's Germany for its Nazi inheritance and its sellout to the United States. But now that Germany had been reunified, with its specters of "Auschwitz" and its additional hordes of narrow-minded Ossies, Adenauer was deemed to have been right after all. Germany needed the West. But the West now needed Germany too, in a way the Germans, particularly the Social Democrats, found deeply troubling.

To bury Germany in the bosom of its Western allies, such as NATO and the EC, was to bury the distrust of Germans. Or so it was hoped. As Europeans they could feel normal, Western, civilized. Germany, the old "land in the middle," the Central European colossus, the power that fretted over its identity and was haunted by its past, had become a Western nation. This blessed state was challenged twice in the space of a year: first reunification and then the Gulf War. The results, as was to be expected, were mixed. The instinctive rejection of uncivilized, un-Western Ossies was one result, the anguished hesitation to join the Western allies in an act of war was another.

It was still snowing on my last night in Bonn. I had a meal of potato dumplings, sausages, and beer with a young political scientist. By young I mean a shade too young to be a 68er. He was not a pacifist. He was critical of his government's wishy-washy support of the allied coalition. He did not seem hampered by a cultural distrust of his country. He was even eager to introduce me to the local food and to the ghastly carnival music played on the jukebox in one or two bars—Gulf War or no Gulf War. The German Army, he said, was a real citizens' army now. Everyone had to serve, which is why debates on conscience and morality were so important. It was everyone's concern. And because German security was tied up in the constitution with that of its allies, military adventures had become virtually impossible. "You see," he said, "we Germans really don't want to do anything on our own again."

It was late. We walked back to my hotel together. It was an old hotel, which in its time put up many distinguished guests, but which somehow overlooked the thirties and early forties in its potted history handed out at the reception desk. We went past Beethoven holding his peace flag, past the "warning post" where young people were holding a candlelit vigil to protest against the war, past the banners that said "No blood for oil" and "German money and German gas are murdering people all over the world." I told him about my plan to write about the memories of war in Germany and Japan. He seemed a little put out, almost shocked, but said nothing. Then, after we had said goodbye, he suddenly turned around and said: "Please, please don't overdo the similarities. We are very different from the Japanese. We don't sleep in our companies to make them more powerful. We are just people, just normal people." He did not say Western people. But he might as well have.

TOKYO

In Tokyo the Gulf War seemed far away. There were no banners, no warning posts, no candlelit vigils or peace demonstrations. The whole notion of war seems more remote in Japan than in Germany, where the ruins and bullet holes are still plain to see. There is nothing much in Tokyo to remind one of the last world war, since virtually the entire city went up in flames in 1945. The hotel that was occupied in the attempted military coup of 1936 had survived the war, but was torn down during the real estate boom of the eighties. The prison where Japan's major war criminals were hanged was replaced by a skyscraper and a shopping mall.

In the seventies and early eighties, you still saw the blind and maimed veterans of the Imperial Army standing on crude artificial limbs in the halls of railway stations or in front of Shinto shrines, wearing white kimonos and dark glasses, playing melancholy old army tunes on their battered accordions, hoping for some spare change. Young people, smartly dressed in the latest American styles, mostly passed them by without a glance, as though these broken men didn't exist, as though they were ghosts visible only to themselves. Older people would sometimes slip them a few coins, a bit furtively, like paying an embarrassing relative to stay out of sight. The ghostlike figures in their white kimonos brought back memories that nobody wanted. And now they too had disappeared forever. The only reminders of the last world war in Tokyo were mere fragments in the air, like the military marches blaring from the pinball parlors.

Roppongi is one of the most fashionable districts in Tokyo. Since 1945 it has always had a slightly Western air. There used to be an American military base there. Now the place smells of luxury. Foreign models rush to fashion studios, young men cruise down the main street in Porsches, and elegant ladies meet for light lunches at northern Italian restaurants. In the midst of all the glitter is a compound of ugly gray cement buildings. They are an oddly unkempt presence, incongruous, as though they shouldn't really be there at all. The ministry of self-defense, housed in here, is not even called a ministry, but an agency, even though its director general carries the portfolio of a cabinet minister. These buildings are among the few reminders of the last war. They used to be occupied by the Imperial Japanese Army, and by the U.S. Army after the war.

Officially Japan has no army, navy, or air force. In 1946 the Japanese, under the eyes of the American occupation, were presented with a constitution which states, in Article Nine, that "the Japanese people forever renounce war as a sovereign right of the nation." And that "land, sea, and air forces, as well as other war potential, will never be maintained." The Self-Defense Forces are a rather shaky compromise. But in fact Japan has a fairly large military, which it is constitutionally unable to dispatch.

When the Cold War began around 1950, the Americans no longer wanted Japan to remain a permanently disarmed model of pacifism. So a National Police Reserve was created. The left protested, but without success. Then a U.S.-Japan Security Treaty was signed, again despite much Japanese protest. Richard Nixon, on a visit to Japan in 1953, said that Article Nine had been a mistake. Many Japanese conservatives agreed, but their view didn't prevail. The Cold War heated up, Japanese business, partly thanks to the Korean War, began to boom, and the left lost more and more ground. The Self-Defense Forces were then legalized under circumstances many Japanese still regard as dubious and unconstitutional.

In the main building of the Self-Defense Agency, as nondescript inside as outside, I had an appointment with Hagi Jiro, deputy director general of the agency. His office was basic, even spartan: a desk, a sofa, a cupboard, and some steel filing cabinets. On the wall was a calendar with pinup pictures of teenage girls on a Pacific beach. Hagi was a thin man dressed in a blue suit. I asked him about Japanese public opinion. What did most people think Japan should do about the Gulf War? He said the majority were against sending any Japanese troops. In November 1990, a special bill proposing just that had to be dropped. Most Japanese, he said, still associated the military with the old Imperial Army. But this varied from generation to generation. People with memories of World War II, he said, were very much opposed to sending Japanese soldiers to fight on any front. People between the ages of thirty and fifty felt less strongly about this. And young people could be swayed easily one way or the other by the mass media.

He mentioned Article Nine of the Japanese constitution. And as so often happened in Germany, the question of trust came up. Hagi said: "The Japanese people do not trust the Self-Defense Forces because they cannot trust themselves as Japanese. This is why they need the constitution to block security efforts."

It was an interesting phrase: cannot trust themselves as Japanese. It came back at the end of our conversation. I told Hagi that I had just arrived from Germany. He smiled and said something unexpected: "I like the Germans very much, but I think they are a dangerous people. I don't know why—perhaps it is race, or culture, or history. Whatever. But we Japanese are the same: we swing from one extreme to the other. As peoples, we Japanese, like the Germans, have strong collective discipline. When our energies are channeled in the right direction, this is fine, but when they are misused, terrible things happen." Here he paused. Then he added: "I also happen to think Japanese and Germans are racists."

This was, of course, what many people believed. It was what I had been taught to believe, that the Germans and Japanese were dangerous peoples, that there was something flawed in their national characters. But it was not what I had expected to hear at the defense headquarters of Japan. Linking the two nations, however, as Hagi had done, was something Germans, in my experience, tended to avoid. I often heard the phrase "typically German" from Germans, almost always in a derogatory sense. ("Typically Japanese," on the other hand, is usually said by Japanese with a mixture of defensiveness and pride.) Yet to be put in the same category as the Japanese—even to be compared—bothered many Germans. (Again, unlike the Japanese, who made the comparison often.) Germans I met often stressed how different they were from the Japanese, just as Wessies emphasized their differences from Ossies. It had occurred to me that the Dorian Gray factor might have been at work. To some West Germans, now so "civilized," so free, so individualistic, so, well, Western, the Japanese, with their group discipline, their deference to authority, their military attitude toward work, might appear too close for comfort to a self-image only just, and perhaps only barely, overcome.

This is not entirely without reason. Japan learned many things from Germany during the nineteenth and twentieth centuries which no longer fit the liberal climate of the Federal Republic. Like Germany, Japan—as represented by its intellectuals and politicians—often felt the need to compensate for a feeling of national inferiority by turning to romantic nationalism. Fichte's theories of organic nationalism were imported to bolster Japanese self-esteem, even as Japan was Westernizing itself to catch up with Western might. Spengler's ideas on the decline of the West were comforting when Japan felt excluded by the Western powers in the 1920s and 1930s. But most of these theories, adapted to Japanese needs, are still widely quoted, on television, at universities, and in popular journals. Fantasies about Jewish conspiracies to dominate the world somehow got frozen in the outer reaches of Japanese folk mythology. And the ideology of pure race, much encouraged before the war by imported German notions, is anything but extinct in Japan.

In Hitler's Germany, Japan was admired for having achieved, instinctively, what German Nazism aspired to. In the words of one Albrecht Fürst von Urach, a Nazi propagandist, Japanese emperor worship was "the most unique fusion in the world of state form, state consciousness, and religious fanaticism." Fanaticism was, of course, a positive word in the Nazi lexicon. Reading Nazi books on Japan, one might think that German propagandists wished to instill in the German people, through propaganda, a culture like the one that was handed down to the Japanese by their ancient gods.

To what extent the behavior of nations, like that of individual people, is determined by history, culture, or character is a question that exercises many Japanese, almost obsessively. There was not much sign of *betroffenheit* on Japanese television during the Gulf War. Nor did one see retired generals explain tactics and strategy. Instead, there were experts from journalism and academe talking in a detached manner about a faraway war which was often presented as a cultural or religious conflict between West and Middle East. The history of Muslim-Christian-Jewish animosity was much discussed. And the American character was analyzed at length to understand the behavior of George Bush and General Schwarzkopf.

The cultural preoccupations cropped up in private conversations too. I met some Japanese friends for a drink in one of the last streets in Tokyo to have remained unchanged since the war. It is in an area called Golden Gai, which used to be a cheap red-light district. We sat in a tiny bar, with room for about ten people. The name of the bar was taken from an avant-garde French film and the voice of Billie Holiday filled the smoky air; the bar prided itself on its intellectual clientele. The majority opinion in the bar was that the Gulf War was fought only for American interests. My friends were all in their early forties, active in the arts. They saw the Gulf War as a question of cultural identity. The Americans wanted to make the Arabs conform to the American view of the world.

What about freedom and democracy? I asked. Weren't those

principles worth defending? Should one allow an aggressive nation to invade another? I knew this was not entirely convincing; Kuwait was hardly a democracy. But I wanted to draw them out. The answer was an interesting variation of anti-Western rhetoric.

"Democracy," said a cartoonist, "is not universal. It is only a Western ideal, which Westerners pretend is universal. That's why this war is wrong: the West is trying to impose its ideas on a non-Western nation. The Americans are not only hypocritical, they are arrogant."

A well-known filmmaker nodded vigorously and said that Japan would have been better off if the Americans had never come. He was referring to the arrival in Japan of Commodore Perry's black ships in 1853. "They have robbed us of our culture," he said. "We hardly know who we are anymore."

I knew him well enough to know that this was said as a provocation. But conversations with Japanese artists and intellectuals often take this turn: the identity question nags in almost any discussion about Japan and the outside world. It leads to odd identifications. In the left-leaning *Asahi Shimbun*, I read the following letter, written by Nakamura Tetsu, a medical doctor of the '68 generation active in the Middle East: "When speaking of the New World Order, we must understand our brethren in Asia whose sense of values and culture is not shared by the West. We must rethink our attitude toward Asia. Only fifty years ago it was we Japanese, caught between our traditional society and Western-style modernization, who suffered a war against America. That war is not concluded yet. It is time to think again about the meaning of the several million [sic] 'sacred spirits' sacrificed in Hiroshima and Nagasaki."

This comes remarkably close in tone and thinking to Pan-Asian Japanese nationalism of the thirties and forties. The idea that Japan had been struggling violently, sometimes clumsily, but still always nobly, against Western domination of Asia since the nineteenth century is not new. It started in the 1860s with the movement to "throw out the barbarians and revere the emperor." It was promoted in Japanese war propaganda. It was defended in a famous book published in 1964 entitled *In Affirmation of the Great East Asian War* by Hayashi Fusao. Hayashi's anti-Western nationalism was the model for right-wing apologetics after the war. But Hayashi was a former Communist. And he wrote that in an ideal world, in which Japan would no longer be divided by international politics, all Japanese would think alike. As he put it: "One Japanese way of thinking will be born." There was nostalgia in these words. During the Pacific War, the Japanese people were told that "a hundred million [Japanese] hearts beat as one."

This ideal world was not yet at hand during the Gulf War. In a public opinion poll conducted by the *Asahi Shimbun*, 70 percent of the people were against using armed force against Iraq, but 29.6 percent of those in their twenties were in favor of it, and at least as many said they were not sure. Nakamura's letter in the *Asahi* was an emotional variation of a common theme among letter writers to that newspaper. A typical one read: "Now, of all times, we Japanese have the right, as well as the duty, to oppose war and tell the world about our own experiences, how our innocent civilians were sacrificed by terrible bombings."

This, to many Japanese, was the point of Article Nine. When the Prime Minister of Japan, Shidehara Kijuro, protested in 1946 to General MacArthur that it was all very well saying that Japan should assume moral leadership in renouncing war, but that in the real world no country would follow this example, MacArthur replied: "Even if no country follows you, Japan will lose nothing. It is those who do not support this who are in the wrong." For a long time most Japanese continued to take this view. The Gulf War put a dent in it.

It was a respectable view, but also one founded on a national myth of betrayal. Japan, according to the myth, had become the unique moral nation of peace, betrayed by the victors who had sat in judgment of Japan's war crimes; betrayed in Vietnam, in Afghanistan, in Nicaragua; betrayed by the arms race, betrayed by the Cold War; Japan had been victimized not only by the "gratuitous," perhaps even "racist," nuclear attacks on Hiroshima and Nagasaki, but by all subsequent military actions taken by the superpowers, including the decision to go to war against Saddam Hussein. The most fervent believers in the myth were men and women of the left, who clung to Article Nine as a priest to his book of prayers.

Several months after the Gulf War had formally ended, a literary critic named Matsumoto Kenichi wrote an article for the *Tokyo Shimbun* in which he compared Saddam's invasion of Kuwait to the Japanese raid on Pearl Harbor. It was the counterpart, in a way, to Enzensberger's comparison of Saddam and Hitler in *Der Spiegel*. Saddam's claim, wrote Matsumoto, that he was fighting for Pan-Arab ideals "eerily echoed the Japanese militarists who, on the eve of Pearl Harbor, arrogantly proclaimed that 'Asia is one.' " Both Iraq and Japan fought "holy wars" against Western imperialism. But the parallel, in Matsumoto's opinion, went further: "Japan and Iraq went to war for virtually identical reasons." Western powers were accused of making war inevitable, by depriving those countries of trade and raw materials. Thus war for Japan and Iraq had supposedly become a matter of survival. "Japan," wrote Matsumoto, "has not atoned for its wartime atrocities. So we can't accuse the Iraqis of using inhuman methods and violating international law without pointing a finger at ourselves."

So far, so good. Introspection of this kind is rare in the mainstream Japanese press. But then the accusing finger suddenly swiveled around: "On the other hand, the response of America's mass media to the initial air attacks on Iraq recalled Japan's euphoric accounts of its early victories in the Pacific . . ." And the conclusion: "The Gulf conflict reminded me once again of the banality and cruelty of war. I was appalled when our Prime Minister, Kaifu Toshiki, expressed his firm support for the multinational coalition and attempted to deploy our Self-Defense Forces to the Middle East. Conservative politicians here appear to have learned little from Japan's own descent into barbarism just fifty years ago."

We are left with the conclusion, then, that all were equally barbarous: wartime Japan, Saddam Hussein, George Bush, Japanese conservative politicians. The pacifist aim may be a virtuous one, and skepticism about the euphoric American press might have been just, but there was something too conveniently indiscriminate about this view. All wars are unjust: it was like the warning post on the market square in Bonn, or the peace professor who thought the bombing of Baghdad was the greatest war crime since 1945. Too much history was thrown into one basket.

But there was one huge difference with Germany: Israel. Japanese did not feel guilty about the Jews; there were no hysterical calls to the Israeli embassy in Tokyo; there was no Japanese Wolf Biermann. For many Germans, the Gulf War recalled visions of the Holocaust; to most Japanese it was just another war, another faraway war, which erupted like a natural disaster. Perhaps if the target of allied bombs had not been Iraq, but China, or even North Korea, Japanese war guilt would have been a factor. But even those Japanese who feel bad about China and Korea do not think of the Japanese war as a Holocaust.

The denial of historical discrimination is not just a way to evade guilt. It is intrinsic to pacifism. To even try to distinguish between wars, to accept that some wars are justified, is already an immoral position. What is so convenient in the cases of Germany and Japan is that pacifism happens to be a high-minded way to dull the pain of historical guilt. Or, conversely, if one wallows in it, pacifism turns national guilt into a virtue, almost a mark of superiority, when compared to the complacency of other nations. It can also be the cause of historical myopia.

Oda Makoto, the father of the anti–Vietnam War movement in Japan and the author of a novel about the bombing of Hiroshima, told me that Japan had to remain a pacifist nation: "Japan, of all nations, must be a conscientious objector." As a military power, Oda said, Japan would be a very dangerous country. And so would Germany. Soon, he thought, Germany would be a pure-race country again. When I expressed some doubt, he said that I, as a Westerner, as a white man, was in no position to judge.

I asked him about the Vietnam War. He saw no difference between the Vietnam War and the Japanese war in Asia. Indeed, it was the Vietnam War that made him reflect on the Japanese conquest of Asia. Nor did he see any difference between European colonialism and the Japanese invasion of China and Southeast Asia. When I pointed out what I thought were differences, he became agitated and raised his voice. "Look," he said, "I have no time to discuss historical distinctions. Colonialism is bad, and that's that." His plump face reddened, his big hands crashed on the table. His Korean-Japanese wife stared silently into her tea. I had been put in my place.

Oda was born in 1932. He remembered how proud he had been, waving his Rising Sun flag after great military victories against the Americans. He could also remember, with particular bitterness, how his native city, Osaka, was bombed a day before the Japanese emperor announced on the radio that the war "had not developed in a way necessarily to Japan's advantage" and that it was time to surrender. Oda did not cry, he said. His real bitterness concerned the way in which the Americans after the war wrecked Japan's chances to break away from the past. It was the Americans who allowed the emperor to remain on his throne. It was the Americans who allowed the same bureaucrats and politicians who had led Japan into the war to continue ruling the country. It was the Americans who made the Japanese undermine their own constitution by building a new army, and it was the Americans who made the Japanese into accomplices of U.S. imperialism in Asia.

His resentment was not without justification, but Oda's ambivalence toward the West was more complicated than political disillusion. It was an ambivalence bordering on hostility. This might have been partly a matter of age. He had been educated, after all, to despise the "Anglo-American demons." And Pan-Asian propaganda was not all that far removed from romantic Third Worldism. But despite Oda's Third Worldist views, his identification with the oppressed was not straightforward either. He also identified with the oppressors. One of the aims of his "Peace for Vietnam" movement had been to help American deserters and antiwar protesters. In Oda's view, the American GIs, like the Japanese Imperial Army soldiers before, were aggressors as well as victims; aggressors because they killed innocent people, victims because they were forced to do so.

Feelings toward the West cannot be other than complex in Japan. On the surface, Japan is the most Westernized country in Asia. Even to Oda Makoto, New York probably feels closer than Beijing (and I daresay Tuscany would be more familiar than Dresden). Even as there was a movement during the nineteenth century to expel the barbarians, there was also a movement to "reject Asia." In woodcuts of turn-of-the-century Japanese wars on the Asian continent, the Japanese are shown as large light-skinned figures in European uniforms, demonstrating their mastery over dwarfish yellow men in pigtails and silk coats.

The ambivalence comes in many varieties, and it emerges in conversations with very different people. The right-wing Liberal Democratic Party politician Kamei Shizuka is in almost every respect the opposite of Oda Makoto. They are roughly the same age, and both are stocky men, with broad peasant features. That is about all they have in common, however. Kamei is a hawk on defense. He wants Article Nine to be scrapped from the constitution. He wants education to be more patriotic, to instill pride in Japanese military heroes, and so on. He does not believe that Japan's war in Asia was all that bad. He wants the emperor to be reinstated in his former status as sacred father of the family state. He wants to revive Shinto as a national cult. He thinks that the Americans after the war robbed Japan of its identity, its pride, its virility.

I visited Kamei in his office in Tokyo, near the Diet building.

His language, like Oda's, was deliberately rough, not so much to express familiarity as to stress a kind of rugged masculinity. Our conversation was interrupted once or twice by telephone calls. Kamei never articulated a word. All I heard were grunts and growls, of affirmation, of negation, of farewell.

I asked him what he thought of the Gulf War. He grunted and said: "We Japanese have a term, *tatemae*, which means official reality, the way you say things are. Then we have *honne*, our real feelings, the way things really are. Now, the *tatemae* is that the Iraqi invasion of Kuwait cannot be allowed. The *honne* is that we Japanese were not consulted before America started the war." The resentment was unmistakable. From the opposite perspective, Kamei was making Oda's point: America had forced Japan to be an accomplice.

"Then," he went on, "there is the question of Israel. You know, we Japanese are well informed. We know what the real face of America is. People here have seen Henry Kissinger on television. He is a Jew. And we know about Jewish influence in America. We know all that. So our *honne* tells us that this war is fought for Israel."

This is fairly standard rhetoric in Japan. It is disturbing, but easy to misinterpret. The main point here is not about Jews, but about America. In ill-informed Japanese minds there is a confusion of Jewish and American interests, a confusion which exists not only in Japan. "America," like "the eternal Jew," is shorthand for rootless cosmopolitanism, international conspiracy, and so on. That Kamei discussed this common paranoia in such odd, Volkish terms could mean several things: that some of the worst European myths got stuck in Japan, that the history of the Holocaust had no impact, or that Japan is in some respects a deeply provincial place. I think all three explanations apply.

"During the nineteenth century," Kamei explained, "Japan was threatened by Western imperialism. The borders in the Middle East were all drawn by Western powers. The British were responsible for Palestine. What Iraq is doing now is no different from what Western powers did until recently. That is my personal impression. Of course, Saddam Hussein is not right. But it cannot be said that Western powers are right and other races are wrong. That cannot be said."

Like Oda, indeed like many people of the left, Kamei thought in racial terms. He used the word *jinshu*, literally race. He did not even use the more usual *minzoku*, which corresponds, in the parlance of Japanese right-wingers, to Volk, or the more neutral *kokumin*, meaning the citizens of a state.

The Japanese government was officially in favor of the Gulf War and paid nine billion dollars toward the allied cause. The Japanese Socialist Party was absolutely opposed to it, far more adamantly so than the German Social Democrats. But the politics were never simple. Kamei explained his party's position: "The *honne* of our party is about the same as that of the Socialists. We are only supporting the war to keep the Americans happy."

Kamei is not a mainstream conservative. He is to the right of his party. Being on the right, he was more prepared to sound anti-American or anti-Western than his government. He could bluster about new alliances in Asia and cutting loose from America. He could say that the Japanese people felt closer to Asia than to the West. I put it to him that German conservatives insisted on being part of the West, that they had made the Western alliance, so to speak, a part of German national identity. I told him about Adenauer's concept of Asia.

Kamei laughed, revealing an even row of gold fillings. "Well," he admitted, "the problem with the U.S.-Japan relationship is difficult. A racial problem, really. Yankees are friendly people, frank people. But, you know, it's hard. You see, we *have* to be friendly . . ."

Again, one felt there was a confusion here, a common one in Japan. Kamei was conflating a political problem and a cultural one, as though they were the same thing. In fact, the reason Japanese officials feel they have to be friendly to the United States has little to do with culture, even less with race, and everything with the peculiarly lopsided security arrangement between the two countries. It is possible, of course, that having different, non-Western cultural traditions has made it harder for Japan to come to terms with the Western world than it has been for West Germany. If there is indeed a border, more unbridgeable than the river Elbe, between Japan and the West, this would help to explain another *idée reçue*: whereas many Germans in the liberal democratic West have tried to deal honestly with their nation's terrible past, the Japanese, being different, have been unable to do so.

It is true that the Japanese, compared with the West Germans, have paid less attention to the suffering they inflicted on others, and shown a greater inclination to shift the blame. And liberal democracy, whatever it may look like on paper, has not been the success in Japan that it was in the German Federal Republic. Cultural differences might account for this. But one can look at these matters in a different, more political way. In his book *The War Against the West*, published in London in 1938, the Hungarian scholar Aurel Kolnai followed the Greeks in his definition of the West: "For the ancient Greeks 'the West' (or 'Europe') meant society with a free constitution and self-government under recognized rules, where 'law is king,' whereas the 'East' (or 'Asia') signified theocratic societies under godlike rulers whom their subjects serve 'like slaves.' "

According to this definition, both Hitler's Germany and prewar Japan were of the East. As the title of Kolnai's book implies, Germany fought a war against the West. Now, it may be so that Adenauer's Germany found its way back to the West. In 1949 the German Basic Law was drawn up by German jurists. In 1954 West Germany formally became a sovereign nation, even though Western powers still kept troops there. An emergency law was passed enabling Germany to take control of its own defense. Except in Berlin, the occupation was formally over. In Japan, in some ways, it is not over yet.

Japan's godlike ruler was told by the Americans to renounce his divinity. Perhaps with a feeling of relief, the lover of rare crustaceans, Mickey Mouse watches, and English breakfasts was swift to comply. And the Americans imposed a constitution which read like translated English and which surrendered the right of Japan to defend itself. Most Japanese were so tired of war and so distrustful of their military commanders that they were happy to do so. Then, when the Cold War prompted the Americans to make the Japanese subvert their constitution by creating an army which was not supposed to exist, the worst of all worlds appeared: sovereignty was not restored, distrust remained, and resentment mounted. Kamei's hawks are angry with the Americans for emasculating Japan; Oda's doves hate the Americans for emasculating the "peace constitution." Both sides dislike being forced accomplices, and both feel victimized, which is one reason Japanese have a harder time than Germans in coming to terms with their wartime past.

If it is possible to draw lessons from history at all, this cannot really be put to the test in Japan. Without formal sovereignty, such questions as whether to appease an aggressor or not make no sense. When I asked a socialist politician in Tokyo to consider whether the German-Japanese war against the West could have been avoided had Western force been applied sooner, he replied: "Perhaps. I don't know. But we deny any solution by military means." When I asked Oda whether one country had the right to help another country defend itself against an aggressor, he said: "No." When I put it to him that in that case the war would have been won by the Axis powers, he replied: "You think as a person educated from the point of view of the victim. I was educated from the point of view of the aggressor."

This was true enough, but it was he, not I, who was still convinced that the Japanese and the Germans were dangerous peoples. There was a great irony here: in their zeal to make Japan part of the West, General MacArthur and his advisers made it impossible for Japan to do so in spirit. For a forced, impotent accomplice is not really an accomplice at all. In recent years, Japan has often been called an economic giant and a political dwarf. But this has less to do with a traditional Japanese mentality—isolationism, pacifism, shyness with foreigners, or whatnot—than with the particular political circumstances after the war that the United States helped to create. To understand the complexity of Japanese memories of its Asian war, one has to understand the conditions that grew from its defeat. One has to return to 1945.

ROMANCE OF THE RUINS

IT IS DIFFICULT TO SAY when the war actually began for the Germans and the Japanese. I cannot think of a single image that fixed the beginning of either war in the public mind. There is the famous picture of German soldiers lifting the barrier on the Polish border in 1939, but was that really the beginning? Or did it actually start with the advance into the Rhineland in 1936, or was it the annexation of the Sudetenland, or Austria, or Czechoslovakia? As far as the war against the Jews is concerned, one might go back to 1933, when Hitler came to power. Or at the latest to 1935, when the race laws were promulgated in Nuremberg. Or perhaps those photographs of burning synagogues on the night of November 9, 1938, truly marked the first stage of the Holocaust. Possibly to avoid these confusions, many Germans prefer to talk about the *Hitlerzeit* (Hitler era) instead of "the war." When people do refer to "the war," they think of soldiers freezing on the eastern front and German cities smashed by bombs.

In Japan, the establishment of a puppet state in Manchuria in 1931 was a hostile harbinger of much to come. But the invasion of China proper began in 1937 with a shoot-out near Beijing, and the Pacific War started with the attack on Pearl Harbor four years later. Incidentally, only Japanese of a liberal disposition call World War II the Pacific War. People who stick to the idea that Japan was fighting a war to liberate Asia from Bolshevism and white colonialism call it the Great East Asian War (*Daitowa Senso*), as in the Great East Asian Co-Prosperity Sphere. People of this opinion separate the world war of 1941–45 from the war in China, which they still insist on calling the China Incident. Liberals and leftists, on the other hand, tend to splice these wars together and call them the Fifteen-Year War (1931–45). Hayashi Fusao, the author of *In Affirmation of the Great East Asian War* and definitely not a liberal, argued that the struggle against Western imperialism actually began in 1853, with the arrival in Japan of Commodore Perry's ships, and spoke of the Hundred-Year War.

If the beginning of the wars is hard to identify, images marking the end are more obvious. The mushroom cloud over Hiroshima, so impressively recorded on film by the American Air Force photographers, and the scratchy radio speech by the Japanese emperor on August 15, telling his sobbing subjects in barely intelligible court language to "bear the unbearable," are described in countless Japanese novels and shown in many films. These are among the great clichés of postwar Japan: shorthand for national defeat, suffering, and humiliation.

The German equivalent, I suppose, would be the picture of Soviet soldiers raising their flag on the roof of the gutted Reichstag in Berlin. An East German once told me that one of the soldiers in the photograph was wearing looted watches on his arm, like a stack of bracelets. Liberation, he remarked wisely, is often mixed with injustice, for the liberators are often no better than the conquered. I looked at the picture again and could not see any watches. Forty years of Soviet rule must have played tricks with his memory, but his instincts were probably right.

If there had been a photograph of Hitler's charred corpse, it, no doubt, would be among the icons of 1945. Instead, we have the photograph of Goebbels and his poisoned family. The contours of his oversized skull, like a misshapen gourd, are still recognizable. Then there is the famous picture of Hitler taking

a last melancholy (or was it merely peeved) peek from the exit
of his bunker at the destruction of his capital. This photograph
has a romantic, even operatic appeal: the evil genius meeting
his doom.

Hitler's doom and the emperor's speech, the end of one
symbol and the odd continuity of another. Whatever their symbolic differences, both would be associated forever with ruins
—ruined cities, ruined people, ruined ideals. The most extraordinary images of 1945 are the silent films of Hiroshima, Berlin,
and Tokyo: acres and acres of burnt-out, bombed-out landscape; Berlin a city of ruined nineteenth-century façades, Tokyo
a city of charred wood and flooded craters.

In the summer of 1945, a month before the bombings of
Hiroshima and Nagasaki, Stephen Spender was sent on a British
government mission to Germany to find out what remained of
its intellectual life. All he found was ruins. Here he is in Cologne:
"The ruin of the city is reflected in the internal ruin of its
inhabitants who, instead of being lives that can form a scar over
the city's wounds, are parasites sucking at a dead carcase, digging among the ruins for hidden food, doing business at their
black market near the cathedral—the commerce of destruction
instead of production . . . The destruction of the city itself, with
all its past as well as its present, is like a reproach to the people
who go on living there. The sermons in the stones of Germany
preach nihilism."

In one of the first German feature films made after the war
—Wolfgang Staudte's *The Murderers Are Among Us* (1946)—we
see the embittered figure of Dr. Mertens scurrying through the
broken streets of Berlin. He is drunk. His eyes look deranged;
a man haunted by terrible visions of the recent past. Rats appear
from the piles of rubble and spurt across his shoes. "Rats," he
whispers, "rats, rats, everywhere."

The Germans called it *Zusammenbruch* (the collapse) or *Stunde
Null* (Zero Hour): everything seemed to have come to an end,
everything had to start all over. The Japanese called it *haisen*
(defeat) or *shusen* (termination of the war). This last term cush-

ioned the blow of failure. The U.S. Army occupation was often called "stationing of U.S. forces," for the same reason. All they had been told to believe in, the Germans and the Japanese, everything from the *Führerprinzip* to the emperor cult, from the samurai spirit to the *Herrenvolk*, from *Lebensraum* to the whole world under one (Japanese) roof, all that lay in ruins too. The only thing that glittered in the burnt remains of Osaka, wrote the novelist Nosaka Akiyuki, was the trail of silver chewing-gum wrappers left by the American Army.

Spender interviewed Konrad Adenauer, who was then the mayor of Cologne. The German people are spiritually starved, Adenauer told him. "The imagination has to be provided for." This was no simple matter, especially in the German language, which had been so thoroughly infected by the jargon of mass murder. How to fashion poetry out of the language of murderers? How to purge this language from what a famous German philologist called the Lingua Tertii Imperii? ". . . the language is no longer lived," wrote George Steiner in 1958, "it is merely spoken."

The Japanese did not really have this problem. The Japanese language itself survived the wreckage relatively unscathed, even though some of the more sensitive members of the wartime generation could no longer hear certain phrases without wincing. The philosopher Yoshimoto Takaaki wrote (in the early 1960s) that "hearing such words as nation, or race, just after our defeat, was like feeling a fresh wound." Still, *kokka* (nation, state) and *minzoku* (race, people) are not quite of the same order as *Sonderbehandlung* (special treatment) or *Einsatzgruppe* (special action squad). The jargon of Japanese imperialism was racist and overblown, but it did not carry the stench of death camps.

There was a problem with Japanese culture, however, which was comparable to but not quite the same as the German predicament. The German problem was Nazism. Although some people believed that the roots of Hitlerism, the peculiar and uniquely German course of history, the *Sonderweg*, went back to Luther, or at least to Herder or Wagner, neither Herder nor

Wagner, let alone the writings of Luther, was ever forbidden. In Germany there was a tradition to fall back on. In the Soviet sector, the left-wing culture of the Weimar Republic was actively revived. In the Western sectors, writers escaped the rats and the ruins by dreaming of Goethe. His name was often invoked to prove that Germany, too, belonged to the humanist, enlightened strain of European civilization.

But in Japan, which never had a Goethe, so far as the occupation authorities knew, and where traditional culture had been bent badly out of shape by many years of chauvinist propaganda, the Americans (and many Japanese leftists) distrusted anything associated with "feudalism," which they took to include much of Japan's premodern past. Feudalism was the enemy of democracy. So not only did the American censors, in their effort to teach the Japanese democracy, forbid sword-fight films and samurai dramas, but at one point ninety-eight Kabuki plays were banned too. Medieval-poetry anthologies were scrutinized for signs of ultranationalist sentiments. Even Mount Fuji, long the object of Shintoist nature worship, was not allowed to be depicted. Nature worship had too often slipped into worship of the Japanese state. So a scene of farmers working on the slopes of Fuji was cut from a feature film in 1946. It was as though Germany—*Sonderweg* or no *Sonderweg*—needed only to be purged of Nazism, while Japan's entire cultural tradition had to be overhauled.

Yet out of defeat and ruin a new school of literature (and cinema) did arise. It is known in Germany as *Trümmerliteratur* (literature of the ruins). Japanese writers who came of age among the ruins called themselves the *yakeato seidai* (burnt-out generation). Much literature of the late forties and fifties was darkened by nihilism and despair. Japanese novelists who had been in the army described the behavior of men in extreme conditions. Cannibalism was a common theme. In his novel *Fires on the Plain*, Ooka Shohei remembered his time in the Philippines, near the end of the war, when starved Japanese soldiers, trapped in the mountains of Luzon, ended up devouring enemies (natives were "black pigs," Americans were "white pigs") as well as each other. Then there were the stories of soldiers coming home to find their wives with other men, and stories about decent women becoming prostitutes, and respectable men scrounging in the black markets.

Humiliation and resentment of the foreign occupation became a popular—and indeed permissible—subject only after the occupation was over. One of the most commercially successful examples in Germany was *Der Fragenbogen* (*The Questionnaire*) by Ernst von Salomon, published in 1951. Salomon was a rather sinister figure who had been involved in the assassination of Walther Rathenau, Germany's Jewish Foreign Minister, in 1922. In *Der Fragenbogen* (the title refers to the questionnaires which Germans had to fill out to show whether they had been Nazis) Salomon describes the Americans as crass, stupid, and virtually as brutal as the Germans had been. "Stupidity," says the main protagonist, "is the most understandable thing in the world. What depresses me is not our defeat, but the fact that our victors made it meaningless."

There was much of this kind of thing in Japan too, perhaps even more than in Germany, since the occupation censors had been so active in suppressing feudalism and anti-American sentiments. In the 1950s there were a number of films about the injustice of war crimes trials and the horror of being torched by American bombs. A new literary genre appeared, describing the effects of the bombs dropped on Hiroshima and Nagasaki. And movie audiences had a pornographic fascination for the seamy side of American military bases: the crime, the prostitution, the raping of innocent Japanese women. If the mushroom cloud and the imperial radio speech are the clichés of defeat, the scene of an American soldier (usually black) raping a Japanese girl (always young, always innocent), usually in a pristine rice field (innocent, pastoral Japan), is a stock image in postwar movies about the occupation.

For most people in Germany and Japan, those first years after the war were a time of pure misery. And yet, what is remarkable about much of the literature of the period, or more precisely, of the literature *about* that time, since much of it was written later, is the deep strain of romanticism, even nostalgia. This colors personal memories of people who grew up just after the war as well. The Japanese playwright Kara Juro, for example, remembered playing in bomb craters near the Sumida River in Tokyo: "You could see the horizon on every side. The skies were so bright that everything looked unnaturally sharp. It was wonderful to play in the ruins. It was like the landscape of dreams."

The novelist and essayist Sakaguchi Ango was already in his forties when the war ended. He had been just a few years too old to be drafted into the army. After the war he became famous for his essays on the bombings and their aftermath. Some call his writing nihilistic. I am not sure this is the right word. In any case, he expressed perfectly the spirit of a defeated nation in ruins. Yet his tone was that of a disenchanted romantic, if one can imagine such a thing. In his famous essay "On Degradation," he described the bombing raids on Tokyo as a grand spectacle, a kind of lethal fireworks display. He enjoyed the "weird beauty of people resigned to their fate." He liked watching young girls moving about the burnt landscape, smiling in the midst of catastrophe.

The immediate postwar period, however, was one of complete depravity. The smiling girlish faces—the "love among the ruins"—were lost: "The youths who had not perished like blossoms for their emperor were black marketeers now." But the depravity is more real and precious to him than the romance of war, which was nothing but a deliberate illusion fostered by political propaganda: the beauty of sacrifice, emperor worship, military valor, a race descended from the gods, and so on. These illusions had to be dashed to make the Japanese human again: "Oh, Japanese people, oh, Japan, I want you all to be depraved. Japan and the Japanese must become degraded! As long as the emperor system persists, as long as such historical devices remain part of the idea of nationhood, they will be manipulated, and we won't be able to develop our lives as human beings in this country."

To Ango, then, as to other writers, the ruins offered hope. At last the Japanese, without "the fake kimono" of traditions and ideals, were reduced to basic human needs; at last they could feel real love, real pain; at last they would be honest. There was no room, among the ruins, for hypocrisy.

It is a common intellectual conceit: the virtue of poverty, the purity of the dispossessed. It was a conceit which, in those early days, was given extra zest by the brief revival of socialist hopes. A few people of the left, including some Communists, were the only ones to have survived the war untainted by the Japanese imperialist adventure. For several years in the 1940s, the American occupation authorities encouraged them to play an active part in Japanese politics. Left-wing parties were founded or revived, trade unions organized. Perhaps, at last, a truly democratic (socialist, of course) Japan would arise from the ruins of war, shaped by the solidarity of an impoverished people.

The writer Wolf Dietrich Schnurre remembered in 1963 how similar hopes in Germany had, in his opinion, actually raised the German people to a higher moral plane: "There was a swell of real, burning hope in ruined Germany. Then, the survivors still had an ear for the silent supplications of the dead. Then, the fresh wind of peace was still blowing through the burnt-out houses. People still had faith. They still saw a neutral, united Germany. The vision of a new Europe was not yet torn to pieces by nationalist rivalry. Freedom was still within our grasp, and antimilitarism and the desire to live were still one."

This was not quite the mood that Stephen Spender found in Germany. But the language is typical of the leftist nostalgia for those years. The novelist Heinrich Böll was about ten years younger than Ango. Like Ooka Shohei, he was a returned soldier. Like Schnurre, he saw a real chance for human salvation in the German rubble. He was an active member of a literary circle called Gruppe 47, which also included Hans Magnus Enzensberger and Günter Grass. What this informal group had in common was a leftist orientation, a liking for Hemingway's sparse reportorial style, and a dislike for romantic escapism. In an article entitled "I Belong to Trümmerliteratur," written in 1952, Böll identified himself with "black marketeers and with their victims, with refugees and all others who have lost a roof over their heads, and above all, of course, with the generation to which we belonged, and which found itself in a strange and memorable situation: the generation that came home."

Like Ango, Böll saw something ennobling in a people stripped of all possessions. He too had a romantic view of the returning soldier, to the point of bringing in Homer as a model for *Trümmerliteratur*: "The name of Homer is unimpeachable in the entire civilized Western world: Homer is the founding father of European epic literature, but his stories are of the Trojan War, of the destruction of Troy and the homecoming of Ulysses. Literature of war, ruins, and coming home—we have no reason to be ashamed of this description."

Now, there may have been an element here of saving pride. Ulysses was perhaps not an entirely fit comparison with Hitler's soldiers. But it was typical of the anxiousness of a German writer to be part of the "civilized Western world." Certainly, in retrospect, those first years were not a time of despair. That came later, for Böll and others who thought like him. Böll was able to be precise about the end of the *Zusammenbruch* and the beginning of bourgeois hypocrisy and moral amnesia. It came on June 20, 1948, the day of the currency reform, the day that Ludwig Erhard, picked by the Americans as Economics Director in the U.S.-British occupation zone, gave birth to the Deutsche Mark. The DM, from then on, would be the new symbol of West German national pride; it also excluded the Easterners living in the Soviet zone. Erhard's motto was "Prosperity for All" (*"Wohlstand für Alle"*). For many who believed in a brand-new world where the human spirit would conquer selfishness and greed, it was the end of a romance.

Böll (in 1960): "Consumers. We are a nation of consumers. Neckties and conformism, shirts and nonconformism, there are consumers for everything. The only important thing is that everything—shirts or conformism—is for sale."

The "inability to mourn," the German disassociation from the piles of corpses strewn all over Central and Eastern Europe, so that the Third Reich, as the Mitscherlichs put it, "faded like a dream," made it easier to identify with the Americans, the victors, the West. If Böll and the Mitscherlichs are to be believed, there was a strong tendency to turn away from reality from the very beginning of the *Zusammenbruch*. The process of willed forgetfulness culminated in the manic effort of reconstruction, in the great rush to prosperity.

The rush, to some extent the amnesia, and definitely the identification with the West, was helped further along by the Cold War. West Germany now found itself on the same side as the Western allies. Their common enemy was the "Asiatic" Soviet empire. Fewer questions needed to be asked. As in the Foreign Legion, what was past, was past. Indeed, to some people the Cold War simply confirmed what they had known all along: Germany always had been on the right side, if only our American friends had realized it earlier. The Cold War came as the final blow for those who had hoped for a pacifist, socialist Germany.

The Mitscherlichs' psychoanalysis of their nation in *The Inability to Mourn* was sweeping—can one really psychoanalyze an entire nation? A little bit of amnesia, some identification with the West, and much energy channeled into economic recovery were perhaps not such bad things. We know what happened when Germany had been humiliated and squeezed roughly three decades before. "Prosperity for All" was probably the best that could have happened to the Germans of the Federal Republic. It took the seed of resentment (and thus future extremism) out of defeat. And the integration of West Germany into a Western alliance was a good thing too. Yet the disgust felt by Böll and others for a people getting fat ("flabby" is the usual term, denoting sloth and decadence) and forgetting about its murderous past was understandable. It cannot have been an edifying spectacle.

The man to hate in Staudte's film *The Murderers Are Among Us* is Brückner, factory owner, family man, and former army officer. Brückner ordered the shooting of more than a hundred Polish men, women, and children on Christmas Day 1942. Dr. Mertens, the embittered veteran dodging the rats in Berlin, was under his command. Mertens tried to stop the killing. He now wants to confront flabby Brückner with his past, and shoot him. He finds him in his factory, celebrating Christmas with his workers. He is just giving a festive speech, celebrating "a Germany we all love, a Germany which will never perish, a Germany where justice will triumph." Dr. Mertens remembers that other Christmas, in 1942, when Brückner was leading his men in a chorus of "Silent Night," even as Polish families were shot in the snow. Dr. Mertens follows Brückner to his house and reminds him of the people whose deaths he had ordered.

"But it was war," says Brückner, his complacency turning to panic. "Different conditions . . . It is peace now . . . Christmas . . . peaceful Christmas . . ."

Dr. Mertens is about to shoot Brückner, but is stopped at the last minute by his lover, Susanne.

S.: "You don't have the right to judge!"

DR. M.: "But we must press charges. In the name of millions of innocent people."

BRÜCKNER: "What do you want from me? I am innocent! I am innocent! I am innocent!" (The sound of his voice echoes as the faces of his victims fade in and out of view.)

This film was made before Erhard's currency reform was even heard of. But it was prescient. The Brückners were the price Germany had to pay for the revival of its fortunes. Indeed, they were often instrumental in it. They were the apparatchik who functioned in any system, the small, efficient fish who voted for Christian conservatives in the West and became Communists in the East. Staudte was clearly troubled by this, as were many Germans, but he offered no easy answers. Perhaps it was better this way: flabby democrats do less harm than vengeful old Nazis. (Dutiful Communists snooping on their neighbors are a different matter.) Some critics, such as Wolf Dietrich Schnurre, thought that Staudte's film was much too weak. It should have ended in a proper war crimes trial, he wrote in 1946, to show just what was to be done about the murderers among us.

Schnurre did not get his wish in real life either. Few Brückners were punished for their deeds, particularly those who had served Hitler well as doctors, lawyers, scientists, or bureaucrats. The early efforts of the occupation forces to "denazify" Germany petered out in the late 1940s, when the beginning of the Cold War set other priorities. This left at least one generation of German writers and artists with the conclusion that the forgetful, prosperous, capitalist Federal Republic of Germany was in many more or less hidden ways a continuation of Hitler's Reich. This perfectly suited the propagandists of the GDR, who would produce from time to time lists of names of former Nazis who were prospering in the West. These lists were often surprisingly accurate.

In a famous film, half fiction, half documentary, made by a number of German writers and filmmakers (including Böll) in 1977, the continuity was made explicit. The film, called *Germany in Autumn* (*Deutschland in Herbst*), was prompted by the official reaction to the murder by Red Army terrorists of Hans-Martin Schleyer, board member of Daimler-Benz (and, incidentally, a former SS officer). The country (or at least the country's intelligentsia) was on the verge of hysteria. Many thought the end of West German democracy was at hand. Now the establishment, so it was thought, would show its true brown color. A recurring image in the film is of Schleyer's funeral in Stuttgart, spliced together with General Rommel's funeral in 1944. The Nazi banners at Rommel's funeral are alternated with shots of the Mercedes-Benz flags fluttering outside the hall where Schleyer's funeral service took place.

Rainer Werner Fassbinder was one of the participants in this film. A year later he made *The Marriage of Maria Braun*. The first years after the war are shown as a kind of miserable idyll; the ruins still glow with human warmth. Maria is prepared to wait for her husband, Hermann, who is missing on the eastern front. This German soldier, by the way, is the only person to emerge from the story with decency and honor. After 1948, the background noise of the jackhammers rebuilding West German cities sounds like machine-gun fire, and Maria becomes ever richer, using and abusing everyone on her way up. The film starts with a portrait of the Führer. It ends with a series of portraits of postwar chancellors, shown in negative film, as though they literally continued in Adolf Hitler's shadow.

Visions of continuity returned in 1990 with the unification of Germany. Even the language was revived. Once again there was a Zero Hour, and a currency reform, when the former subjects of the Communist Party state were handed one Deutsche Mark for every Eastern one. And again there was an outcry among intellectuals about missed opportunities, material greed, and historical amnesia. When the wall was finally pried open in the winter of 1989, the East German writer Stefan Heym was not the only one to sneer at the "materialism" of people who wanted, for the first time in their lives, to enjoy, if only vicariously at first, the affluence of the West, which Heym, as a privileged writer had been enjoying all along. Have they really learned nothing, he wondered aloud, nothing at all, after forty years of socialist education? Günter Grass called the unification an "*Anschluss*," and West German entrepreneurs were compared to the Stuka planes that dive-bombed Poland in 1939. Soon, said Heym, the slogan "One People" will become "One Reich, One People, One Führer." To lifelong "antifascists" who had always believed that the Federal Republic was the heir to Nazi Germany, unification seemed—so they said—almost like a restoration of 1933. The irony was that many Wessies saw their new

Eastern compatriots as embarrassing reminders of the same unfortunate past.

It explains, at any rate, why the unification of the two Germanys was considered a defeat by antifascists on both sides of the former border. While Günter Grass used "Auschwitz" as an argument against unification, the East German playwright Heiner Müller said in countless interviews that capitalism—"selection"—and the logic of technological and industrial progress led straight to Auschwitz and Hiroshima. Perhaps inevitably, the symbols of memory had become tools of political polemics. Rarely was the word "Auschwitz" heard more often than during the time of unification, partly as an always salutary reminder that Germans must not forget, but partly as an expression of pique that the illusion of a better, antifascist, anticapitalist, idealistic Germany, born in the ruins of 1945, and continued catastrophically for forty years in the East, had now been dashed forever.

Ludwig Erhard's almost exact counterpart in Japan was Ikeda Hayato, Minister of Finance from 1949 and Prime Minister from 1960 to 1964. His version of Erhard's "Prosperity for All" was the Double Your Incomes policy, which promised to make the Japanese twice as rich in ten years. Japan had an average growth rate of 11 percent during the 1960s. Ikeda, advised by the Detroit banker Joseph Dodge, had already succeeded by then in undoing the inflationary policies of the New Dealers who arrived in Japan with "the stationing" of General MacArthur's troops. He also had managed to deprive the Japanese trade unions of some of their considerable new powers. And he had helped to prepare the peace treaty with the United States and fifty other nations that was signed in San Francisco in 1951. These nations did not include China, which had suffered so badly from the Japanese war, or North Korea or the Soviet Union. For they were the new enemies once again, in a war that did wonders for the Japanese economy, as did the next Asian war, in Vietnam.

In 1960, hundreds of thousands demonstrated in Tokyo and other cities against the ratification of a new security pact with the United States. The pact actually reduced American powers in Japan, but it was seen as an example of American intervention nonetheless. People thought, not without reason, that the United States, in collusion with the conservative Japanese elite, was undermining the peace constitution. Ikeda's predecessor as Prime Minister, Kishi Nobusuke, forced the bill through the Japanese parliament anyway. The public temper became so heated that President Eisenhower was forced to postpone a visit to Japan, even though "patriotic" gangsters had volunteered to guard his route into town.

The point of all this is that Ikeda's promise of riches was the final stage of what came to be known as the "reverse course," the turn away from a leftist, pacifist, neutral Japan—a Japan that would never again be involved in any wars, that would resist any form of imperialism, that had, in short, turned its back for good on its bloody past. The Double Your Incomes policy was a deliberate ploy to draw public attention away from constitutional issues. And so the time of ruins was seen by people on the left as a time of missed chances and betrayal. Far from achieving a pacifist utopia of popular solidarity, they ended up with a country driven by materialism, conservatism, and selective historical amnesia. They also felt, even more than was the case in Germany, a real sense of déjà vu. Prime Minister Kishi had never been an architect, but otherwise his wartime career had been quite similar to Albert Speer's: Vice-Minister of Industry and Commerce during the 1930s, and Vice-Minister of Munitions during the war. He was arrested as a Class A war criminal but was released in 1948. His political comeback was not really remarkable at all. Very few wartime bureaucrats had been purged. Most ministries remained intact. Instead it was the Communists, who had welcomed the Americans as liberators, who were purged after 1949, the year China was "lost." In June 1951, a West German diplomat returned from Tokyo and wrote the following letter to a Minister for Economic Affairs in Bonn: "All those who were purged from their jobs in 1945–46 for political or other reasons have now resumed their work in complete freedom. In other words, everything in Japan that corresponded to what was done in Germany under the name of denazification has been laid aside. I have absolutely no doubt that in one year we will see a complete change of personnel in Japanese politics. Because of their superior discipline, a large number of our old friends will once again be taking up leading positions."

Before this happened, the Communists, and leftists in general, had been the most active advocates of purges themselves: political opponents were quickly branded as war criminals. And the Communists were absolutely opposed to what they called the emperor system. But their own dedication to democracy was not always apparent. Nor did a succession of violent strikes do much for their public image in Japan. Nonetheless, the "red purges" of 1949 and 1950 and the return to power of men whose democratic credentials were not much better helped to turn many potential Japanese friends of the United States into enemies. For the Americans were seen as promoters of the right-wing revival and the crackdown on the left. This is one reason why, of all the historical symbols to haunt future generations, Hiroshima, as an American "war crime," would be the most powerful.

Continuity is always a problem after a disastrous regime. An absolutely clean break is impossible. Zero Hour is an illusion. Cultural habits and prejudices, resulting from political propaganda, religion, or whatnot, are never easy to change, particularly when the agents of change are foreign occupiers who might not always know what they are doing. It is easier to change political institutions and hope that habits and prejudices will follow. This, however, was more easily done in Germany than in Japan. For exactly twelve years Germany was in the hands of a criminal regime, a bunch of political gangsters who had started a movement. Removing this regime was half the battle. In Japan there was never a clear break between a fascist and a prefascist past. In fact, Japan was never really a fascist state at all. There was no fascist or National Socialist ruling party, and no Führer either. The closest thing to it would have been the emperor, and whatever else he may have been, he was not a fascist dictator. Many of the men who governed Japan before the war (the war in China as well as the Pacific War) continued to do so during the war, and remained when it was over. These were discreetly autocratic bureaucrats and conservative politicians, none of whom had any of the thuggish swagger of a Göring or a Goebbels. One might say that the armed forces actually ruled Japan, but if so, the question is which armed forces, or even who in the armed forces. The chain of command was by no means clear. So, whereas after the war Germany lost its Nazi leaders, Japan lost only its admirals and generals.

There had not been a cultural break either in Japan. There were no exiled writers and artists who could return to haunt the consciences of those who had stayed. There was no Japanese Thomas Mann or Alfred Döblin. In Japan, everyone had stayed. Many former leftists officially recanted their political views during the 1930s in a formal manner known as *Tenko*, literally conversion, only to revert to their Marxism as soon as the war was over. There were writers, such as Nagai Kafu, who were privately appalled about the state of wartime Japan and scoffed in their diaries at the vulgarity of militarism. But "inner emigration" was about as close as any Japanese writer—the odd Communist aside—came to registering any kind of protest.

Among the many photographs of life in the ruins of Japan, there is one particularly striking picture. It was taken in Tokyo in 1945 by the photographer Kimura Ihei. In the foreground are three people, two women and one man, bowing in the direction of the main gate, or *torii*, of the Yasukuni Shrine. Between the bowing people and the gate is a wooden sign that says: "Off-Limits to All Allied Personnel and Vehicles." The occupation authorities had tried to suppress activities at this shrine, where the souls of men and women (mostly men) who had died for the emperor were worshipped. Enshrined here, among the spirits of millions of soldiers who had never asked to die, were the souls of men who had massacred civilians in Nanking and Manila, tortured POWs, and murdered slave workers. Yasukuni was the holiest shrine of the militarized emperor cult.

In front of the main shrine are two huge bronze lanterns, engraved with the figures of Japanese war heroes and scenes of celebrated battles. In a way that was typical of the American occupation, the shrine's keepers were ordered to deface the lanterns, even as the main object of their veneration, the emperor himself, was kept in place and carefully protected from historical scrutiny. The Shinto priests dutifully covered the reliefs with cement, which they removed without any problem in 1957. The emperor himself resumed his annual visits to the shrine in 1948, the year Kishi Nobusuke was released from jail. And here they were, this man and two women, in the cold winter of 1945, worshipping the very symbol that had brought them, and millions of others, such grief.

Yet nothing had stayed entirely the same in Japan. The trouble was that virtually all the changes were made on American orders. This was, of course, the victor's prerogative, and many changes were beneficial. But the systematic subservience of Japan meant that the country never really grew up. There is a Japanese fixation on America, an obsession which goes deeper, I believe, than German anti-Americanism, which often goes deep enough. Germany was occupied by several powers, including two European ones. Japan was effectively occupied only by the Americans. West Germany was part of NATO and the European Community, and the GDR was in the Soviet empire. Japan's only formal alliance is with the United States, through a security treaty that many Japanese have opposed. By renouncing national sovereignty, Japan became entirely dependent on the U.S. for its security. So there is still a great deal of unfinished business

with the Americans, whose political domination is keenly felt.
By now, when Japanese talk about the war at all, they usually
mean the war against the United States. Many Japanese who
had deep reservations about the war in China felt a sense of
patriotic pride when Japan attacked the United States in 1941.
Guilt about the Nanking Massacre by no means implies a similar
feeling of guilt about Pearl Harbor. Whereas the Germans are
told over and over to remember the Nazis and the Holocaust,
young Japanese think of Hiroshima and Nagasaki—and possibly Nanking, but only when prompted by liberal schoolteachers and journalists. The war in Southeast Asia is hardly
remembered at all. Older Japanese do, however, remember the
occupation, the first foreign army occupation in their national
history. But it was, for the Japanese, a very unusual army.
Whereas the Japanese armies in Asia had brought little but
death, rape, and destruction, this one came with Glenn Miller
music, chewing gum, and lessons in democracy. These blessings
left a legacy of gratitude, rivalry, and shame.

You get an idea of what it must have felt like in fiction. *American Hijiki*, a novella by Nosaka Akiyuki, is, to my mind, a masterpiece in the short history of Japanese *Trümmerliteratur*.
Nosaka was a teenager when the war ended and so was his main
character, an advertising man named Toshio. Toshio's memories of 1945 are of those chewing-gum papers glittering in the
sun, of GIs with big behinds wrapped in tight gabardine trousers, of jeeps with aerials sticking up like fishing rods, of free
food and squirts of DDT, of being tipped to provide the foreign
soldiers with girls, of saying "San-Q" (thank you) at every opportunity, of parachute drops of crates filled with tea, which
the Japanese mistook for seaweed (Hijiki) and ate with aston-
ishment at foreign eating habits. To a Japanese of Toshio's
generation, the total American victory was not just a military
disaster, it was a racial humiliation.

" 'Gibu me shigaretto, chocoreto, san-Q. No one who's had
the experience of begging from a soldier could carry on a free-
and-easy conversation with an American, I know it. Look at

those guys with their monkey faces, and the Americans with their high-bridged noses and deep-set eyes. And now all of a sudden you hear people saying the Japanese have interesting faces, beautiful skin—can they be serious? Often in a beer hall I'll see a sailor at a nearby table, or some foreigner who seems shabby if you just look at his clothes, but his face is all civilization and I catch myself staring at his three-dimensional features. Compared to the Japanese all around him, he's a shining star. Look at those muscular arms, the massive chest. How can you not feel ashamed next to him?' "

Toshio's wife, like many modern Japanese women, is less neurotic about foreigners. She made friends with an American couple on holiday in Hawaii and invited them to Tokyo. The husband, a big, bluff man named Higgins, turns out to have been in Japan before: during the occupation. He even speaks a few words of Japanese. Toshio thinks he ought to find Higgins a girl.

" 'What is it that makes me perform such service for this old man? When I'm around him, what makes me feel that I have to give everything I've got to make him happy? He comes from the country that killed my father, but I don't resent him at all. Far from it, I feel nostalgically close to him. What am I doing when I buy him drinks and women? Trying to cancel out a fourteen-year-old's terror at the sight of those huge Occupation soldiers? Paying him back for the food they sent when we were so hungry we couldn't stand it?' "

Toshio hears about a special entertainment, a sex show in which the man with the biggest penis in Japan will perform. This he must show Higgins. For surely this will impress the American guest. And so they gather in a hotel room in Sugamo, very near the place where the leading Japanese war criminals were hanged. Japan's Number One is about Toshio's age. His name is Yot-chan. His partner is about twenty-five, and presumably attractive. Still, things do not turn out well. Number One has trouble with his performance, no matter how hard he and the girl try.

"Before he knew it, Toshio was straining as if he himself had been struck impotent. 'What the hell are you doing? You're numbah one, aren't you? Come on, show this American. That huge thing of yours is the pride of Japan. Knock him out with it! Scare the shit out of him!' It was a matter of pecker nationalism: his thing had to stand, or it would mean dishonor to the race."

But it is all to no avail. Toshio understands the situation perfectly: " 'This man they call Yot-chan must be in his mid-thirties, and if so, Higgins might well have been the cause of his sudden impotence. If Yot-chan had the same sort of experience that I did in the Occupation—and he must have, whatever the differences between Tokyo and Osaka-Kobe—if he has memories of "Gibu me chewingamu," if he can recall being frightened by the soldiers' huge builds, then it's no wonder he shriveled up like that.' "

The film director Oshima Nagisa is about the same age as Nosaka and Japan's Number One. He remembers how hungry the Japanese were after the war for entertainment, anything from the outside world, where people had money, ate plenty of food, and lived in big houses, instead of among the ruins. They wanted to see America, if only in flickering images on a torn and dirty screen. But did these films teach the Japanese democracy? Oshima thinks not. Instead, he believes, Japan learned the values of "progress" and "development." Japan wanted to be just as rich as America—no, even richer: "And if we think about the extraordinary speed of postwar progress and development in Japan, perhaps we should say that the route upon which we traveled was that Union Pacific railway line which we saw in those Westerns several decades ago."

PART TWO

AUSCHWITZ

IN AN INTERVIEW with a popular German magazine, the Polish film director Andrzej Wajda made the following statement: "Germany will continue to mean, among many other things, Auschwitz. That is to say: Goethe and genocide, Beethoven and gas chambers, Kant and jackboots. All this belongs indelibly to the German heritage."

Many German intellectuals would nod their heads in agreement. Auschwitz is the past that refuses to go away, the dark blot on the national psyche. It is not just a German problem; it is part of Germany itself. The past, wrote the West German historian Christian Meier, is in our bones. "For a nation to appropriate its history," he argued, "is to look at it through the eyes of identity." What we have "internalized," he concluded, is Auschwitz.

All this rests on the assumption that there is such a thing as a national psyche. And to assume that is to believe in national community as an organic mass with history coursing through its veins. I think it is a romantic assumption, based less on history than on myth; a religious notion, expressed less through scholarship than through monuments, memorials, and historical sites turned into sacred grounds. Auschwitz is such a place, a sacred symbol of identity for Jews, Poles, and perhaps even Germans.

The question is what or whom Germans are supposed to identify with.

Like millions of others—pilgrims, tourists, identity seekers, and the merely curious—I visited Auschwitz, the museum, as well as the remains of the extermination camp of Birkenau. I was there on a warm spring day. Accounts of visits to Auschwitz rarely fail to mention nasty weather: harsh frost, or continuous, depressing drizzle, or sticky heat. But I was there on a perfectly pleasant day. The landscape was neither especially beautiful nor sinister.

I tried to imagine what it had been like inside those wooden barracks of Birkenau—hundreds of people stuffed into primitive military stables with barely room for forty. I found it impossible. It was like trying to imagine extreme hunger or having your fingernails ripped out. I knew about the suffering, but could not imagine it. The air smelled too clean, the grass outside was too fresh, the wooden bunks, crammed between thin walls—six people to one bunk, with space for two—were too neat. There were no lice, there was no mud, there was no crying, no cursing, above all no fear. (Perhaps that is why lousy weather is a cliché of Auschwitz descriptions; at least you can imagine that.)

The idea that visiting the relics of history brings the past closer is usually an illusion. The opposite is more often true. The area of the former ghetto in Warsaw was more evocative, to me, than Auschwitz, precisely because there was nothing left. The past had been obliterated. There were new, drab apartment blocks there now and patches of dirty grass. Hidden away in a grimy corner was Natan Rapoport's monument of the 1943 uprising: a bronze sculpture faced with stone blocks. (The blocks, supposed to recall the Western Wall in Jerusalem, had been meant for a different purpose. Hitler had wanted them for a victory monument in Berlin.) Someone had daubed a swastika on the monument. Someone else had tried unsuccessfully to wipe it off. There was a man with vodka on his breath selling maps of the ghetto. He was playing scratchy tunes of Israeli folk songs on a small cassette machine. In this desolation, the imagination was unhindered by relics. This is where it happened. One could imagine that, even if one couldn't imagine what it had been like.

Auschwitz, though, with the tourists taking holiday snapshots in front of the iron gate with the famous words *"Arbeit Macht Frei"* ("Freedom Through Labor"), was different. Here the past had fossilized into something monumental or, as Adorno would have put it, *museal*. I tried to search for at least a clue of what had happened. Inside those dark barracks of Birkenau, my eyes were drawn to the wooden beams supporting the crudely made roofs. Many of them had proverbs written on them in German, the kind of thing you see on walls of Bavarian farmhouses or old-fashioned beer mugs, often in Gothic script—"Cleanliness is next to godliness"—and so on. I don't know whether these maxims, to be read by people whose only duty was to die, were meant as a joke. Perhaps not. Perhaps the folkish sentimentality was part of the culture of violence and death. The SS officers liked to hear music—waltzes, tangos, light opera tunes—as they murdered their slaves. The roads to many German concentration camps had signposts with traditionally styled wood carvings, the kind that normally depict fairy-tale characters or forest gnomes. Only, these showed SS men beating bearded Jews.

George Steiner, in an essay on Günter Grass, wrote: "One comes to understand how the sheer grossness of German pleasures—the bursting sausages and flowered chamber pots, the beer-warmers and the fat men in tight leather shorts—was the ideal terrain for the sadistic-sentimental brew of Nazism."

Stephen Spender, writing in 1945, made a slightly more subtle point: "These *Sprichwörter* [proverbs] are characteristic of German seriousness, German piety, German good intentions, German self-congratulation, the desire to label every environment with a few inches of thought sliced out of the Bible or the Poets or the Classics, the desire at the same time to reduce thought to a common denominator of banality, the desire, at the worst, of the devil to quote scripture."

Were the crimes of Auschwitz, then, part of the German "identity"? Was genocide a product of some ghastly flaw in German culture, the key to which might be found in the sentimental proverbs, the cruel fairy tales, the tight leather shorts? The danger here is to confuse the forms of German atrocities with their causes. It is, of course, generally true that mawkishness and brutality go together. Sentimentality, after all, is a substitute for feeling. Banal homilies and a beery sense of fun certainly lent a grotesque air to German crimes, but do they really explain them?

As I read the proverbs inside the Birkenau barracks, I noticed something curious about them: they appeared to have been freshly painted, almost as though the camp had only just been vacated. Was this for the benefit of the tourists? A touch of authenticity, like the reconstructed barracks in Buchenwald ("absolutely real," assured my guide, as he pressed his heels onto the squeaky wooden floorboards)? Later I realized what had happened: a few months before I visited the camp, it had been used as a location for a Hollywood film production. One of the stars in that production, Willem Dafoe, said in an interview that he had grown accustomed to the place: ". . . it becomes where you work. It becomes a movie set."

Kitsch is forever waiting to spring its trap in Auschwitz-Birkenau. Kitsch puffs up the banal by injecting it with the hot air of religiosity. Kitsch emotions are always false. To visit the site of suffering, any description of which cannot adequately express the horror, is upsetting, not because one gets closer to knowing what it was actually like to be a victim, but because such visits stir up emotions one cannot trust. It is tempting to take on the warm moral glow of identification—so easily done and so presumptuous—with the victims: there but for the grace of God go I, and so on. Places of horror hold a fascination which can all too easily slip into a form of masochistic pleasure. The imagination turns toward a morbid desire to be horrified. It is perhaps the hardest form of kitsch to resist, especially if one was brought up, as Oda Makoto, the peace activist, put it, from the point of view of the victims.

And yet the imagination is the only way to identify with the past. Only in the imagination—not through statistics, documents, or even photographs—do people come alive as individuals, do stories emerge, instead of History. The inevitable gap between what happened and its representation through the imagination can result in kitsch, to be sure. But is the fear of kitsch, so often voiced by German artists and intellectuals, a sign of moral fastidiousness where Auschwitz is concerned, or does it point to a fear of identification—with the aggressors or with the culture that nurtured them?

Kitsch can, of course, be a deliberate ploy, as in the films of Hans-Jürgen Syberberg. He believes that "in kitsch, in banality, in triviality and their popularity lie the remaining rudiments and germ cells of the vanished traditions of our myths . . ." Hitler, he argues, understood this and knew how to activate the latent power of mythical kitsch. Syberberg, whose movie *Hitler: A Film from Germany* is a kind of delirious ode to such kitsch, thinks that the denial of German irrationalism and kitschy mythology robs Germany of its identity: "Hitler is to be fought, not with the statistics of Auschwitz or with sociological analyses of the Nazi economy, but with Richard Wagner and Mozart."

In the midst of much woolly nonsense, Syberberg has hit upon one insight (perhaps he even exemplifies it): it is still difficult to sever in our minds the banal horror of Auschwitz from the kitschy glamour of the Nazi style. Syberberg expresses the legacy of Auschwitz by wallowing in the style, as though German *Kultur* can be saved, as it were, by deconstructing the mythology, by purifying it of its bloodstained history. He is trying to redefine the German identity, rather in the way that Mishima Yukio did in Japan. But, as with Mishima's suicidal fantasies, his films leave you with the uneasy feeling that he identifies rather too readily with the ideals that at one time made the Germans such a dangerous people.

But Hans-Jürgen Syberberg is a maverick in Germany. His anguished rescue operation of the German identity from the greedy clutches of Americanized materialists and rootless Jews finds favor in the rancid pages of the extreme right-wing *National-Zeitung*. His collected essays were recommended together with picture books of Stukas and tanks—an odd place to be for this romantic aesthete. But he is shunned by the liberal intelligentsia. The temptation for those who grew up among the aggressors would not be to seek identification, but, on the contrary, to keep a distance, through silence, cliché, denial, abstraction, scholarship, busyness, or gestures of ritualized penance.

Peter Weiss visited Auschwitz in 1964 as part of a group of West German judges and prosecutors who were collecting data for the Auschwitz trial in Frankfurt. Their brief was to check up on the witness accounts. Men busily took out tape measures to determine the exact width of the railway ramp, or the precise distance from the ramp to the wash barracks of the women's camp. One witness claimed she had heard prisoners screaming in the punishment cells. These "standing cells" (height: 2 meters; size: 50 by 50 cm; air vent: 5 by 8 cm) guaranteed a slow death through starvation and lack of air. The bodies of the dead had to be scraped out of the cells with iron pitchforks. Some of the victims had eaten their own fingers.

To check the plausibility of the witness's claim, a judge ordered his assistant to wriggle into a standing cell and make a noise. Perhaps, the judge suggested through the tiny air vent, he could sing something. The young man, dressed in a neat suit, did as he was told. His voice was clearly audible: he sang Schubert's "Sah ein Knab' ein Röslein stehn."

The judges were doing their work. Distance was built into their job. They were not there to do penance, to deal with "Auschwitz" as a metaphor, to be tourists, or to empathize with the victims. They were there to sift the evidence, to decide whether the view of the crematorium from one of the prisoners' blocks was obstructed or not, to determine whether a charred tree proved that bodies had been burned (or, as the protocol had to say, allegedly burned) in an adjacent pit. They were there to measure the past in centimeters.

Twenty-seven years later I wandered around that very same spot. It was now part of the Auschwitz museum, in what used to be the main camp, the one whose solid brick buildings fooled the Red Cross into thinking conditions weren't so bad, really. The museum was divided into blocks, each containing an exhibition of photographs and memorabilia having to do with the Nazi occupation of specific nations. There was a Polish block, a Hungarian block, a Soviet block, a Dutch block, etc.

The Polish exhibition was the most harrowing, though for me perhaps not the most poignant. The photographs of Dutch Jews being rounded up and deported affected me most. But not because they were particularly gruesome. There was nothing in the Dutch block like the photographs of the Warsaw ghetto going up in flames, with grinning SS men in the foreground watching burning people jump to their deaths. Rather, it was the normality, the banal familiarity of the scenery, the streets, the houses, the railway stations, that struck me with such force. The people being herded into the trains looked familiar. I had grown up in those streets. Here again identification plays tricks upon the imagination. There seemed to be something particularly outrageous about the fact that these well-dressed, well-educated, middle-class Dutch Jews were being treated in this manner.

I wondered what it must be like for a German to see these pictures. What pitfalls of the imagination lay in wait for one who was told to "internalize" Auschwitz, without being able to identify so easily with the victims, for one whose father might have been one of those smirking SS men in the ghetto. A German acquaintance of roughly my age, a post-68er, told me that his visit, in 1974, had been the worst day of his life. That, he said, as well as his Christian education, had made him refuse to serve in the army.

As I walked from photograph to photograph in the Polish block, wondering what had happened in these rooms long before they were converted to the clean, white-walled museum rooms of today, I encountered a group of German tourists, mostly people in their fifties and sixties. They would have been teenagers during the war. A Polish woman in her thirties was guiding them. The photographs spoke for themselves. Yet the guide quietly explained in fluent German what people were seeing: giggling soldiers watching elderly rabbis crawling on their knees, Himmler peering through an eyehole to inspect the efficacy of the gas chambers, children driven through the ghetto with rifle butts, bony corpses piled high. The tourists looked stricken as they silently shuffled from one outrage to the next. Suddenly one of them became agitated. She was a woman of about sixty, in a green hat, a beige twin set, and thick brown shoes. She went up to the guide and clutched her arm: "You must understand," she said, "we knew nothing about this, *wir haben nichts gewusst . . .*" The guide looked at the woman and said, quietly and contemptuously: "I'm sorry, but I cannot believe you. I honestly cannot believe you."

"But you must," said the woman, "you must. We really didn't know . . ."

She may have been right. She may not have known anything. Perhaps it even showed a measure of decency that she was so anxious for the Polish guide to realize this. That she was there at all must have been proof of some willingness to face the past. One only wished she had remained silent, instead of using the words which too many Germans had used before.

Auschwitz is a museum, but it is also much more than that. The Polish institution responsible for the site, under the Communist regime, was called the Council for the Preservation of Monuments to Resistance and Martyrdom. We know what was meant by resistance: the brave struggle against fascism by patriotic Communists. And those who fell in this struggle were the official martyrs of fascism. Auschwitz was turned into a museum by a Polish government decree on July 2, 1947: "On the site of the former Nazi concentration camp a Monument of the Martyrdom of the Polish Nation and of Other Nations is to be erected for all times to come."

There were monuments to the antifascist resistance all over the Communist world. The monument at Buchenwald, near Weimar, in the former German Democratic Republic, is one of the most grandiose examples: heroic stone figures breaking the chains of fascist slavery and forging ahead toward a glorious future of peace and brotherly solidarity. The Rapoport monument in Warsaw shows, on a more modest scale, a similar configuration of muscles and chains. The leader of the uprising, Mordechai Anielewicz, is cast in bronze as a typical proletarian hero: bare-chested, rolled-up sleeves, a hand grenade held up like a hammer. On the rear of the monument is a different image: Jewish martyrs, including a rabbi holding a Torah, marching passively to their deaths. The dedication, inscribed at the base in Hebrew, is to "The Jewish People, Its Heroes and Martyrs."

There is nothing heroic at Auschwitz. The focus is on martyrdom. The prison cells in Block 11, where many died of torture, have become shrines to martyrdom. Wreaths and candles commemorate the martyrs—mostly Communists, until the post-Communist government began to change the focus of the museum. Martyrdom implies faith, in an ideal, in nationhood, in God. A martyr's death is terrible but it is instilled with deep meaning. Primo Levi's nightmare of surviving in a silent world which refuses to listen is bad enough. The idea of millions of people murdered for nothing is unbearable. The temptation is to invent meaning, by calling them martyrs, by erecting crosses, by engaging in religious ritual.

The ritual can be quite specific, but it can also be oddly abstract. I spent some time inside the crematorium of the main camp, examining, as many had done before me, the primitive oven. Later, more efficient ovens were installed in the Birkenau death camp designed by J. A. Topf & Sons. The firm had applied to the German government in 1942 for a patent for their "crematory oven for massive requirements, functioning without interruption." The patent was finally granted, after a renewed application, in 1953.

I was standing around with several tourists, mostly Americans. No one said much. A couple whispered, as though we were in a chapel. The silence was broken by a peculiar noise which seemed to be coming our way from the outside, something that sounded like "ushoi! ushoi!" The noise grew louder and then stopped. A tall man stepped into the crematorium, brandishing a feathered staff. He looked Oriental, Mongolian perhaps. He was followed by a group of mostly young people. Among them were several Germans and Japanese. One Japanese woman in denim overalls played softly on a tambourine. A banner was unfurled. "Walking for peace," it read. Leaflets were handed out, showing the route of the peace walk through Europe. Various atrocities were mentioned, for which we were told to atone: the extermination of Native Americans, the Vietnam War, Hiroshima. The leader of the group, the tall man with the feathered staff, was a Native American, named, I believe, Red Hawk. When the group had assembled inside, Red Hawk lifted his staff and in a deep voice began to chant a kind of prayer. The tambourine played, feathers fluttered, eyes closed in devotion.

Just outside the walls of the main camp, near this crematorium, stood a large wooden cross. It was erected by Carmelite nuns in 1989, next to a drab red-brick building, which the nuns had turned into a convent. The building, built in 1914, used to be called the Theater. Entertainments were staged there for Austro-Hungarian soldiers stationed in the barracks next door. The Nazis used it to store Zyklon B gas canisters. The intention of the Carmelites, a devout Catholic told me, was to pray for all the victims, Jewish and Gentile. But this so outraged a New York rabbi named Avraham Weiss that he turned up with six of his followers to protest. They had dressed up in striped prayer shawls and tried to storm the convent. Polish workers then sprayed the protesters with cold water and tore off their skullcaps. This image swiftly went around the world. Auschwitz, the *anus mundi*, had become a squalid battlefield where people fought over the symbols of martyrdom.

Rabbi Weiss is a supporter of Gush Emunim, an association of religious settlers in Israel, settlers, that is, who believe in their right to claim land for religious reasons. History to him is symbolic,˙ mythical, an indispensable compass in the continuing search for national identity. His view of history is exclusive. The Carmelites, in his opinion, were intruders in a place that has unique significance as the supreme symbol of Jewish suffering. The Christian cross—under which so much of this suffering was not only condoned but encouraged—was seen as an affront to the memory of the Holocaust.

But it was not quite the struggle between national or Jewish identity and the universal values claimed by the Carmelite nuns. Auschwitz, said the Archbishop of Brussels, is on "Polish Christian ground." To Jozef Cardinal Glemp, the Primate of Poland, a Pole was almost by definition a Christian. After Rabbi Weiss took on the nuns, Glemp said that "Polish feelings and our hard-won Polish sovereignty had been offended" by Jews who "control the mass media in many countries."

The Germans have no religious symbols of identity at Auschwitz. That is only for those who can claim the victims as their own. But there are other ways in which Germans can pray at the shrine. They can help to pay for its upkeep. The Auschwitz museum is fraying at the edges: the piles of shoes that once belonged to Jewish children are covered with mold, the crematorium is rusting. So a German television program called *Panorama* asked its viewers to donate money to preserve the camp as a warning to future generations. About 110,000 marks was collected. This may not seem much, compared with some other fund-raising efforts on television, but it must be one of the few cases where money was collected for the sake of memory alone. There were, however, also letters addressed to the television producer, such as this one, anonymous of course: "I too am in favor of preserving Auschwitz. I would like it to be made fully operative again, so people like you can be 'freed through labor.' We can also find a solution for all these political asylum seekers. I volunteer to donate 50 kg of gas [Zyklon B]."

In the first two decades after the war, few Germans were keen to preserve the sites of Nazi crimes at all. But there are many Germans now, especially in the West, who regard the maintenance of former concentration camps as a sacred duty. A number of the main camps have become *Gedenkstätte* (places of remembrance). Like Auschwitz, they are museums, shrines, and tourist spots, all in one.

When you drive into Fürstenberg, a pretty, run-down little town in Brandenburg north of Berlin, you are greeted by two signs. One reads: "Fürstenberg greets its visitors." The other shows the way to the town's main attraction, the former Ravensbrück concentration camp, where 130,000 people, mostly women and children, were imprisoned between 1939 and 1945. Half of them died.

The National Warning and Memorial Place Ravensbrück was a monument, as my guidebook still stated, in pure East German style, to "our dead sisters, the immortal heroines of the antifascist struggle, who gave their lives for the freedom and independence of their countries and a happy future of all peoples."

In 1992 most of the camp was out of bounds, since it was still a Russian Army base. Troops from the former Soviet Union were selling their uniforms and other junk from their former lives to tourists outside the main gate. The former SS homes were occupied by officers and their families. The privates lived in the barracks of the old camp.

Along the cobblestoned road to the camp, about half a mile from the main gate, stood Sylvia's Sauna and Fitness Center. Opposite Sylvia's Sauna was a half-finished modern building. It was meant to be a brand-new supermarket, the first ever in Fürstenberg. But Gertrud Müller, chairwoman of the German Camp Society Ravensbrück, protested: "This memorial place must never be desecrated." She used the word *entweihen* (to rob something of its sacred nature). More protest followed, almost entirely from the western part of Germany, and the supermarket project had to be abandoned. The government of Brandenburg took swift action to avoid further embarrassment. A new supermarket was to be built elsewhere. A pleasant spot was selected near a large cemetery and crematorium on the other side of town. The controversy died. Later on, one of the guards of the cemetery told a German magazine reporter that this pleasant spot was where the SS had burned the bodies of their prisoners, when Ravensbrück still lacked its own ovens.

"It is barbarous to write a poem after Auschwitz," wrote Theodor Adorno. People have interpreted this in different ways. What I think he meant was that the poet, wrapped up in "private and complacent contemplation," could never find words to express the mechanized, soulless, industrial brutality of Auschwitz. Besides, poetry is a creation of pleasure and beauty and thus inappropriate as an expression of mass murder.

There is much to be said against Adorno's statement, which, in any case, he revised himself in later years. But it does appear as though German artists—filmmakers, playwrights, novelists, as well as poets—have, with very few exceptions, taken his words to heart. There are hardly any novels, plays, or films that deal directly with the Holocaust, neither in East Germany, where there were political reasons, nor in the West, where there were none. I do not mean documentaries, history books, exhibitions, or witness accounts. There has been no lack of these, in the former Federal Republic at any rate. I am speaking only about works of the imagination.

The exceptions are interesting for what they reveal about the silent or at best the oblique mainstream. The most famous poem about the death camps is "Todesfuge" ("Death Fugue," 1945) by Paul Celan. It is written in the lilting rhythm of a dance tune, echoing the cruel game played by the camp *Kommandant* in the poem, who orders Jews to play music as others dig their own graves: "Jab your spades deeper there, you others play on for the dance."

"Todesfuge" has become a classic, published in West German schoolbooks. Every educated German knows the famous line: *"Der Tod ist ein Meister aus Deutschland"* ("Death is a master from Germany"). But its reception in Germany has been ambivalent. Was the poem perhaps a bit too lyrical, a bit too pleasurable to the ear? Did it not end up sweetening the horror instead of expressing it? Paul Celan himself felt ambivalent, and in the late 1960s he asked editors to remove it from anthologies. And yet Celan's poem remains, for me, the most moving statement on the Holocaust. Its beauty as a poem does not anesthetize the sense of horror it conveys. On the contrary, it makes us feel it all the more.

Paul Celan was not only outside the mainstream of postwar German literature because of his work; he was not even German. He was born in Romania of Jewish parents. His mother taught him German, the language of those who would later order her death. Celan said that German passed "through the thousand darknesses of death-dealing utterance." He traveled to Germany, to visit friends, to collect prizes. But language really was his only link, language and history, of the most devastating kind. In 1970, he killed himself in Paris.

Peter Weiss wrote a play based on the testimonies in the Auschwitz trial, entitled *Die Ermittlung* (*The Investigation*, 1965). It is a kind of prose poem, using mostly documentary material. But although it describes in detail the atrocities that took place, it is written from a Marxist point of view. The specific suffering of the Jews is dissolved into a general narrative of class struggle. The words "Jew" and "Jewish" (let alone "Gypsy") are not mentioned anywhere. As Peter Demetz puts it in his book *After the Fires*, Weiss has reduced "Auschwitz to a place without Jews."

Like Celan, Weiss was Jewish. And like Celan's, his relationship with Germany was tenuous. Weiss lived abroad much of his life and for some time wrote in Swedish. He did not, in his work at least, identify with the victims of Auschwitz as a Jew. Nor, ostensibly, did he regard Auschwitz as a specifically German crime. He was too much of a Marxist for that: he thought in terms of structures, economics, and class interests, not nations or cultures. But he was interested in the postwar German "identity" nonetheless. Weiss saw structural and philosophical continuities of the Third Reich spilling into the Federal Republic. He wanted his play to be the beginning of a mass movement in West Germany. Only through years of massive "spiritual labor," he thought, could the German people free themselves from their "psychosis." Weiss, then, did believe in a national psyche.

One of the most famous plays about the destruction of the Jews, *Der Stellvertreter* (*The Deputy*, 1963), was written by Rolf Hochhuth, a German Gentile and a Protestant. It is a flawed piece, in which the Jews are mere pawns in a bitter critique of the Vatican's complicity in their murder. The theme is not so much historical, cultural, or national as theological: the struggle between God and the devil in the hearts of priests. The scenes set in Auschwitz, in which Dr. Mengele is cast as a seductive Mephistopheles in a black silk cape, are clumsy. And yet the play was a rare and brave attempt at imagining Auschwitz, which in Germany received a frosty critical reception. One of Hochhuth's few literary supporters at the time, the critic Marcel Reich-Ranicki, wrote that German writers had been reduced to an uncomfortable silence by Hochhuth's play, because they were aware of their own failure to address the theme at all.

But it is also true that, as Peter Demetz says, "there is not a single aspect of German life and letters that remains unaffected by the legacy of Auschwitz." At least it was true of the Federal Republic. There are many references to the Holocaust in postwar German fiction, but most are oblique or metaphorical. Writers in the 1950s and 1960s, such as Heinrich Böll and Siegfried Lenz, were even reluctant to refer to the Nazis by their name. Böll called them "the buffalo eaters" and their victims "the lambs." Lenz, in his novel *Deutschstunde* (*The German Lesson*,

1968), wrote about "the men in leather coats" or simply "the authorities in Berlin." In 1964, Alexander Kluge, a filmmaker and writer of the early postwar generation, talked about his difficulty in depicting the Holocaust: "One cannot really describe it," he said. "However, it is possible, even terribly necessary to take stock. Make inventories. I attempt to erect fences. I hope that the reader's imagination can move between those fences."

Certainly a well-chosen metaphor can stir the imagination more than a direct description. The sudden whistle of a train on the sidings of the Oswiecim (Auschwitz) railway station evokes more menace than a tour of the museum. But the reluctance in German fiction to look Auschwitz in the face, the almost universal refusal to deal with the Final Solution outside the shrine, the museum, or the schoolroom, suggests a fear of committing sacrilege. It is as though the *anus mundi* were the face of God, as though any attempt to draw the image of the unimaginable or inexpressible would trivialize its sacred nature. It is all right to let the witnesses speak, in the courtroom, in the museums, on videotape (Claude Lanzmann's *Shoah* has been shown many times on German television), but it is not all right for German artists to use their imagination.

In the winter of 1992 a film entitled *Hitlerjunge Salomon* (*Hitler Youth Salomon*) was shown in Germany. This movie, entitled *Europa, Europa* elsewhere, was a success in the United States. The story was based on a true survivor's tale.

Salomon Perel was born in Germany as the son of a Polish Jew. He escaped to Poland with his family and survived the war by pretending to be an overseas German, a *Volksdeutsche*. He was adopted by a Nazi officer, who placed him in a Nazi elite school. There is some wallowing in Nazi kitsch here: absurd uniforms and demented speeches, forest love scenes with blond Nazi maidens, and Hitler Youth singing about Jewish blood splattering from German knives. But much of this was true to the facts.

During his school holidays, Salomon tried to get a glimpse of his lost parents by riding a tram through the Lodz ghetto, where he thought they might be. The tram windows were painted white, so that German passengers were spared the sight of dying Jews, but Salomon manages to see through the cracks, and so does the audience. What we see is neither a cliché nor kitsch, but an impression of reconstructed hell. The picture ends with an appearance of the real Salomon Perel, in Israel, where he now lives. He sings a Hebrew song. (Now, *this* was kitsch.)

Hitlerjunge Salomon did not have much success in Germany. The filmmaker Volker Schlöndorff saw this as proof of a silent boycott. When it was turned down as the official German entry for the Oscar competition, the Polish director of the film, Agnieszka Holland, was outraged. It was a German production, she said, and the refusal to enter the picture was yet another German attempt to deny the past. *Der Spiegel* thought the film might have embarrassed people because it "broke a German taboo." Salomon's character didn't fit the philosemitic image of the good Jew, a stock figure in much postwar German fiction.

It was, in fact, never clear why the film was not entered for the Oscars. The German selection committee said that since the director was Polish, the film was not technically German. The leftish *Frankfurter Rundschau* newspaper called this argument "formalism," reminiscent of the "formalism of pure race."

Perhaps the committee was being bureaucratic, or maybe the theme was too embarrassing. But it is striking how often, in conversation with Germans who had seen the film, I heard the fear of kitsch expressed. The *Frankfurter Allgemeine Zeitung*, usually quick on the draw when German honor is impugned, ran an article saying that *Hitlerjunge Salomon* was simply a bad film. It was a cheap melodrama, the critic wrote, a travesty of innocent-abroad stories. The schmaltzy music and tawdry sets were not up to the theme. But what is up to the theme? There is a point at which aesthetic fastidiousness becomes an alibi for not depicting the theme at all.

But beneath the fear of bad taste or sacrilege may lie a deeper problem. To imagine people in the past as people of flesh and blood, not as hammy devils in silk capes, is to humanize them. To humanize is not necessarily to excuse or to sympathize, but it does demolish the barriers of abstraction between us and them. We could, under certain circumstances, have been them. This is not a great problem for an artist (or an audience) who identifies naturally with the victims. For a Jewish writer to imagine an SS officer at Auschwitz is not to run the risk of contamination. For a non-Jewish German, told to internalize Auschwitz as a German crime, the problem is real. It is one thing to do as many German authors, from Günter Grass in the West to Christa Wolf in the East, have done: to humanize small Nazi functionaries in provincial towns far removed from the centers of mass murder; it is quite another thing to find something in common with the butchers themselves. To pull this off one would first have to imagine the past from the point of view of the victim.

In his preface to *Das Brandopfer* (*The Burnt Offering*, 1954), "one of the very few pieces of high literature to concern itself with the full horror of the past" (George Steiner), the author, Albrecht Goes, made the following remarkable statement: "As the teller of this story . . . I shall never as long as I live cease to shudder at the thought that all those death orders (by Heydrich, Eichmann, et al.) were issued in the language in which I think, speak, write, and dream. Despite this, I have told my story in a hushed voice, but not without a certain strength. It is a borrowed strength, certainly—one peculiar to Israel. It is based on the bond, which has enabled the 'children of Israel,' also known as the 'children of Zion,' to survive in this world: a bond which they know lasts forever."

The story, about a pregnant Jewish woman who is forced, on the eve of her arrest, to leave the baby carriage of her unborn child to a Gentile shopkeeper's wife, is indeed exceptional in its choice of subject. (*Das Brandopfer* is the literal German translation of Shoah, or Holocaust.) But its philosemitism is not at all unusual for a German of the author's generation. The heroine, or rather the victim, of his story is not simply a German

Jewish woman; she is "a child of the prophets." It is as though to tell the story of the Holocaust, Goes had to adopt the mythical identity of the victims.

Perhaps even more remarkable is the novel by Wolfgang Koeppen entitled *Jacob Littners Aufzeichnungen aus einem Erdloch* (*Jacob Littner's Notes from a Hole in the Ground*). It was published in 1948 under the name of Jacob Littner, and republished in 1992 under Koeppen's own name. Koeppen also wrote three famous novels in the 1950s about Nazi traumas in postwar Germany.

Jacob Littner was in fact more than a literary character. He was a Jewish stamp dealer in Munich who survived the war and the "liquidation" of the ghetto of Zbaraz in Poland by bribing a Polish antisemite to allow him to live—if that is the right word—in a dark, stinking hole under the Pole's house. He told his story to a publisher in Munich, before moving to New York. The publisher took a few notes, which formed the basis of Koeppen's novel. Koeppen was paid for his work by Littner himself, who sent him food parcels from New York. Here, then, is a German Gentile who literally adopted a Jewish identity to tell the story of the Holocaust.

Maybe it could not—certainly in those early days—have been done in any other way. But even under a Jewish name, the author could not resist the temptation to end on an abstract, religious note. Throughout most of the book, the language is sober, the descriptions of the horror are concrete. But it ends like this: "Hate is a terrible word . . . I hate no one. I don't even hate the guilty. I have suffered their persecution, but I do not presume to be their judge. My refusal and inability to act as a judge also means this, however: I must not forgive, I must not exonerate the guilty. What they did, in my opinion, is beyond human judgment. Only God is able to judge inhuman crimes . . ."

Three years after the war it was not up to Germans to ask for the suspension of human judgment. Only the victims could do that. But the flight into religious abstraction was to be all too common among Germans of the Nazi generation, as well as their children; not, as is so often the case with Jews, to lend mystique to a new identity, as a patriotic Zionist, but on the contrary to escape from being the heir to a peculiarly German crime, to get away from having to "internalize" Auschwitz, or indeed from being German at all.

Then came *Holocaust*. The virtual taboo against depicting Auschwitz was broken, not by German artists, but by a Hollywood soap opera, a work of skillful pop, which penetrated the German imagination in a way nothing had before. *Holocaust* was first shown in Germany in January 1979. It was seen by 20 million people, about half the adult population of the Federal Republic; 58 percent wanted it to be repeated; 12,000 letters, telegrams, and postcards were sent to the broadcasting stations; 5,200 called the stations by telephone after the first showing; 72.5 percent were positive, 7.3 percent negative. An article by Heinz Hoehne in *Der Spiegel* said it all: "An American television series, made in a trivial style, produced more for commercial than for moral reasons, more for entertainment than for enlightenment, accomplished what hundreds of books, plays, films, and television programs, thousands of documents, and all the concentration camp trials have failed to do in the more than three decades since the end of the war: to inform Germans about crimes against Jews committed in their name, so that millions were emotionally touched and moved."

Holocaust was never shown in the German Democratic Republic, but people in the border areas could tune in to the Western stations. And they did, even though it was officially forbidden. In 1992 I asked a schoolteacher in what used to be East Berlin whether she had seen the series. She said she had. Was it discussed at school? No, it was not, for then teachers and pupils would have had to admit that they had broken the law. So people pretended they had not seen *Holocaust*? Yes, said the history teacher, but in any case "the Jewish problem did not exist for our children. Now we have to teach them about it, but they don't even understand what made the Jews special, or why Hitler wanted to exterminate them. You see, over here we are not very knowledgeable about the Bible, neither the Old nor the New Testament."

In the Federal Republic, *Holocaust* shocked and angered a number of West German intellectuals. It was the usual fear of kitsch, as well as a suspicion of "Hollywood values," often short-hand for "Amerika." The *Frankfurter Rundschau* worried that it commercialized the horrors of the past: Auschwitz as "an article of consumption." Edgar Reitz, the director of the far more sophisticated soap opera *Heimat*, complained that "the Americans have stolen our history through *Holocaust*," because films in the style of *Holocaust* prevented Germans from "taking narrative possession of our past, from breaking free of the world of judgments." In fact, *Holocaust* had done no such thing. German artists themselves had failed to find a narrative for Auschwitz.

There were hate letters sent to the broadcasters, usually anonymously, which called *Holocaust* a pack of Jewish lies. The whole thing was a Jewish trick to make money by having the Germans look bad. The late Prime Minister of Bavaria, Franz Josef Strauss, was of this opinion, or at least he said he was. But so, from a different angle, were some leftist intellectuals, to whom Hollywood commercialism was the root of all evil. There is a school of thought in Germany whose explanation for Auschwitz is based on a contempt for commercialism and what is loosely termed "modernity"—post-Enlightenment rationalism, mass production, capitalism, etc. "Auschwitz," said the East German playwright Heiner Müller in an interview, "is the last stage of the Enlightenment." More than that, "Auschwitz is the altar of capitalism. Rationality as the only binding criterion reduces man to his material worth." Once again, forms and substance are confused: even if the methods of the Holocaust could be called industrial, even rational, the reasons for it certainly could not.

Intellectuals such as Müller or Syberberg or Adorno were right to be awed by the power of mass culture. Yet the impact of *Holocaust* in Germany, in particular, is not hard to explain. The Auschwitz of the courtroom, the chapel, or the museum had been an abstraction, a metaphor, a bunch of unimaginable statistics, the death of millions with no name. With *The Diary of Anne Frank* it was as though one of the nameless dead had risen from the mass grave and assumed an identity. The family of Dr. Josef Weiss, even in the incarnation of American soap opera characters, had an identity every German could recognize: solid, educated, middle-class. They could have been your neighbors; in fact, they *were* your neighbors, if you were of a certain age.

Holocaust proved that metaphors and allusions were not enough to bring history alive. The Weiss family had to be invented, the past reenacted. The soap opera form had such a powerful effect because it was the opposite of Brechtian alienation: emotions are boosted, identification is enforced. We feel we know personally our favorite soap opera characters, just as we feel on intimate terms with a popular talk show host. Yet it is precisely that kind of identification that much postwar German art and literature has shied away from. Identification with the Jewish victims could not be done with real conviction; identification with the persecutors—that is, with your parents, your grandparents, or yourself—was too painful.

How German viewers, or most non-German viewers for that matter, would have taken to *Holocaust* had the main characters not been educated, middle-class Germans, but, let us say, poor Romanian Gypsies, is an interesting question. I rather doubt that the impact would have been the same. Identification clearly has its limits.

"After *Holocaust*," wrote a West German woman to her local television station, "I feel deep contempt for those beasts of the Third Reich. I am twenty-nine years old and a mother of three children. When I think of the many mothers and children sent to the gas chambers, I have to cry. (Even today the Jews are not left in peace. We Germans have the duty to work every day for peace in Israel.) I bow to the victims of the Nazis, and I am ashamed to be a German."

Judging from the many letters published after *Holocaust*, this was a fairly typical response. A good number of people born after the war felt ashamed to be German. It would appear to confirm Christian Meier's thesis that history is "in our bones," that we carry the sins of our fathers on our backs, that history is in our blood. It is true that Germans were responsible for Auschwitz. But is shame in future generations of Germans a suitable or even a useful response? The novelist Martin Walser, who was a child during the war, believes, like Meier, that Auschwitz binds the German people, as does the language of Goethe. When a Frenchman or an American sees pictures of Auschwitz, "he doesn't have to think: We human beings! He can think: Those Germans! Can we think: Those Nazis! I for one cannot . . ."

This is the language of a man who is troubled by national identity. Adorno, a German Jew who wished to save high German culture, on whose legacy the Nazis left their bloody finger marks, resisted the idea that Auschwitz was a German crime. To him it was a matter of modern pathology, the sickness of the "authoritarian personality," of the dehumanized SS guards, those inhumane cogs in a vast industrial wheel. Is there no alternative to these opposing views? I believe there is.

Auschwitz was a German crime, to be sure. "Death is a master from Germany." But it was a different Germany. To insist on viewing history through the "eyes of identity," to repeat the historian Christian Meier's phrase, is to resist the idea of change. Can one internalize Auschwitz from the point of view of the aggressors without falling prey to kitsch emotions of false guilt or even false pride? To assume that Auschwitz was caused by some awful flaw in the German identity, just as a streak of collective German genius produced Goethe and Brahms, is to perpetuate a kind of neurotic narcissism: at best a constant worry that the Germans are a dangerous people, at worst a perverse pride in an almost tribal capacity for sublime music and unspeakable crimes.

HIROSHIMA

BETWEEN THE FORMER Japanese and Italian embassies in Berlin, both built in the 1930s in the pompous classico-fascist style of Hitler's dream city of Germania, runs a short, narrow street that used to be called the Graf-Spee-Strasse, after the German admiral, who died in 1914, in a battle with the British Navy off the Falkland Islands. Like many streets and squares in Berlin —Adolf-Hitler-Platz, Hermann-Göring-Strasse, etc.—it was renamed after the war. It is now called the Hiroshimastrasse.

This choice of name, said to have annoyed the Italians considerably, had nothing to do with the Japanese. The left-wing Berlin senate chose it as an expression of its pacifism. But even if the Japanese had no part in this, it perfectly caught the prevailing *Geist* of postwar Japan. To the majority of Japanese, Hiroshima is the supreme symbol of the Pacific War. All the suffering of the Japanese people is encapsulated in that almost sacred word: Hiroshima. But it is more than a symbol of national martyrdom; Hiroshima is a symbol of absolute evil, often compared to Auschwitz. There is a Hiroshima-Auschwitz Committee in Hiroshima. In at least one novel about Hiroshima, the Japanese and the Jews are singled out as the prime victims of white racism. There was even a plan, in the late 1980s, to build an Auschwitz memorial in a small town near Hiroshima.

The atom bomb attack on August 6, 1945, was, in the words

of a Hiroshima University professor, Saika Tadayoshi, "the worst sin committed in the twentieth century." Professor Saika was the author of the famous inscription on the A-Bomb Cenotaph in Hiroshima Peace Park, built around a stone coffin containing the names of A-bomb victims: "Let all the souls here rest in peace; for we shall not repeat the evil."

The phrasing is deliberately vague. But lest visitors to the Peace Park think that "we" refers exclusively to the Japanese government during the war, a sign was put up in the early 1980s to clarify the matter, in English and Japanese: "It summons people everywhere to pray for the repose of the souls of the deceased A-bomb victims and to join in the pledge never to repeat the evil of war. It thus expresses the 'heart of Hiroshima,' which, enduring past grief and overcoming hatred, yearns for the realization of world peace."

Hiroshima (the name is often written in the phonetic characters used to transcribe foreign names, to make the place sound more international, more universal) has the atmosphere of a religious center. It has martyrs, but no single god. It has prayers, and it has a ready-made myth about the fall of man. Hiroshima, says a booklet entitled *Hiroshima Peace Reader*, published by the Hiroshima Peace Culture Foundation, "is no longer merely a Japanese city. It has become recognized throughout the world as a Mecca of world peace."

The great hall of the main railway station is always full of uniformed schoolchildren, Boy Scout groups, old-age pensioners, foreign tourists, dignitaries, and country folk, following the flags of their guides. They are among the millions of people who make their pilgrimage to Hiroshima each year. All visit Peace Park, the site of a thriving commercial district before it was demolished by the bomb, which exploded overhead. It is now the center of the Hiroshima cult.

It is even harder to imagine what happened in Hiroshima than it is at Auschwitz, for the horror of Hiroshima was compressed into one singular event, which left hardly a visual trace. In a sense, of course, the entire modern city of Hiroshima is evidence of the bomb. The slick shopping streets, the public parks, the baseball stadium, the high-rise hotels, even the old castle, rebuilt in concrete—none of this was there before August 6, 1945. It is as if the scene of the crime, as it were, had been utterly erased, or rather, buried under a brand-new city, like a modern Troy, or the former Warsaw ghetto.

And yet, for the visitor, especially a Caucasian, who is always assumed to be a foreigner, and usually an American, it is hard to forget the legacy of the bomb. This is not just because of the many monuments, plaques, and memorials, which are indeed impossible to miss, but also because you cannot walk through Peace Park without feeling self-conscious. No Japanese will be so crass as to come up to you and say: "You did this, you are guilty of mass murder." But when schoolchildren approach you, prompted by their teachers, to ask what you think of peace, you feel that some gesture of atonement, or at least a word of regret, is demanded. You are asked to declare peace in the name of your race, the white race, the one that many Japanese blame for dropping the bomb.

The park is a veritable Lourdes of shrines, monuments, stones, bells, fountains, and temples, commemorating the dead and offering prayers for peace. The shops in Peace Park sell key rings, ballpoint pens, T-shirts, coasters, postcards, books, cups, Buddhist rosaries, chopsticks, etc., all with prayers for peace. Most of these souvenirs bear a picture of the bombed shell of the former Hiroshima Prefecture Industrial Promotion Hall, now known as the A-Bomb Dome. The real thing stands just across the river that runs at one end of the park, as a permanent reminder of the evil that was done. Ceremonies are held there, and paper lanterns are floated in the river as symbols of the souls of the dead. Gray and white peace doves, hundreds of them, flutter around the trees, planted, so the guide explained, "by individuals and groups, both inside and outside Japan, who wanted to remember the souls of the victims and pray for peace." There is a sign near the cenotaph that reads:

"If you touch the doves, please rinse your mouth and wash your hands to prevent the disease they carry."

Behind the cenotaph is the Flame of Peace, donated by the Japan Junior Chamber of Commerce. It represents two hands opened to the skies. The flame was lit with torches carried by religious groups and representatives of various Japanese corporations. Next to it is the Monument of Prayer, a statue of a man, woman, and child. If you step on the stone placed in front of the pedestal, a musical box plays a tune entitled "Spirits, do not weep beneath the ground."

Visitors behave at the cenotaph in the way people usually do at Japanese shrines, when there are no special ceremonies to perform. They pray, they toss coins in the Pond of Peace behind the stone coffin, and they take photographs of one another to commemorate the occasion. Schoolchildren in navy-blue and black uniforms file past, laughing and yawning and slouching. They are instructed by their teachers to copy the words of the inscription in their notebooks. The atmosphere is not at all solemn; it rarely is at Japanese religious sites. The only somber note, droning through the children's voices, is the sound of the Peace Bell nearby. It is inside a concrete dome, which, my guidebook said, "expresses the universe."

Watching the laughing schoolkids, I was reminded of another memorial site I had visited, some years before. Then, too, I was struck by the casualness of Japanese visitors to a blood-soaked place. It was on Saipan, a small island in the Pacific, next to Tinian, an even smaller island, whence the *Enola Gay* took off for Hiroshima. Saipan had been a thriving Japanese colony, and when the U.S. Marines landed in 1944, the fighting was so fierce that at least 25,000 Japanese and nearly 4,000 Americans died in just a few days. But the worst of it was the mass suicides of hundreds of civilians, mostly women and children, who threw themselves off a cliff. Some who hesitated were shot in the back by Japanese snipers. This melancholy spot is marked by a sign, which says, in Japanese and English: "Suicide Cliff." Young

Japanese tourists, mostly girls, giggled and took snapshots of one another.

It is only when hierarchy is involved that people in Japan become almost oppressively solemn. The day after I visited Hiroshima, I had half an hour to spare in Fukuoka, the biggest city in Kyushu. In front of the main railway station, I watched a ceremony in aid of road safety. Young girls in uniforms, with bands saying "Miss Road Safety Fukuoka 1992," stood in identical poses, white-gloved hands folded, feet pressed together, as old men in black suits held forth gloomily about obeying traffic regulations. A brass band stood in attendance, stiff, in straight rows, like Prussian soldiers. And the various city dignitaries, wearing the bands and badges of their respective offices, were lined up behind the speakers, like generals at a parade. There was not a smile to be seen, not a whisper to be heard. Here, everyone knew his place, and order ruled, here where the point was not the killing of hundreds of thousands in war, but the promotion of safe driving in peace.

What is interesting about Hiroshima—the Mecca rather than the modern Japanese city, which is prosperous and rather dull—is the tension between its universal aspirations and its status as the exclusive site of Japanese victimhood. Tucked away in a corner, outside the park, is a monument to the Koreans who died from the A-bomb attack. Many of them had been forced to work in Japan during the war. The monument, erected in 1970 by the South Korean residents' association in Japan, stands on a large stone tortoise, the mark of a Korean grave. The tortoise is covered with wreaths, flowers, and paper cranes, bearing the names of various Korean organizations. Next to the grave marker is a sign, in English and Korean. It tells the story of 20,000 Koreans whose "sacred lives" were "suddenly taken from our midst." They were given no funerals or memorial services, so "their spirits hovered for years, unable to pass on to heaven." They were not enshrined in the Japanese park, and later attempts by local Koreans to have the monument moved into Peace Park failed. There could only be one cenotaph, said the Hiroshima municipal authorities. And the cenotaph did not include Koreans.

At the beginning of 1946, the governor of Hiroshima Prefecture invited a number of distinguished local people to offer ideas on how to reconstruct their city, which had virtually disappeared. Ota Yoko, a novelist, who survived the A-bomb, wanted many trees to be planted in the new Hiroshima. "I would like to interweave dream and reality in harmony to enrich the citizens' lives," she said. Another person felt that a rich cultural life was needed. Yet another (an abbot) wanted many Buddhist temples scattered about the city. But the most remarkable suggestion came from the deputy mayor of Kure, a port outside Hiroshima, where many of the battleships were built during the war. He wanted "to keep the vast expanse of the burnt-out area intact as a memorial graveyard for the sake of everlasting world peace."

Some people regret that this never came to pass. Starting in the 1980s, a former high school teacher from Osaka named Uno Masami has written a series of popular books about the need to learn from the Jews, specifically from the ways they dominate the world. These books sold in the hundreds of thousands. One of them, entitled *The Day the Dollar Becomes Paper*, has a chapter on Hiroshima. Hiroshima, Uno wrote, should have been left as it was, in ruins, just as Auschwitz, so he claims, was deliberately preserved by the Jews. By reminding the world of their martyrdom, he said, the Jews have kept their racial identity intact and restored their virility. The Japanese, in contrast, were duped by the Americans into believing that the traces of Japanese suffering should be swept away by the immediate reconstruction of Hiroshima. As a result, the postwar Japanese lack an identity and their racial virility has been sapped by American propaganda about Japanese war guilt.

This is an extreme position. Few Japanese would go so far, even though, as readers, they might find it pleasantly provocative. But if one leaves aside the antisemitism and the idea of keeping Hiroshima in ruins, it is an opinion widely held by

Japanese nationalists. The right always has been concerned with the debilitating effects on the Japanese identity of war guilt imposed by American propaganda. However, right-wing nationalists care less about Hiroshima than about the idée fixe that the "Great East Asian War" was to a large extent justified.

The left has its own variation of Japanese martyrdom, in which Hiroshima plays a central role. It is widely believed, for instance, that countless Japanese civilians fell victim to either a wicked military experiment or to the first strike in the Cold War, or both. The A-bomb, in this version, was dropped to scare the Soviets away from invading Japan. This at least is an arguable position. But the idea that the bomb was a racist experiment is less plausible, since the bomb was developed for use against Nazi Germany. Yet many Japanese believe it. One of the more eccentric books on this topic was written by Koochi Akira, a former employee of the United Nations, who argued that the bomb was a deliberate form of genocide planned by white racists. Uno Masami, who holds similar views, has claimed that these racists were Jews. Again, such opinions are extreme. But, judging from what appears in Japanese periodicals and on best-seller lists, not *that* far from the mainstream.

There is another view, however, held by leftists and liberals, who would not dream of defending the "Fifteen-Year War." In this view, the A-bomb was a kind of divine punishment for Japanese militarism. And having learned their lesson through this unique suffering, having been purified through hellfire and purgatory, so to speak, the Japanese people have earned the right, indeed have the sacred duty, to sit in judgment of others, specifically the United States, whenever they show signs of sinning against the "Hiroshima spirit." This is at the heart of what is known as Peace Education, which has been much encouraged by the leftist Japan Teachers' Union and has been regarded with suspicion by the conservative government. Peace Education has traditionally meant pacifism, anti-Americanism, and a strong sympathy for Communist states, especially China.

"World Peace begins in Hiroshima" was the slogan on the

flags and banners, draped in black, carried by A-bomb survivors praying at a Shinto shrine on the first anniversary of the bombing. "The world is still controlled by 'the philosophy of power,' " said the mayor of Hiroshima on August 6, 1987. "We must convert the world to the Hiroshima spirit." This means that whenever America, with logistical and financial help from its Japanese ally, uses military force—in Korea, for example, or in Vietnam, or the Persian Gulf—it is seen as a betrayal of the A-bomb victims, a stab in the heart of Hiroshima.

In one respect, at least, left-wing pacifism in Japan has something in common with the romantic nationalism usually associated with the right: it shares the right's resentment about being robbed by the Americans of what might be called a collective memory. The romantic nationalists think that the U.S. occupation after the war deliberately destroyed sacred traditions, such as the imperial cult, without which the Japanese could have no identity. The romantic pacifists believe that the United States, to hide its own guilt and to rekindle Japanese militarism in aid of the Cold War, tried to wipe out the memory of Hiroshima.

Kurosawa Akira made a rather mawkish film, entitled *Rhapsody in August*, about the spiritual scars left by the A-bomb in Nagasaki. The film is a lament, not just for the bombing but for the way memory passes into history and history is swiftly forgotten. In an interview with Gabriel García Márquez, published in a Berlin newspaper, Kurosawa was asked by the writer what "this historical amnesia meant to the future of Japan and the Japanese identity." Kurosawa answered that the Japanese didn't like to talk openly about the bombing. "Our politicians, in particular, remain silent about it, perhaps out of fear of the Americans." Until the United States apologizes to the Japanese people, said Kurosawa, "the drama won't be over."

It is true that, during the occupation, the American authorities did not want the Japanese to dwell on the A-bomb attacks.

They didn't want the Japanese to feel victimized. In the first years after the war only scientific texts about the A-bomb were allowed to be published. As late as 1949 a film project initiated by the city of Hiroshima, to be called *No More Hiroshimas*, was canceled because the occupation authorities objected to scenes of "the destruction and human misery which resulted from the atom bomb." In 1950, just one year before the end of the occupation, the title of a painting by Maruki Iri and Maruki Toshi had to be changed from *Atomic Bomb* to *August 6, 1945*.

But Kurosawa was wrong nonetheless. For few events in World War II have been described, analyzed, lamented, reenacted, re-created, depicted, and exhibited so much and so often as the bombing of Hiroshima and, to a much lesser extent, Nagasaki. The problem with Nagasaki was not just that Hiroshima came first but also that Nagasaki had more military targets than Hiroshima. The Mitsubishi factories in Nagasaki produced the bulk of Japanese armaments. There was also something else, which is not often mentioned: the Nagasaki bomb exploded right over the area where outcasts and Christians lived. And unlike in Hiroshima, much of the rest of the city was spared the worst. So discussing the bombing in detail can prove awkward and is best avoided. But novels about Hiroshima were written, if not published, almost as soon as the war was over. In 1983, a compendium of Japanese atom bomb literature was published in fifteen volumes.

Censorship during the occupation was one reason, I suppose, for the anti-American tone of many A-bomb books and films that appeared once the occupation was over. At last the forbidden could speak its name. Another reason was the political background of filmmakers and novelists. Some had always been ardent nationalists, filled with distrust of the West, and America in particular. Others had been Marxists before the war who were forced by the military authorities to recant and pledge allegiance to the imperial cause. But even when they reverted to their former faith after the war, this did not necessarily constitute a major shift. The enemy—the greedy, materialistic, individualistic, imperialistic, racialist United States—remained the same.

So you had films like *Hiroshima*, made in 1953 by Sekigawa Hideo, which ends with a scene of American tourists buying souvenir bones of the victims. Even more spiteful was a comic book that appeared in 1969 entitled *In the Stream of the Black River*. It is about a beautiful young woman who survived the bomb but is dying of radiation disease. Before she goes, however, she wants to have her revenge on the "white pigs." She becomes a *pansuke*, a whore specializing in GIs, the lowest kind of prostitute, "drenched in the stink of disgusting foreigners." She will give all those "warmongers who still use military bases in Japan a souvenir." She will infect them with syphilis. That will teach them! "Why weren't those war criminals put on trial?" she exclaims to a sympathetic policeman who took her off the streets. "Always remember how that A-bomb tortured your mother," she tells her wide-eyed little son. This story was published in *Manga Punch*, a comic magazine with a circulation of millions.

And yet, despite these diatribes, the myth of Hiroshima and its pacifist cult is based less on American wickedness than on the image of martyred innocence and visions of the apocalypse. One moment there was normal life—laughing children, young girls singing, housewives cleaning, good men working—then, in an instant, all was turned to ash. The comparison between Hiroshima and Auschwitz is based on this notion; the idea, namely, that Hiroshima, like the Holocaust, was not part of the war, not even connected with it, but "something that occurs at the end of the world . . ." The words are those of Ota Yoko, the novelist, who wrote about her experience as a Hiroshima survivor in *City of Corpses*. "We had been flattened by a force—arbitrary and violent—that wasn't war." It was, perhaps, "the latest cosmic phenomenon." Ota, by the way, had been one of the many Japanese who rejoiced at the attack on Pearl Harbor. She had "felt a fresh new flame."

All the quasi-religious elements of the Hiroshima myth from

a leftist perspective are there in Oda Makoto's novel *The Bomb*. The bomb explodes on page 168, just as a sweet young Japanese woman is about to offer a bunch of flowers to a sick Malayan student in his hospital room. It is a gesture of beauty and innocence. Then "followed an unearthly roar, as though the heavens were collapsing." A Japanese soldier, versed in European history, recalls the wrath of the gods in the *Iliad*.

Every white American in Oda's novel spouts racist filth: " 'All scholars are Jews,' said Will. Those words seemed to fan Ken's dislike of Jews, for he let out a tirade of invective. The worst people in the world were the Japs, followed by the Jews." Hence the reader is left to conclude that the bombing of Hiroshima was a racist act. But the Japanese in Oda's account are racist too, toward Koreans and other Asians. The only truly decent and wise characters in the story are members of a Native American tribe. They are forbidden by tribal tradition to take up arms. Their elders, sitting in the desert, can see the apocalypse coming. Is this really the end of the world? asks George, one of the tribal brothers. " 'The end, brother,' Ron replied with conviction. 'Doesn't the world look as red as the sun—or a fireball hundreds of times brighter? The people are being burned alive, becoming charred corpses.' "

This is the imagery of Buddhist hell scrolls, full of bloodied figures enveloped in bright red flames. Hara Tamiki was, like Ota Yoko, a Hiroshima survivor. He wrote a story entitled "Summer Flowers." His vision of the end is preceded by a description of the weather, which has all the spectacular ominousness of a Hollywood epic or a Leni Riefenstahl production: "Against the darkening sky the mountains displayed an ever more brilliant green; the islands of the Inland Sea too stood out in bold relief. The waves, the calm blue waves, seemed at any moment about to rage, stirred up by the fiercest of storms." This sets the scene for an almost Wagnerian apocalypse that ends "in the dreadfully gloomy faint green light of the medieval paintings of Buddhist hell." In 1951, possibly depressed over the Korean War, Hara threw himself in front of a train.

In the 1950s, the artists Maruki Iri and Maruki Toshi painted a modern version of a hell scroll, entitled *The Atom Bomb—Hiroshima* (not the same work as *August 6, 1945*). I went to see it at the modern art museum in Hiroshima. The painting, on four panels, like a Japanese screen, has traditional Japanese elements, but it also contains images of the fall of man that could just as well be Christian. Dead bodies, horribly scarred or burned, literally fall from the upper end of the painting amid lightning bolts that suggest divine wrath. Rabid dogs carry dead babies in their bloody maws. Charred corpses are tied in ropes. Crows pick at mutilated bodies. A mass of faceless humanity marches on in charcoal ranks, as though on the way to purgatory.

On the white wall displaying the Maruki painting was a sign that read "Hiroshima and modern art: 'the heart of Hiroshima,' the universal theme of mankind." I looked at some of the other exhibits. It was clear that the art of Anselm Kiefer had left its mark. But while Kiefer sifted through the shards of German history and *Kultur* in the postwar ruins of his country, his admirers in the Hiroshima museum were preoccupied solely with the Hiroshima spirit. There was, for example, Araki Takako's ceramic book—rather like Kiefer's tomes of lead—entitled *Atomic Bomb Bible*. The scorched text was in Hebrew. There was also a silk-paneled screen (unlike anything by Kiefer), by Ueno Yasuo, called *6-8-1945*, showing people in the throes of death, painted in red speckled with gold.

Missing from all these works was any sense of a wider world beyond August 6, 1945. Hiroshima stood in complete isolation. This was noticed by one of the contributors to the catalogue, Kuwabara Sumio, a professor of art. He quoted the words of Kazuki Yasuo, whose harrowing paintings of Japanese POWs in Siberia were not in the Hiroshima museum. Kazuki's works on the war are the only ones in Japan to approach Kiefer's in depth. He was a POW in Siberia himself, but instead of indulging in self-pity, his dark, almost abstract paintings—for example, of handprints, like bloodstains on a torture cell's walls—offer a vision of cruelty and suffering that goes beyond specific events. On his way to a Siberian POW camp, Kazuki saw a corpse soaked in blood. It was the body of a Japanese soldier whose brutal behavior had led to his lynching by an enraged Chinese mob. He compared this "red corpse" to the "black corpses" of victims of the bomb.

"The story of the black bodies," he said, "has been told and retold in these past twenty years. Hiroshima and Auschwitz have become the symbols of World War II, the deaths of these particular innocents symbolizing the general cruelty of war. The black corpses made the Japanese feel that they were the main victims of the war. In unison they shouted: 'No more Hiroshimas!' It almost seemed as though there had been no war apart from the dropping of the A-bomb. A deeper insight into the real nature of war, and the only true basis for the antiwar movement, must come, not from the black corpses, but from the red one."

This is true. And yet I do not think the religious metaphors and hellish visions of Hiroshima (the bombing of which, after all, was hellish) can be reduced to Japanese self-pity alone. Buddhist hell scrolls had a function which many Christians— Pietists in particular—would recognize. It was believed that the contemplation of evil would lead to salvation. Hell is transcended by staring at it. Those who succeed are lifted to a higher moral plane, from where it becomes possible, among other things, to preach the gospel of universal peace. This is a notion that most religions with universal aspirations have in common, East and West.

It is easier, to be sure, to look at a hell that is not of your own making. Japanese can identify with the victims of Hiroshima, but it is impossible for Germans to feel victimized by Auschwitz. Japanese sins are dissolved in the sins of mankind. This allows the Japanese to take two routes at once, a national one, as unique victims of the A-bomb, and a universal one, as the apostles of the Hiroshima spirit. This, then, is how Japanese pacifists, engaged in Peace Education, define the Japanese identity. But still

I wonder whether it is really so different from the position of many Germans who wish to "internalize" Auschwitz, who see Auschwitz "through the eyes of identity." In either case, nationality has come to be based less on citizenship than on history, morality, and a religious spirit.

The problem with this quasi-religious view of history is that it makes it hard to discuss past events in anything but nonsecular terms. Visions of absolute evil are unique, and they are beyond human explanation or even comprehension. To explain is hubristic and amoral. If this is true of Auschwitz, it is even more true of Hiroshima. The irony is that while there can be no justification for Auschwitz unless one believes in Hitler's murderous ideology, the case for Hiroshima is at least open to debate. The A-bomb *might* have saved lives; it *might* have shortened the war. But such arguments are incompatible with the Hiroshima spirit.

In July 1992 a United Nations Conference on Disarmament Issues was held in Hiroshima. This was the result of years of Japanese lobbying to hold this annual conference in "the world's first atom-bombed city." All went well, apparently, until an American Harvard professor argued that the Hiroshima bombing "ended World War II and saved a million Japanese lives." He also added that the horror of this event had helped to prevent nuclear wars ever since, and thus in effect Hiroshima and Nagasaki saved millions more lives. The Japanese were outraged. Newspaper editorials fulminated against the professor for failing to understand the point of view of the victims. The *Asahi Shimbun* felt "disgusted once again," and observed that "unless the United States disentangled itself from this kind of view," it would run into a great deal of opposition from nonnuclear countries.

But still, the *Asahi* went on, the conference must be counted a success, since the participants, many of whom visited Hiroshima for the first time, "had all expressed shock at the displays and relics in the Peace Memorial Museum." They had also participated in "the singing of 'The Prayer of Hiroshima.' " Only a British writer, Alan Booth, commenting on the affair in the *Asahi*'s English edition, pointed out that prayers, ceremonies, and uniformity of views were not what conferences were usually for.

The point of view of the victims is jealously guarded in Hiroshima. Their essential innocence is insisted upon. Yet in the history of Japan's foreign wars, the city of Hiroshima is far from innocent. When Japan went to war with China in 1894, the troops set off for the battlefronts from Hiroshima, and the Meiji emperor moved his headquarters there. The city grew wealthy as a result. It grew even wealthier when Japan went to war with Russia eleven years later, and Hiroshima once again became the center of military operations. As the *Hiroshima Peace Reader* puts it with admirable conciseness, "Hiroshima, secure in its position as a military city, became more populous and prosperous as wars and incidents occurred throughout the Meiji and Taisho periods." At the time of the bombing, Hiroshima was the base of the Second General Headquarters of the Imperial Army (the First was in Tokyo). In short, the city was swarming with soldiers.

One of the few literary masterpieces to emerge from the A-bomb attack, Ibuse Masuji's novel *Black Rain*, is set against this background of militarism and political oppression. The book begins with a scene set on a bridge near the epicenter of the A-bomb. Moments before the blast, junior high school children were made to listen to a military harangue and sing a patriotic song. And near the end of the book, after the actual bombing has been described over and over in all its horror, the governor of Hiroshima Prefecture issues an order to fight on: "Citizens of Hiroshima—the losses may be great, but this is war!"

The citizens of Hiroshima were indeed victims, primarily of their own military rulers. But when a local group of peace activists petitioned the city of Hiroshima in 1987 to incorporate the history of Japanese aggression into the Peace Memorial

Museum, the request was turned down. The petition for an "Aggressors' Corner" was prompted by junior high school students from Osaka, who had embarrassed Peace Museum officials by asking for an explanation about Japanese responsibility for the war. Like millions of others (60,000 children a year), they were shown the grisly relics of the A-bomb: the bottles bent out of shape by the heat, the photos of the mushroom cloud, the torn bits of clothing, the weird shadow imprinted on a doorstep by radiation, and the life-sized tableaux of horribly mangled people staggering through the rubble with their skins dripping like molten wax.

Presumably with some prompting from their teachers, the junior high school students from Osaka wanted more than this chamber of horrors. They wanted to know what happened before. They also demanded an official recognition of the fact that some of the Korean victims of the bomb had been slave laborers. (Osaka, like Kyoto and Hiroshima, still has a large Korean population.) Both requests were denied. So a group called Peace Link was formed, from local people, many of whom were Christians, antinuclear activists, or involved with discriminated-against minorities. The group, naturally, was opposed by right-wing nationalist organizations, such as the Japan Patriotic Party, which rallied around the Peace Park, blaring patriotic songs through loudspeakers mounted on trucks. The patriots appear to have won. But according to one of the peace activists, the municipal government of Hiroshima had been against the idea of an "Aggressors' Corner" anyway.

One of the ironies of the affair was that the antinuclear activists regarded the A-bomb attack as a crime, whereas one of their right-wing opponents did not. Maeda Kazuyoshi, head of the Yukoku Ishinkai (Society for Lament and National Restoration), thought the bombing had saved Japan from total destruction. But he insisted that Japan could not be held solely responsible for the war. The war, he said, had simply been part of the "flow of history."

I asked the director of the Peace Memorial Museum, Kawamoto Yoshitaka, why the suggestion to build an "Aggressors' Corner" had been rejected. Kawamoto, a polite municipal bu-reaucrat in a blue serge suit, smiled patiently and said: "We couldn't have such a thing here. The aggressors were in Tokyo. Our only aim is to show what happened on August 6, 1945."

In his conversation, Kawamoto switched back and forth from universals ("mankind," "world peace") to the specifically na-tional. I sensed that he was used to explaining the Japanese national character to foreign visitors. The Japanese laugh when they feel sad, he said. The Japanese can communicate with one another without speaking. The Japanese think only from a sub-jective point of view. The Japanese understand the essential sadness of things (*mono no aware*). And so on and so forth. What about young Japanese? I asked.

"The younger generation no longer know the art of endur-ance," he said. "And they don't understand what life was like for us. You see, they come here and tell me that Japanese also committed war crimes, but they don't know what they are talking about. They just repeat what their left-wing teachers say."

It was important, he went on, to explain the past on a level that the young could understand. The young, he said, no longer read, so you have to present them with visual information. Yes, but shouldn't they be taught about the history of the war as well as the A-bomb? Of course, he said, of course. But that was not what this museum was for. So I asked him what it was for.

He smiled, feeling that he was on safer ground. "You see, this museum was not really intended to be a museum. It was built by survivors as a place of prayer for the victims and for world peace. Mankind must build a better world. That is why Hiroshima must persist. We must go back to the basic roots. We must think of human solidarity and world peace. Otherwise we just end up arguing about history."

The history of the war, or indeed any history, is indeed not what the Hiroshima spirit is about. This is why Auschwitz is the only comparison that is officially condoned. Anything else is too controversial, too much part of the "flow of history." The plan to build an Auschwitz memorial in a small town between Hiroshima and Kure was proposed in the late 1980s by the mayor of Kure. The mayor of Hiroshima thought it was a good idea. And the pacifist citizens' groups were not against it either, but they insisted that a memorial to the Nanking Massacre should form a major part of such an enterprise. The plan was quietly dropped.

There is, nonetheless, a place, not far from Hiroshima, about an hour and a half by train and forty minutes by ferryboat, that serves as a reminder that there was another side to Japanese history, not unrelated to what happened on August 6, 1945. Okunojima is a tiny island in the Inland Sea. The first things you see as you disembark from the ferry are rabbits. They run all over the neat paths and pleasant lawns, like bits of white fluff dotting the landscape. They are so tame you can stroke them. There is not much else on the island, except a large hotel, which looks like a hospital, a few ruins of late-nineteenth- and early-twentieth-century buildings, and an old gun emplacement facing the mainland across the water. There is also a small concrete building near the jetty. It is called the Okunojima Toxic Gas Museum.

The tame bunnies are the descendants of laboratory animals used for experiments with mustard gas and other lethal substances in what was the largest toxic gas factory in the Japanese Empire. More than 5,000 people worked there during the war, many of them women and schoolchildren. About 1,600 died of exposure to hydrocyanic acid gas, nausea gas, and lewisite. Some were damaged for life. Official Chinese sources claim that more than 80,000 Chinese fell victim to gases produced at the factory. The army was so secretive about the place that the island simply disappeared from Japanese maps.

Little of this was known after the war. When the Americans arrived in 1945, they took away the data, dumped large quantities of gas into the sea, and torched the plant. The hotel now stands on the site of the main factory. You still can see the ruins of the electric generator and some of the storage buildings. Only when a young Japanese history professor named Yoshimi Yoshiaki dug up a report in American archives in the 1980s did it become known that the Japanese had stored 15,000 tons of chemical weapons on and near the island and that a 200-kilogram container of mustard gas was buried under Hiroshima.

Surviving workers from the factory, many of whom suffered from chronic lung diseases, asked for official recognition of their plight in the 1950s. But the government turned them down. If the government had compensated the workers, it would have been an official admission that the Japanese Army had engaged in an illegal enterprise. When a brief mention of chemical warfare crept into Japanese school textbooks, the Ministry of Education swiftly took it out.

Yet the memory of the toxic gas plant never completely disappeared. In 1975, survivors who could prove they had been harmed by gases were finally paid some compensation. In 1985 a small memorial was erected for the workers who died on the island during the war. And in 1988, through the efforts of survivors, the small museum was built, "to pass on," in the words of the museum guide, "the historical truth to future generations."

The curator of the one-room museum is a short, wiry man named Murakami Hatsuichi. He looked tough, hardened, like a former prizefighter. Murakami first started working at the factory in 1940 as a fourteen-year-old janitor. The money was good and he was "filled with a spirit of self-sacrifice" to help Japan win the war. It was also a way to gain promotion in the army. Murakami showed me around the sinister exhibits: a wooden horse wearing a gas mask; pictures of gas attack victims, their skins disfigured by festering scars and boils; old gas canisters; drawings of schoolgirls practicing swordsmanship in the factory yard; group photographs of army officers grinning in the sun.

Murakami's explanation was matter-of-fact. He did not sermonize or moralize. Nor was he interested in explaining the Japanese national character. He struck me as an honest man.

He told me that he would not have remembered the place in such detail if he had not been shown the documents returned from America. I asked him about the purpose of the museum. He said: "Before shouting 'no more war,' I want people to see what it was really like. To simply look at the past from the point of view of the victim is to encourage hatred."

What did he think of the Peace Museum in Hiroshima? "At the Hiroshima museum it is easy to feel victimized," he said. "But we must realize that we were aggressors too. We were educated to fight for our country. We made toxic gas for our country. We lived to fight the war. To win the war was our only goal." Murakami looked more and more like a prizefighter, narrowing his eyes and punching his fist into his palm. "Look," he said, "when you fight another man, and hit him and kick him, he will hit and kick back. One side will win. How will this be remembered? Do we recall that we were kicked, or that we started the kicking ourselves? Without considering this question, we cannot have peace."

I thought of Murakami's words when I walked around Hiroshima again the next day. They didn't make me feel any less awkward when asked by the schoolkids what I thought of peace. The fact that Japanese had buried poison gas under Hiroshima did not lessen the horror of the A-bomb. But it put Peace Park, with all its shrines, in a more historical perspective. It took the past away from God and put it in the fallible hands of man.

NANKING

THE RAPE OF NANKING, or the Nanking Massacre, took place after the Japanese Imperial Army captured the city in the middle of December 1937. This was less than half a year after Japanese troops invaded China proper. Nanking, as the capital of the Nationalist government, was the greatest prize in the attempted conquest of China. Its fall was greeted in Japan with banner headlines and nationwide celebration. For six weeks Japanese Army officers allowed their men to run amok. The figures are imprecise, but tens of thousands, perhaps hundreds of thousands (the Chinese say 300,000) of Chinese soldiers and civilians, many of them refugees from other towns, were killed. And thousands of women between the ages of about nine and seventy-five were raped, mutilated, and often murdered.

But the numbers don't convey the savagery of what happened in Nanking, and in many other Chinese villages, towns, and cities as well. Nor do they explain why it was allowed to happen. Was it a deliberate policy to terrorize the Chinese into submission? The complicity of the officers suggests there was something to this. But it might also have been a kind of payoff to the Japanese troops for slogging through China in the freezing winter without decent pay or rations. Or was it largely a matter of a peasant army running out of control? Or just the inevitable consequence of war, as many Japanese maintain?

I was given a booklet in Japan entitled *Nanking Atrocities*. Although the booklet was in Japanese, the English word "atrocities," transcribed as *aturoshitees*, was used in the title, as though there was no corresponding Japanese word. There are, in fact, many Japanese expressions for cruelty, violence, murder, or massacre. But the word "atrocity" conveys more than the inevitable cruelty of war. An atrocity is a willful act of criminal brutality, an act that violates the law as well as any code of human decency. It isn't that the Japanese lack such codes or are morally incapable of grasping the concept. But "atrocity," like "human rights," is part of a modern terminology which came from the West, along with "feminism," say, or "war crimes." To rightwing nationalists it has a leftist ring, something subversive, something almost anti-Japanese.

The booklet was edited and published by a group of high school teachers who had visited Nanking to find out more about the Massacre. It contains Chinese witness accounts, maps of the main execution grounds, and some of the photographs displayed at the memorial museum in Nanking. The Japanese did not leave a copious visual record of their atrocities, even though they were keen photographers. Censorship was tight. But there is enough in the way of photographs and even film footage (mostly taken by Western missionaries) to give an impression. There are pictures, some taken by Japanese photographers and some by Chinese or foreign witnesses, of Chinese men being used for bayonet practice, of people being machine-gunned into open pits, of terrified women, huddling naked in rice paddies, trying to shield their private parts, of Japanese soldiers chopping off heads with their long swords, of corpses piled high on the banks of the Yangtze River, and of dead women with bamboo sticks rammed up their vaginas.

Some of these images, taken from newsreels, were used in Bernardo Bertolucci's film *The Last Emperor* (1987). When it was shown in Japan, the Japanese distributors, Shochiku Fuji, decided to delete these scenes without telling the director. When Bertolucci found out, the distributors claimed that the British producer of the film had asked for the cuts—probably, so the distributors presumed, because he thought the footage "would be too grisly for Japanese taste." Bertolucci and his British producer were furious, the cuts were restored, and Shochiku Fuji apologized for the "big misunderstanding."

There is no evidence that the distributors were pressured by the government, or anybody else, to make the cuts. The most plausible explanation for their behavior is that they wished to avoid any negative publicity. Extreme right-wing groups can be very intimidating. And since controversy in Japan is always embarrassing, and sometimes even dangerous, it takes a certain courage to delve into issues which might bring unwanted attention.

The Nanking Massacre is such an issue. It has become the prime symbol of Japanese savagery during the war in Asia. During the Tokyo War Crimes Tribunal, Nanking had the same resonance as Auschwitz had in Nuremberg. And being a symbol, the Nanking Massacre is as vulnerable to mythology and manipulation as Auschwitz and Hiroshima.

In Japanese schools the controversy is officially killed by silence. All it says in a typical textbook for high school students is: "In December [1937] Japanese troops occupied Nanking." A footnote explains: "At this time Japanese troops were reported to have killed many Chinese, including civilians, and Japan was the target of international criticism." This is all. But even this was too much for some conservative bureaucrats and politicians, who wanted the passage to be deleted altogether.

No wonder, then, that the middle school students were shocked when their teacher, Mori Masataka, one of the editors of *Nanking Atrocities*, showed them a documentary video about the Massacre. He asked them to write down their thoughts after seeing the film. The responses were remarkably uniform. This, for example, from a thirteen-year-old girl named Ritsuko: "I always associated the war with Hiroshima and Nagasaki. But the nuclear bombings happened after 1940. Before that, Japan did things which were even worse. Watching the video, it seemed almost unreal. Before this, I could only think of Japan as the loser in the war, but we Japanese must know what happened before 1940. What impressed me more than anything else, seeing this video, was the scene of Japanese soldiers laughing as they watched Chinese people being killed. How could they have done that? I cannot understand the feelings of the Japanese at that time . . ."

For the first time the students were made aware of the Japanese as aggressors. This was the intended shock effect. Mori, like most, if not all, teachers involved in Peace Education, has left-wing views. Although he can count on many sympathizers among the rank and file of the once powerful Japan Teachers' Union, few are as actively engaged as he is. He told me that most of his colleagues were not so much against him as indifferent. Most shy away from controversy. His video and his booklet on wartime history are distributed privately to a small network of like-minded teachers, as an alternative to the official, evasive, summary interpretation of history presented in school textbooks vetted by the Ministry of Education.

They reflect a political view which is necessarily simplified. The Japanese were "aggressors," they "invaded" China, their behavior was "criminal and cruel." The Chinese were all either "brave resisters" or "innocent victims." In one of his pamphlets Mori writes about a visit to Nanking, where he "felt the painful necessity to review history from the point of view of the aggressor." This, then, is what the students are asked to do: to replace their sense of Japanese victimhood with the aggressors' point of view.

Here is Yasuko, fourteen years old (in 1991): "We often hear about the terrible ways in which Nazis murdered their victims, but the Japanese were pretty bad too. What about those creepy smiles on the faces of Japanese as they cut off the heads of Chinese people? How could they laugh when they were killing people? I felt like averting my eyes when I saw those severed heads stuck on poles . . ."

The point of the film is not primarily historical. The militant racial chauvinism of "the emperor system" is clearly blamed for the war and its atrocities. But it was those creepy smiles that impressed Mori's students. Official evasion about the past is challenged by a vision of evil perpetrated by "the Japanese at that time"—their fathers and grandfathers—smiling. By contemplating "the hell of Nanking," by looking at history through the eyes of identity (the identity of the aggressor), they could, in their teacher's words, "build the history of tomorrow and link hands with the peoples of Asia."

This is a political view, as I said, but Mori's attitude also raises doubts about Ruth Benedict's distinction between Christian "guilt culture" and Confucian "shame culture." She made this distinction in *The Chrysanthemum and the Sword*, a book she wrote during the war to help American intelligence officers understand the Japanese mind. In her opinion, a "society that inculcates absolute standards of morality and relies on man's developing a conscience is a guilt culture by definition . . ." But in "a culture where shame is a major sanction, people are chagrined about acts which we expect people to feel guilty about." However, this "chagrin cannot be relieved, as guilt can be, by confession and atonement . . ." A "man does not experience relief when he makes his fault public even to a confessor. So long as his bad behaviour does not 'get out into the world' he need not be troubled and confession appears to him merely a way of courting trouble."

This is a mechanistic view of human behavior, typical of the social anthropologist. It is not entirely false, yet it is a limited explanation at best: there are too many exceptions, too many Germans who don't have the slightest wish to confess, and too many Japanese, like Mori, whose efforts to make public the "sins" of their country are definitely meant as gestures of atonement. That is why they travel to China and Southeast Asia to apologize to former victims. Guilt and shame are in any case not as easy to distinguish as Ruth Benedict suggests. Is the exaggerated philosemitism of certain Germans a matter of personal guilt, or national shame? Is it any different from the effusive behavior of elderly Japanese tourists in China who greet every Chinese they meet as a long-lost friend? And did the Mitscherlichs not argue in *The Inability to Mourn* that "the process of denial extended in the same way to the occasions for guilt, mourning, and shame"? If memory was admitted at all, the Mitscherlichs wrote about Germans in the 1950s, "it was only in order to balance one's own guilt against that of others. Many horrors had been unavoidable, it was claimed, because they had been dictated by crimes committed by the adversary." This was precisely what many Japanese claimed, and still do claim. And it is why Mori insists on making his pupils view the past from the perspective of the aggressors.

Clearly the children were shocked. The playfulness of extreme violence is always especially shocking. SS guards delighted in calling their routine torture of concentration camp inmates "sport." Submitting old, sick men to murderous physical exercises was "sport." Making rabbis ride each other piggyback as they were beaten to death was "sport." Playfulness enters into the business of killing when the victim must be humiliated as well as destroyed. Inventiveness in torture and murder becomes in itself a form of sport. It is probably no coincidence that the most infamous story of the Nanking Massacre should be a sporting feat. It is not the worst atrocity story, but it has all the mythical elements to appeal to the imagination. It is a story of omnipotence and epic wickedness. It became the subject of a furious "debate" in Japan more than forty years after the event allegedly took place.

Two young Japanese officers, Lieutenant N. and Lieutenant M., were on their way to Nanking and decided to test their swordsmanship: the first to cut off one hundred Chinese heads would be the winner. And thus they slashed their way through Chinese ranks, taking scalps in true samurai style. Lieutenant M. got 106, and Lieutenant N. bagged 105.

The story made a snappy headline in a major Tokyo newspaper: "Who Will Get There First! Two Lieutenants Already Claimed 80." In the Nanking museum is a newspaper photograph of the two friends, glowing with youthful high spirits. Lieutenant N. boasted in the report that he had cut the necks off 56 men without even denting the blade of his ancestral sword. The next report carried the headline: "Fast Pitching Progress!" This was before such dangerous Americana as baseball terms were forbidden by the government censors.

Later, back in Japan, Lieutenant M. began to revise his story. Speaking at his old high school, he said that in fact he had beheaded only four or five men in actual combat. As for the rest . . . "After we occupied the city, I stood facing a ditch, and told the Chinese prisoners to step forward. Since Chinese soldiers are stupid, they shuffled over to the ditch, one by one, and I cleanly cut off their heads." But even that may have been a false boast. I was told by a Japanese veteran who had fought in Nanking that such stories were commonly made up or at least exaggerated by Japanese reporters, who were ordered to entertain the home front with tales of heroism.

The story of the hundred heads was, in any case, soon forgotten in Japan. But it became part of the wartime lore in China. Honda Katsuichi, a famous *Asahi Shimbun* reporter, was told the story in Nanking. He wrote it up in a series of articles, later collected in a book entitled *A Journey to China*, published in 1981. This was the book that inspired Mori Masataka to take a deeper interest in the Japanese war. It also caused a stir in right-wing nationalist circles. Yamamoto Shichihei, well known for his books comparing the Japanese and the Jews, wrote a series of articles attacking Honda's reports. The attack was joined by other intellectuals who invariably come forth when national face must be defended, and the whole thing developed into the *Nankin Ronso*, or Nanking Debate. In 1984, an anti-Honda book came out, by Tanaka Masaaki, entitled *The Fabrication of the "Nanking Massacre."*

The nationalist intellectuals are called *goyo gakusha* by their critics. It is a difficult term to translate, but the implied meaning is "official scholars," who do the government's bidding. These men (almost all are men) may not be highly respected by the academic establishment, particularly among historians, many of whom are still avidly Marxist, but they have considerable influence on public opinion, as television commentators, lecturers, and contributors to popular magazines. Virtually none of them are professional historians. Tanaka is a retired journalist.

Indeed, the debate on the Japanese war is conducted almost entirely outside Japanese universities, by journalists, amateur historians, political columnists, civil rights activists, and so forth. This means that the zanier theories of the likes of Tanaka Masaaki are never seriously contested by professional historians. One reason is that there are very few modern historians in Japan. Until the end of the war, it would have been dangerously subversive, even blasphemous, for a critical scholar to write about modern history. The emperor system, after all, was sacred. The other reason was that modern history was not considered academically respectable. It was too fluid, too political, too controversial. Until 1955, there was not one modern historian on the staff of Tokyo University. History stopped around the middle of the nineteenth century. And even now, modern history is considered by senior historians to be something best left to journalists.

The arguments against the Nanking Massacre are not very sophisticated. Tanaka and others have pointed out that it is physically impossible for one man to cut off a hundred heads with one blade, and that for the same reason Japanese troops could never have killed more than 100,000 people in a few weeks. Besides, wrote Tanaka, none of the Japanese newspapers reported any massacre at the time, so why did it suddenly come up in the Tokyo War Crimes Tribunal? He admits that a few innocent people got killed in the cross fire, but these deaths were incidental. Some soldiers were doubtless a bit rough, but that was due to "the psychology of war." In any case, so the argument invariably ends, Hiroshima, having been planned in cold blood, was a far worse crime. "Unlike in Europe or China," writes Tanaka, "you won't find one instance of planned, systematic murder in the entire history of Japan." This is because the Japanese have "a different sense of values" from the Chinese or the Westerners.

Leaving aside, for the moment, the more delicate Japanese sense of values, Tanaka's point about systematic murder deserves attention. Since Nanking, as a symbol of atrocity, is regarded by some as the Japanese Holocaust, it is important to make distinctions. The point that it was not systematic was made by leftist opponents of the official scholars too. The historian Ienaga Saburo, for example, wrote that the Nanking Massacre, whose scale and horror he does not deny, "may have been a reaction to the fierce Chinese resistance after the Shanghai fighting." Ienaga's credentials as a fierce critic of orthodox conservative views are beyond reproach—something that has not necessarily helped his academic career. But even he defends an argument that all the apologists make too: "On the battlefield men face the ultimate extremes of human existence, life or death. Extreme conduct, although still ethically impermissible, may be psychologically inevitable. However, atrocities carried out far from the battlefield dangers and imperatives and according to a rational plan were acts of evil barbarism. The Auschwitz gas chambers of our 'ally' Germany and the atomic bombing of our enemy America are classic examples of rational atrocities."

Some Marxists, and not just in Japan, carry this argument even further. Heiner Müller observed—along with his remark that Auschwitz was the "last stage of the Enlightenment"—that the A-bomb was "the scientific substitute for the Last Judgment." The answer, in Müller's opinion, was to humanize warfare, to substitute man-to-man combat for scientific killing, for "war is contact, war is dialogue, war is free time."

Another way of putting this is that war is sport. If the hundred-heads contest is the metaphor for the Nanking Massacre, this would make it a more humane or at least a more human atrocity than gas chambers and A-bombs. Well, perhaps. Nanking was not a supernatural apocalypse or part of an effort to annihilate an entire race. Yet the question remains whether the raping and killing of thousands of women, and the massacre of thousands, perhaps hundreds of thousands, of other unarmed people, in the course of six weeks, can still be called extreme conduct in the heat of battle. The question is pertinent, particularly when such extreme violence is justified by an ideology which teaches the aggressors that killing an inferior race is in accordance with the will of their divine emperor.

It is this last point that right-wing nationalists are particularly loath to admit. And it is one that left-wing teachers, activists, and scholars wish to emphasize. Mori's video starts with an image of the imperial chrysanthemum and the sound of marching military boots. The Nanking Massacre, for leftists and many liberals too, is the main symbol of Japanese militarism, supported by the imperial (and imperialist) cult. Which is why it is a keystone of postwar pacifism. Article Nine of the constitution is necessary to avoid another Nanking Massacre. The nationalist right takes the opposite view. To restore the true identity of Japan, the emperor must be reinstated as a religious head of state, and Article Nine must be revised to make Japan a legitimate military power again. For this reason, the Nanking Massacre, or any other example of extreme Japanese aggression, has to be ignored, softened, or denied.

The politics behind the symbol are so divided and so deeply entrenched that it hinders a rational historical debate about what actually happened in 1937. The more one side insists on Japanese guilt, the more the other insists on denying it. The rhetoric in the Nanking Debate, particularly on the side of the revisionists, is both irrational and unhistorical. In his book *The Fabrication of the "Nanking Massacre,"* Tanaka Masaaki accuses Honda Katsuichi and his liberal newspaper of spreading "enemy propaganda." Watanabe Shoichi, another prominent revisionist, wrote a foreword to Tanaka's book. Like Tanaka, he is not a historian, but a professor of English literature. Watanabe attacked Honda for propagating the "Tokyo Trial View of History," which foisted guilt "not only on the Japanese officers and men of the time, but on all Japanese, indeed on our children yet to be born."

Despite their somewhat second-rank intellectual status, the Nanking Massacre revisionists cannot be dismissed as unsavory crackpots, for unlike those who argue that the Holocaust never happened, they are not confined to an extremist fringe. They have a large audience and are supported by powerful right-wing politicians. Ishihara Shintaro, a popular and articulate politician and former cabinet minister, cooperated with Watanabe Shoichi on a book, entitled *A Japan That Can Say "No,"* which denied that anything out of the ordinary had taken place in Nanking. When Ishihara was asked in a *Playboy* interview what he thought of the Nanking Massacre, he said: "People say that the Japanese made a holocaust there, but that is not true. It is a story made up by the Chinese. It has tarnished the image of Japan, but it is a lie."

The liberal left was naturally outraged and the usual minority of activists tried to make a fuss. A group was formed called the Society of Kyoto Citizens Who Will Not Tolerate the Ishihara Statement. They published a pamphlet which included Ishihara's response to the society's criticism. He tried to be accommodating: It was true, he wrote, that the Taiwanese and Koreans who had been killed by the A-bombs, after being forced to come and work in Japan, were innocent victims. But he saw no need to revise his statement on Nanking. The Japanese, he said, should see their history through their own eyes, for "if we rely on the information of aliens and alien countries, who use history for the sake of propaganda, then we are in danger of losing the sense of our own history." Yet another variation of seeing history through the eyes of identity.

Ishihara Shintaro's remarks were one reason why I came to be sitting in a stuffy hotel room in Nanking during the summer of 1991. The hotel was on a busy street lined with trees, in an

area where the Western embassies and hospitals used to be—
known in 1937 as the Safety Zone, which was never really safe.
Japanese troops would come in and round up Chinese men to
find hidden soldiers. Those with callused hands were let go.
They were assumed to be peasants or workers. The others were
classified as soldiers and taken away for execution. Their bodies
were dumped in the river.

We were a motley group, gathered in the hotel to attend a
conference on the Massacre. The main organizers were two
Chinese Americans. One was a businessman, the other a dentist
living in New York. The dentist was born after the war, and
the businessman was a child in 1937. They said they had become
involved out of patriotism. Other participants included Chinese
from various parts of the People's Republic. Among them were
a schoolteacher, a lawyer, several university professors, and,
curiously, a policeman in civilian clothes. There was also an
elderly American whose father had been a reporter in China
during the Japanese war. He carried a large piece of cardboard
around with him, on which he had pasted old newspaper photographs of Japanese atrocities. He would unveil his treasure if
he thought you were worthy of a viewing, glancing over his
shoulder all the while. Finally, there were various Japanese
groups, men and women, many of them schoolteachers. One
of them was Mori Masataka.

It was meant to be a larger conference, with many more
delegates, to be held in a proper hall at Nanking University.
But the Chinese government had refused at the last minute to
give permission. Or so we were told by the Chinese Americans.
The assumed reason was an unexpected visit to Beijing by
the Japanese Prime Minister. Since the Chinese had put in
a request for favorable loans, a conference on Japanese war
crimes was not opportune. But an informal gathering of en-
thusiasts appeared to be permissible. A small prick in the
Japanese conscience was, perhaps, not entirely inopportune.

We drank tea and waited for the arrival of some of the survivors of the Massacre, who had promised to give us their per-

sonal accounts. The Japanese took photographs of us and of one another. Most of them were in their forties. Some of the men wore their hair long. Most of the women were in jeans. None spoke English or Chinese. The interpreter was the Chinese American dentist, who had studied in Japan.

After some delay, the survivors arrived, one woman and three men. They had the tanned, leathery skin of people who had worked outside all their lives. They wore simple blue clothes. The men wore Mao caps. One of them smiled much of the time, revealing a virtually toothless mouth. He told the first story. The Japanese, he said, had amused themselves by tossing a hand grenade in the river and making him retrieve the dead fish. Then they would "dry" him by holding torches to his skin. He was later shot into the river by a machine gun, but managed to survive. It was the duty of the Japanese government, he said, to pay him compensation money.

Then it was the woman's turn. She rolled up one trouser leg to reveal a long, brown scar. Some of the Japanese came closer to take photographs. The woman was two years old at the time, she said, and the Japanese had stabbed her with bayonets. She could not say more, since the memories were too painful, but she did want to stress that the Japanese government should pay her compensation.

A small, tough-looking man spoke up. He was seventeen in 1937 when he was dragged from his house, taken to a sawmill with several others, stripped, and forced on his knees. One by one, the Chinese men were struck with an ax. Somehow he managed to get away, badly wounded in his neck, only to find that his house had been burned down. He showed us his scar and said the Japanese should pay compensation.

Mori began to ask questions. He was interested to hear more details. Exactly when had all this taken place? At what time? Where? A map was produced. What had the weather been like? The questions may have struck some people as impertinent, or too insistent, but I admired his tenacity. Facts were more important to him than a show of emotions.

The fourth survivor told us how he had been taken to the river with about five thousand other men. His voice sounded weary, as though he had already told the same story too many times. His eyes weren't focused. Yet he gave a startling account. The men, he said, were lined up by Japanese officers sitting on horseback. He could remember the long samurai swords dangling from their sides. Then the shooting began. It came from a machine gun on the riverbank. He held his younger brother by the hand, and his father stood behind them. Both his father and his brother died, as did all the other men. The Japanese made sure of this by plunging their bayonets into anything that still moved. The man survived by pretending to be dead. For three hours he lay absolutely still among the bleeding corpses. When the Japanese poured gasoline over him and the other bodies, he managed to crawl free just before the corpses caught fire.

There was a moment of silence. One of the Japanese women dabbed her eyes with a pink handkerchief. A Japanese teacher, representing—according to his name card—the Forum to Reflect upon the War Victims in the Asia-Pacific Region and Engrave It in Our Minds, stood up and made a speech in Japanese, which was translated into Chinese. "We want to show," he said, "that the past cannot be blamed only on militarism. We ourselves bear a responsibility today. That is why we have decided to visit Nanking every year on the fifteenth of August, for we feel that we can only talk about peace if we are inspired by the souls of the victims. By hearing you talk, we feel that a friendship between the Chinese and Japanese peoples can be built. By listening to your stories, we can work toward world peace."

A doctor from Nanking closed his eyes and sang a song, clapping his hands to the rhythm. The witnesses smiled and other Chinese joined in. It was an old song, commemorating the "September 19 Incident" of 1931, when Japan began its annexation of Manchuria. This was followed by impassioned speeches. A Chinese lawyer attacked "Japanese militarism" and professed his love of peace. The politician Ishihara Shintaro, he said, had offended the Chinese people, especially the people of Nanking: "We want the support of all peace-loving people to resist the revival of Japanese militarism."

The shabby room was hot and overcrowded. The air was thick with cigarette smoke. I felt squeamish about inspecting the scars, which the survivors were eager to display. And although I agreed that the Japanese government should be obliged to come clean about the past and had been ungenerous about compensation, I was irritated by the clichéd language of self-righteousness, all the talk of a Japanese militarist revival in a country whose leaders had just turned the army on its own people. The tone of the conference suggested that militarism was a continuing, perhaps even congenitally Japanese, problem.

I asked one of the survivors when he had started to speak in public about his wartime experiences. In 1982, he said. Why only then? He mentioned the Japanese textbook scandal. After news reached China in 1982 that the Japanese Education Ministry had made changes in schoolbooks to deny Japanese responsibility for an aggressive war, survivors in Nanking had been selected by the Chinese government to come forward and tell their stories. Before that no official notice had been taken of them. There was a reason for this, which the survivors didn't mention: Nanking had been the capital of Chiang Kai-shek's Nationalists, far removed from the Communist struggle against Japanese fascism. "Perhaps," said the man, "there was a political reason. But we still feel the same."

The schoolbook story in 1982, as reported in the Japanese newspapers, was that the word "invasion" (of China) had been changed to "advance into" (China) and that references to the Nanking Massacre had been deleted. The story was in fact wrong. Such changes had been made some years before, not without controversy in Japan. But the 1982 textbook story was baseless. The conservative *Sankei* newspaper apologized to its readers for the error. The *Asahi* did not. But the controversy came at a good time for the Chinese government. Deng Xiao-ping was being criticized by the army and by rivals in the Communist Party for being soft on the United States and Taiwan. And a Japanese trade delegation had visited Taipei just before the Japanese Prime Minister's planned visit to Beijing. So it was in Deng's interest to embarrass the Japanese, to twist the knife a little.

The textbook issue afforded a useful opportunity to bring up the Nanking Massacre. The Chinese government decided to commemorate it by building a special museum. It is a sad, ill-maintained place in a poor suburb. The villages surrounding the site cannot have changed much since the Japanese were there: low houses made of brick and mud, narrow lanes filled with children playing in the dirt, people riding their bicycles to the market with squawking chickens suspended by their necks from the handlebars. Massacres were said to have taken place here. I was told there were human bones under the dusty earth.

The museum is a concrete building surrounded by a large rock garden. The rocks, in various shapes and sizes, are inscribed with the names of massacre sites and the numbers of people killed there. Above the main entrance to the museum is a large inscription, in Chinese and English: "Victims: 300,000." On both sides of the corridor, just inside the building, are long sandboxes protected by glass. Bones and skulls, allegedly the remains of Chinese victims, are arranged in the sand. Curtains of dust and cobwebs hang from the damp ceilings. A sign inside the main room explains that the museum was built "to commemorate the victory of the Chinese people in the anti-Japanese war." And that its purpose is "to educate the people, to encourage them to redouble their efforts to strengthen China and support its foreign policy of peace and independence, and promote the friendship between the Japanese and Chinese peoples, and the struggle for world peace."

The most interesting exhibits are the official Japanese Army documents, dispatches from commanding officers on the scene. The language is more revealing than the smudged photographs of atrocities. The most common expressions for murdering large numbers of people are "tidying up" (*katazukeru*) and "treatment" (*shori*), as in "special treatment." I was shown a video of documentary footage I had seen before: the bodies being dumped into pits, the disemboweled women, the laughing executioners. The film ended with the statement that "Nanking had suffered much and had contributed greatly to the world struggle against fascism."

When I came out of the museum, I saw one of the young Japanese teachers. He had changed into the garb of a Buddhist priest and was praying for the dead, fingering his rosary. One of the other teachers was taking photographs of him. I was handed a pamphlet by a young woman of the same group. It was an interesting document, since it contained accounts by members of the group who had visited Nanking on a previous occasion. Again, their emotions were often quite at odds with the idea of "shame culture" versus "guilt culture." Even where the word for shame, *hazukashii*, was used, its meaning was impossible to distinguish from the Western notion of guilt.

"I knew it was going to be tough," one of the Japanese visitors wrote, "but after we arrived on the spot, I felt haunted by the sadness and anger of the Chinese, who had suffered such unspeakable atrocities. I felt crushed by the knowledge that I was the descendant of those Japanese. I felt confused, but nonetheless I kept thinking that the dead should speak! The victims of Nanking should rise and attack us Japanese! For we, who have lived after the war without coming clean about our past, we will not be able to forge a fresh view of history without experiencing shame."

My last stop in Nanking was a place called Yu Hua Tai, where a battle had raged for three days. There is an ugly monument marking the spot of one of the worst massacres. It is a great phallic tower divided by trees from a monumental sculpture of proletarian Chinese heroes standing up to fascism. It was also the place where Lieutenants M. and N. were executed, after being tried by a Chinese war crimes court for their deadly game of swordsmanship.

Lieutenant M.'s daughter published a long article in one of the nationalist magazines that are forever attacking the Tokyo Trial View of History. She thought it was shameless of Honda Katsuichi to have ruined the reputation of her father. Had he no sensitivity toward the surviving family members at all? Her father had wished for nothing more than peace and harmony between Japan and China. How could he rest in peace when lies were being spread? After speaking to her father's spirit, Miss M. was called by her tour guide. The bus was waiting. It was time to go to the next stop. "Then," she said, "I scooped up some of the red earth and folded it in my handkerchief. I felt as though this earth had absorbed the smell of my father."

In the second half of the 1980s, between the textbook affairs and Emperor Hirohito's death, something interesting happened in Japan. A small number of Japanese Imperial Army veterans began to talk in public about their war experiences. Their testimonies were recorded on videotape and shown at privately organized exhibitions, such as the Exhibition of War for Peace held in a Catholic church in Tokyo. The men were in their seventies and eighties. Most had been privates or junior officers. Perhaps it was the proximity of death that made them want to talk, or perhaps it was because most of their superior officers were no longer alive; there was less pressure to keep quiet, less face to be preserved. The same thing happened after the death of Emperor Hirohito; it was as though forbidden subjects could suddenly be aired. As a young historian put it to me, the emperor was the highest superior officer of all.

One of these veterans was a businessman from Kyoto Prefecture named Azuma Shiro. He first spoke in public in 1987, and caused a sensation. Television crews and newspaper reporters came down to his small town on the coast to record his testimony. Right-wing patriots threatened to kill him. He was blackballed from his veterans' association. Yet he could no longer keep quiet. Indeed, he talked and talked, as though the rest of his life depended on it. Azuma Shiro had been in Nanking in the winter of 1937.

In 1992, when he picked me up at the station of a small town to the east of Kyoto, Azuma was eighty-one. A stocky man with a square face and hair dyed a purple shade of black, he looked younger than his age. He was proud of this. He asked me several times to guess his age. I said about sixty-five. While driving from the station to his house, through a pretty landscape of rice paddies surrounded by mountains, he opened the glove compartment of his car and produced a brass knuckle-duster. "In case the right-wingers try anything," he said, fitting the metal brace on his hand.

Azuma's house, built in traditional Japanese style with tatami mats and papered screen doors, was filled with Chinese art. There were Chinese scrolls on the walls, and the sliding screen doors were decorated with Chinese landscapes done by a painter in Beijing. Some of these were presents, Azuma said, from a senior official in the Chinese Communist Party. Azuma had done him a favor by taking care of his son, who was studying in Japan.

We had tea, served by Azuma's wife. He began to talk about his life. Azuma was born in this same small town on the coast, where his father ran a successful business. He had been a spoiled child and led a dissolute schoolboy life, spending his pocket money at local brothels. When he was drafted into the army in 1937, he was suffering from a venereal disease.

Army life was harsh, but he never questioned the reasons for going to war. It was the imperial will, and victory was justified by any means. He did, however, resent his superior officers. They were "cowards," he said. To be a coward was the worst thing he could say about people. His platoon commander, a young man named Mori, who graduated from the military academy, was a coward. He put on airs, but had had no stomach for combat. In fact, Azuma had not felt he had much in common with any of his comrades, except one, an engineering student named Higuchi. Higuchi was the only one who read books, who didn't "have mud on his boots." But he died one night in China, shot in a panic by friendly fire. Azuma cradled his friend as his brains spilled onto his lap.

Azuma had always loved books. Apart from Higuchi, he said, he had been the only one in the platoon who read books. I asked him what books he read in China. "Pearl Buck's *The Good Earth* and Adolf Hitler's *Mein Kampf*," he said. He had much enjoyed both. Even *Mein Kampf*? Yes, he said. He had worshipped Adolf Hitler. He was particularly impressed by a story he had heard that German soldiers were not allowed to rape foreign women, lest they sully the purity of the German race. This, he said, was not something that bothered the Japanese troops in China.

"Sexual desire is human," he said. "Since I suffered from a venereal disease, I never actually did it with Chinese women. But I did peep at their private parts. We'd always order them to drop their trousers. They never wore any underwear, you know. But the others did it with any woman that crossed our path. That wasn't so bad in itself. But then they killed them. You see, rape was against military regulations, so we had to destroy the evidence. While the women were fucked, they were considered human, but when we killed them, they were just pigs. We felt no shame about it, no guilt. If we had, we couldn't have done it.

"Whenever we would enter a village, the first thing we'd do was steal food, then we'd take the women and rape them, and finally we'd kill all the men, women, and children to make sure they couldn't slip away and tell the Chinese troops where we were. Otherwise we wouldn't have been able to sleep at night."

Clearly, then, the Nanking Massacre had been the culmination of countless massacres on a smaller scale. But it had been mass murder without a genocidal ideology. It was barbaric, but to Azuma and his comrades, barbarism was part of war. This is a theme mulled over by many Japanese novelists, even during the war: the transformation of normal men into savage killers. Ishikawa Tatsuzo witnessed the Nanking Massacre and wrote a novella about it in 1938, entitled *Living Soldiers*. It contains such

sentences as this: "Killing enemy soldiers was for Corporal Ka-
sahara exactly the same thing as killing carp."

Azuma resumed his story: "One of the worst moments I can
remember was the killing of an old man and his grandson. The
child was bayoneted and the grandfather started to suck the
boy's blood, as though to conserve his grandson's life a bit
longer. We watched a while and then killed both. Again, I felt
no guilt, but I was bothered by this kind of thing. I felt confused.
So I decided to keep a diary. I thought it might help me think
straight."

Nanking itself—although he later referred to it as a "theater
of hell"—was not particularly eventful for Azuma. He said he
spent most of the time playing cards. Once in a while his platoon
would have to go in search of hidden Chinese soldiers, but he
never took part in any executions. I asked him why not. I wanted
to know why some Japanese were involved in mass arrests and
killings and others were not. He said it depended on the platoon
commander. His commander, Mori, was a coward. Did he mean
that Mori was too squeamish for executions? This surely was a
good thing. Azuma grunted. "Well, maybe so . . ."

He did have friends, however, who took part in the killings.
One of them, Masuda Rokusuke, killed five hundred men by
the Yangtze River with his machine gun. Azuma visited his
friend in the hospital just before he died in the late 1980s.
Masuda was worried about going to hell. Azuma tried to reas-
sure him that he was only following orders. But Masuda remained convinced that he was going to hell.

Not long after his spell in Nanking, Azuma fell ill and was
repatriated. He managed to keep his diary with him, even
though such diaries were usually confiscated by the military
police. During his stay in Japan, he transcribed his notes into
a more coherent account, which he wanted to leave to his future
children. He still had no doubt that the war was just and that
it had to be won at all costs, but he wanted to put on record
what violence ordinary men were capable of.

The account was wrapped up and stored in a cupboard, where

it stayed until 1987. He eventually had five children, but none of them had shown the slightest interest in their father's war experiences. "It was never discussed," Azuma said. He did have a brother, who also served in China, but he took to drink and died in a car crash the week before I saw Azuma. His brother never talked about the war either. What about his old comrades? I asked. How did they discuss the war?

"Oh," said Azuma, "we wouldn't talk about it much. When we did, it was to justify it. The Chinese resisted us, so we had to do what we did, and so on. None of us felt any remorse. And I include myself."

Azuma showed me some photographs of his veterans' association. They were taken on annual outings to various country hotels. The men would stand or sit in strict hierarchical order. Mori, a small, delicate-looking man, sat in the middle of the front row. The earliest picture was taken in the late 1940s. The men looked young and, with their coarse features, short-cropped hair, and tight military expressions, rather menacing. The latest one was taken in 1984. Some of the faces had dropped out. The survivors looked like retired bank managers.

Azuma's memories, his diaries, everything about his past would no doubt have been forgotten if there had not been a plan to build a new war museum in Kyoto. The curators of the new museum at Ritsumeikan University were looking for wartime diaries and had been told about Azuma. The diary was removed from the cupboard, dusted off, and sent to the university. The curators were so impressed by the material that they asked Azuma to give a press conference. He agreed, and it changed his life. The press conference, held in his house, was not in the form of a confession—there is no evidence that Azuma feared the prospect of hell. Nor did it contain a political message—Azuma is not a pacifist. He just spoke about what he had seen and done during the war in China.

The reaction was swift. Accused of hurting the pride of his old regiment, he was threatened with "punishment" by his veterans' association. Letters arrived through the mail—anonymous letters, or signed "A Japanese Patriot"—threatening him with death. But there were other letters, signed by individual citizens, expressing support. He was encouraged by the support, but fired up by the threats. "I always believed it had been a just war. But the threats, the abusive phone calls, the letters, they made me furious. I was just telling the truth. And they wanted to stop me. I was damned if I couldn't tell the truth!"

Azuma began to write ferociously about the war, about military education, about the emperor's responsibility, about the Tokyo war crimes tribunal. The trials had been a good thing, he said, but the Japanese ought to have held their own tribunal. The emperor was a coward, the greatest coward of all, he said, for ducking his responsibility. Azuma had been particularly upset when a document known as the "Emperor's Monologue," recorded in 1946, was published in 1991. It showed the emperor to have been well informed, belligerent, and self-serving. Azuma said, "We went to war for him, my friends died for him, and he never even apologized."

It was getting late. We had our supper sitting on the tatami floor. The landscape outside—the pine trees, the rice paddies, the distant mountains—was screened by darkness. Azuma poured hot sake into my cup. He got more and more agitated. "They turned the emperor into a living god, a false idol, like the Ayatollah in Iran or like Kim Il Sung. Because we believed in the divine emperor, we were prepared to do anything, anything at all, kill, rape, anything. But I know he fucked his wife every night, just like we do . . ."

He paused and lowered his voice. "But you know we cannot say this in Japan, even today. It is impossible in this country to tell the truth."

Again, he told me the story of his friend Higuchi. He had forgotten that he had already told it once. He described what he had felt when his only friend died, his brains spilling out. Azuma dabbed his eyes with the back of his hand. "That damned emperor . . . !" he said.

We repaired to the inn where I was to stay the night. It was a traditional country inn near the small harbor. We had both had too much to drink and staggered in. The innkeeper, a large, rather lugubrious man, led us to my room. But first he wanted to show us something. His brother-in-law had just finished painting the screen walls. We simply had to see this. So there we stood, unsteady on our feet, in the middle of a large Japanese room, surrounded by the local landscape in Japanese ink. There was the harbor and there the mountains and there the rocks in the bay, sprouting pine trees.

"Now let me show you something interesting," said the innkeeper. "See that rock?" We nodded. "Looks large, doesn't it?" We nodded again. "Now walk to the opposite corner of the room—go on . . ." We did. "Suddenly looks small now, doesn't it?" he said. "It's called perspective."

PART THREE

HISTORY ON TRIAL

STUTTGART

THERE WAS NOTHING in the physical appearance of Josef Schwammberger that marked him as a mass murderer. He had the pale, mottled skin of an old man who had spent too much time indoors—an elderly concierge of an apartment building perhaps. He wore brown slacks and a beige leisure jacket. He tended to shuffle, as though wearing a pair of old slippers. His eyes were a dull shade of gray. He was eighty years old in the spring of 1992, when he was sentenced to life in prison.

The trial of Josef Schwammberger, conducted in the state court at Stuttgart, was probably the last Nazi trial to be held in Germany. Schwammberger was accused of being responsible for the murder of at least 3,000 Jews. But the surviving witnesses were few and the evidence often vague, so he was convicted of personally killing 25 people and of being an accessory to the murder of at least 641.

The Israeli ambassador to Bonn visited the court and took the opportunity to remind the German people of their collective responsibility for the past. He told the German press that one could not separate the cultural heritage of Goethe, Schiller, Bach, and Beethoven from the terror of the Nazi regime. Schwammberger, in other words, was part of the national heritage, one more stone in the mosaic of German identity. Neo-Nazi youths staged a demonstration outside the court, claiming that German war guilt was all a Jewish lie.

Schwammberger's Nazi career could be described as a modest success. Born in South Tirol in 1912, he became a party member in 1933, which put him in the class of opportunistic joiners rather than early believers. Sent to Cracow in 1939 as a low-ranking SS officer, he became *Kommandant* of a slave-labor camp, which was closed in 1942. The 200 surviving slaves were shot. He was promoted to the rank of *Oberscharrführer* and became ruler of the ghetto in Przemysl, whose inhabitants were transported at regular intervals to Belzec and Auschwitz. His cruelty and sense of fun were not unusual for a man of his position: his favorite Alsatian, Prinz, was often set upon the Jewish prisoners and he was fond of killing people in front of their families.

His postwar life was not untypical either, for a man of his ilk: he was helped by Catholic priests to escape to Argentina, where he lived in peace, devoting his time to beekeeping. He was only brought back to Germany in 1990; his trial began the following year.

Schwammberger's presence in the court was oddly ephemeral; he was there, yet he seemed not to be there. Everybody—the judges, the lawyers, the witnesses, the public—talked about him, yet he remained absolutely still. Once in a while, he would work his mouth, like a lizard. He hardly spoke at all. It was impossible to tell whether he even heard anything. His thin-lipped face remained blank, even when one of the witnesses, an eighty-one-year-old man, told the court how he and several others had been treated after trying to escape from the ghetto. They were ordered to lie on their backs and open their mouths for Ukrainian guards to piss in. Schwammberger, said the witness, had found this terribly amusing.

Another witness, a man named Nussbaum, had come from Kansas City accompanied by his son and grandchildren. Nussbaum had been a plumber. He fixed up Schwammberger's house in the ghetto. In a sense, Schwammberger had saved his life, by pulling him out of a crowd destined for Auschwitz; somebody had to bolt the doors of the cattle cars; that somebody was Nussbaum. He realized later that one of the cattle cars had contained his own family.

Nussbaum had been waiting for this day. He had always kept his memories to himself. Even his son knew nothing about them. "Your honor," he said in a thick Polish accent, "there are so many stories I could tell you . . ." Like the one about the rabbi on Yom Kippur in 1942 who insisted on praying instead of doing hard labor; Schwammberger made everybody watch as he shot him in the head.

Nussbaum's memory seemed clear and his manner was spirited. He told us outside the courtroom that Schwammberger was an animal. "No, he was worse than an animal. An animal kills to eat. He, he, he, I have no word for it, he is a cold killer. If I were able to, I would tear off his right arm, not kill him, mind you, just take off his right arm, the one he used to shoot with, and put it in his left hand."

The judges and counsel had gone to Przemysl to see for themselves. They had measured the distance from the *Kommandant*'s former house to the site of one of his alleged murders. They needed to test the witness's memory in the courtroom. So everybody huddled around the ghetto map, as Nussbaum pointed out the old landmarks. He still remembered everything. Even Schwammberger could not contain his curiosity and shuffled across to peer over his former plumber's shoulder.

After he had shuffled back again, Schwammberger was asked by the judge whether he could remember the witness. Schwammberger's mouth moved. The judge asked him to speak up. A soft "*nein*" was heard. The judge showed signs of impatience. He asked how it was possible that he had forgotten all the witnesses, even though they could remember him in detail. Schwammberger mumbled that 50,000 people might remember him, but he could not possibly remember 50,000 people. The judge said he was simply trying to establish some kind of contact with the defendant. "I'm trying to get you to say something.

Some of the witnesses knew you well. Why, one of them even groomed your dog." For the first time, Schwammberger came to life. In a rasping voice, which hinted at the man who had once, long ago, been accustomed to giving orders, he said: "It would be utterly illogical for me to hand over the care of my dog to some stranger!"

This unexpected little outburst caught Schwammberger's counsel by surprise. He said that his client was too exhausted to carry on. His heart was weak. He needed a rest. The judge rolled his eyes but declared the court adjourned.

The setting of the mini-drama I had witnessed was undramatic. The courtroom was modern, functional, almost wholly without the trappings of traditional judicial authority, such as the wigs and other pomp one finds in British courts. There was no theater about the proceedings, no ceremony. Documents, measurements, maps were what mattered, not oratory. And the public at the proceedings consisted entirely of German high school students. They had come all the way from Bad Wimpfen, a small spa town near Heidelberg, with their history teacher, a bearded 68er named Bernd Wetzka.

Outside the courtroom, Mr. Nussbaum spoke to American reporters. The students crowded around the defense lawyer, a man of roughly the same age as their history teacher. They were puzzled by his plea for an acquittal. They asked him whether he really believed that Schwammberger was innocent. "Belief," the lawyer answered, "belongs in church. My duty is to make sure my client gets a fair trial and that the witnesses are credible." This, he explained, was complicated, since the alleged crimes took place such a long time ago. He said it would take more courage for the judge to deliver a not-guilty verdict, in the face of public opinion, than to declare his client guilty.

The teenagers looked grave and nodded. Wetzka snorted and said: "Yes, our judges have really showed such courage in the past, haven't they? And what about the Nazi judges who were never purged after the war . . . ?"

One of the students, a girl with a punk haircut, asked whether it was possible for a witness to have only heard what he now claims to have seen. The lawyer began to answer, but Wetzka snorted again and said the testimonies had been much too detailed to be able to believe that.

There were signs here of a generational difference. The teacher was angry, he felt personally involved, there was little room for skepticism. He later told me his own parents had been Nazis. He had often quarreled with them about the past. They still insisted that it had not been all bad, that they had been idealists, that the stories about the Jews were exaggerated. He had heard all the excuses and they still made him angry. His pupils were less emotionally involved. Their questions showed an intelligent interest in the proceedings. Schwammberger could not have been *their* father.

Wetzka told me that this visit to the trial had meant a lot to his pupils. They had already been to see two former concentration camps, Natzweiler-Struthof and Dachau, but the Schwammberger case had left a greater impression. The history of the Nazi period was already remote to them, something they read about in books, but this trial really brought those distant events to life, he said. Months later, one of the pupils wrote a report for the school magazine: "After hearing in detail from witnesses what cruelties he had committed, it was easier to understand the verdict."

No doubt it was. Nor is there any doubt that the trial was good for Mr. Nussbaum. His memories were released. It was perhaps a personal catharsis. It was moving to see at least one survivor confronting his torturer in a German court. But not all witnesses were as tough as Nussbaum. The experience proved too much for one man, who died of a heart attack in court. Still, the demand for retribution, even if it was only a little splash in an ocean of evil, was satisfied. Perhaps, as Simon Wiesenthal hoped, it would serve as a warning. In any case, it was hard to feel sorry for Schwammberger, despite his pathetic state.

And yet, I felt uneasy sitting in that court in Stuttgart. I felt especially uneasy about those students, in their colorful anoraks, filling the public gallery. My first instinct was to applaud West German education. Things had come a long way since 1968. There had been no school classes at Nuremberg, or even at the Auschwitz trial in Frankfurt from 1963 till 1965. Good for the teacher, I thought. Let them hear what was done. But I began to have doubts. Just as belief belongs in church, surely history education belongs in school. When the court of law is used for history lessons, then the risk of show trials cannot be far off. It may be that show trials can be good politics—though I have my doubts about this too. But good politics don't necessarily serve the truth.

Forty-four years before Schwammberger's trial, another German of far higher rank was tried in Nuremberg. Ernst von Weiszäcker was Under Secretary for Foreign Affairs when Germany conquered most of Europe. Since 1943, he had served as ambassador to the Vatican—a rather crucial posting, since the Germans wanted to make sure the pope kept silent about the Final Solution. Whether or not this was due to Weiszäcker's diplomatic skills, the pope did not disappoint them. Ernst von Weiszäcker's son Richard was the later President who spoke more than any other politician about the burdens of Germany's guilt.

There is a story about the young Richard when he was in Nuremberg at the time of the war crimes trials. He is said to have turned to a friend and to have remarked, in his best Wehrmacht officer style, that they should storm the court and release the prisoners. The friend, rather astonished, asked why on earth they should do such a thing. "So that we can try them ourselves" was Weiszäcker's alleged response. His wish came true only many years later, when German courts prosecuted much smaller fry. Meanwhile, he elected to be a junior member of his father's defense team.

Ernst von Weiszäcker was accused of planning to wage an

aggressive war and complicity in the deportation of Jews from various occupied countries. He was acquitted on the first count, but found guilty on the latter. He had signed a document which stated that the Foreign Ministry had no objections to a planned deportation of Jews. His chief defense counsel, Hellmut Becker, argued that Weiszäcker was an old-fashioned patriot who had done what he could under very difficult circumstances to stop the Nazis from doing their worst. Since he had failed to do so, Weiszäcker admitted his guilt in the eyes of God, but not according to the laws drawn up by the Allied powers at Nuremberg.

In 1950, Becker wrote that "few things have done more to hinder true historical self-knowledge in Germany than the war crimes trials." He stuck to this belief. Becker must be taken seriously, for he is not a right-wing apologist for the Nazi past, but an eminent liberal. I visited him at his office in Berlin. One wall was decorated with fine military prints. On the other was an Israeli calendar.

Becker was not against holding trials as such. But he believed that existing German laws should have been applied, instead of retroactive laws about crimes against peace (preparing, planning, or waging an aggressive war). He mentioned the fact that Stalin's judge on the Nuremberg tribunal wished to have it clarified that what was to be condemned was not aggressive war in general, but Nazi aggression in particular. The Soviet occupation of the Baltic States or parts of Poland was not to be a crime against peace. The *tu quoque* principle was expressly forbidden in any discussion of war crimes: the bombing of Dresden, say, or the expulsion of German-speaking civilians from their homes in Eastern and Central Europe in 1945 was deemed to be irrelevant to the trial.

It was to avoid a travesty of the legal process that the British had been in favor of simply executing the Nazi leaders without a trial. The British were afraid that a long trial might change public opinion. The trial, in the words of one British diplomat, might be seen as a "put-up job." There was also concern that international law might not apply to many of the alleged crimes. If revenge was the point, why drag the law into it? Why not take a political decision to punish? This was what Becker, in his office, called the Italian solution: "You kill as many people as you can in the first six weeks, and then you forget about it: not very legal, but for the purposes of purification, well . . ." The British only backed down from their position in May 1945, after Hitler and Goebbels had killed themselves. Only then did the British agree to a trial of the remaining Nazi leaders.

Due process or revenge. This problem had preoccupied the ancient Greek tragedians. To break the cycle of vendetta, Orestes had to be tried by the Athens court for the murder of his mother. Without a formal trial, the vengeful Furies would continue to haunt the living.

The aspect of revenge might have been avoided had the trial been held by German judges. There was a precedent for this, but it was not a happy one. German courts had been allowed to try alleged war criminals after World War I. Despite strong evidence against them, virtually all were acquitted, and the foreign delegates were abused by local mobs. Besides, Wetzka was right: German judges had collaborated with the Nazi regime; they could hardly be expected to be impartial. So it was left to the victors to see that justice was done.

The question is how to achieve justice without distorting the law, and how to stage a trial by victors over the vanquished without distorting history. A possibility would have been to make victors' justice explicit, by letting military courts try the former enemies. This would have avoided much hypocrisy and done less damage to the due process of law in civilian life. But if the intention was to teach Germans a history lesson, a military court would have run into the same problems as a civilian one. And judging from statements made at the time, history teaching was undoubtedly one of the aims of the war crimes trials.

Robert M. Kempner, the German American prosecutor in the Weiszäcker trial, wrote that the "trials with their devastating

collections of German documents were the greatest history seminar ever held in the history of the world." When the American
chief prosecutor in Nuremberg, Robert H. Jackson, was asked
by the British judge, Lord Justice Lawrence, what he thought
the purpose of the trials should be, Jackson answered that they
were to prove to the world that the German conduct of the war
had been unjustified and illegal, and to demonstrate to the
German people that this conduct deserved severe punishment
and to prepare them for it.

The Nuremberg trials were to be a history lesson, then, as
well as a symbolic punishment of the German people—a moral
history lesson cloaked in all the ceremonial trappings of due
legal process. They were the closest that man, or at least the
men belonging to the victorious powers, could come to dispens-
ing divine justice. This was certainly the way some German
writers felt about it. Some welcomed it with the enthusiasm of
pious sinners on their way to confession. They were the fore-
runners of the *betroffen* generation of 1968. All were men of the
left. Some were Communists.

Erik Reger, the novelist, for example: "The less the Nuremberg tribunal dresses itself up in the robes of formal law, the
more honestly the political element will be expressed. Its judgment before history will be all the greater then, and all the more
instructive. And the trial will not take place in an atmosphere
of contrived symbolism, but in one of moral force, through
which evil can be overcome."

A reporter for the *Süddeutschen Zeitung*, W. E. Süskind, not,
so far as I know, a Communist, described the trial as an *"Ur-
Prozess"*—"a trial never seen before on this earth, and thus a
truly historic moment."

What becomes clear from this kind of language is that law,
politics, and religion became confused: Nuremberg became a
morality play, in which Göring, Kaltenbrunner, Keitel, and the
others were cast in the leading roles. It was a play that claimed
to deliver justice, truth, and the defeat of evil. The documents,

the testimony, the high seriousness of the occasion were meant to vouchsafe the truth. This was used to great effect by playwrights, who re-created the trials on the stage.

Rolf Schneider, a leftist writer who lived in the German Democratic Republic, wrote a so-called documentary play entitled *Trial in Nuremberg (Prozess in Nürnberg)*. He re-created the events by editing testimonies and cross-examinations. The documentary play, he wrote in the preface, was an invention of the German-language theater: "It arose from memories of history and dissatisfaction with the present, which includes the present descriptions of the past." He also wrote: "One reason for re-creating this trial on the stage is simple information: important because, among other things, this trial was the model for later trials of this kind, in Nuremberg, Jerusalem, Frankfurt . . ."

There is indeed much information there. The cross-examinations of Göring, Schacht, and Keitel are fascinating. But the intention was not to present the historical facts as objectively as possible. For the play was as political as the trial itself, though with a different twist. Schneider was clever enough to put most of his political points in the mouths of the British and American prosecutors. The British prosecutor, for example, is quoted as saying that the "German industrialists were guilty to exactly the same extent" as the political and military defendants. This was, of course, the classic GDR line: fascism as the last defense of capitalism.

Then he had the American prosecutor, in effect, defend the Nazi left wing, led by Ernst Röhm and Gregor Strasser. Göring said they had to be destroyed for their disloyalty to Hitler. The American prosecutor said in the play: "These people represented social goals. They brought you supporters because of that. And you did away with the social aims of all those supporters when you made common cause with German big industry."

This, then, took care of the awkward problem of proletarian support for the Nazi movement. It is not an utterly false representation of the facts, but a biased one. The political purpose for presenting the trial in this way is clear. To lend legitimacy to the antifascist Communist state, capitalists and industrialists had to be seen as the puppeteers of fascist thugs. The play ends with a statement by the American prosecutor on crimes against peace (not crimes against humanity, which concerned racial persecution and genocide, which never fitted so snugly into official antifascist ideology). We now have this law on our books, the prosecutor said: "It will be used against the German aggressor this time. But the four powers, who are conducting this trial in the name of twenty-three nations, know this law and declare: Tomorrow we shall be judged before history by the same yardstick by which we judge these defendants today."

Again, not unreasonable. That was indeed the way Robert Jackson saw things then. But what was the main reason for this ending? The play was written in 1968, at the height of the Vietnam War. It was the era in which German intellectuals, in the GDR and the Federal Republic, wrote such sentences as these (by Christian Geissler): "One of the four chief prosecutors at the international tribunal back then brought his case in the name of the United States of America. And for us naive people of that time, this meant that he was stating his case in the name of justice, freedom, and humanity.

"We had seen through the amorality of the Nazis, and wanted to rid ourselves of it. It was from the moral seriousness of the American prosecution that we wished to learn sensible political thinking.

"And we did learn.

"And we allowed ourselves to apply this thinking to the present time. For example, we will use it now to take quite literally the morality of those American prosecutors. *Oradour and Lidice—today they are cities in South Vietnam.*" (Italics in the original text.)

The tables were neatly turned. The *tu quoque* argument—however inappropriate in this case—was finally put to use. We are all guilty. A playwright, or any writer for that matter, is of course perfectly entitled to do this. But to say that the documentary play offered simple information was disingenuous, as disingenuous, or indeed as foolish, as the idea that political trials are suitable vehicles for moral history lessons. For such trials do not pacify the Furies.

Twenty years after the Nuremberg trials began, a German court in Frankfurt tried some of the officers and guards of Auschwitz for crimes against humanity. It was not quite the first German trial of this kind. In 1957 an SS officer was charged with having led a murder squad on the Lithuanian border. But this had been an exception. The Nuremberg judges had applied the new law against genocide and racial persecution only to crimes committed during the war itself, as though the Holocaust were simply another war crime. In presenting his case, the French chief prosecutor, François de Menthon, hardly mentioned the Jews at all.

At any rate, after Nuremberg, most Germans were tired of war crimes. And until the mid-1950s German courts were permitted to deal only with crimes committed by Germans against other Germans. It took the bracing example of the Eichmann trial in Jerusalem to jolt German complacency—that, and the fact that crimes committed before 1946 would no longer be subject to prosecution after 1965. (It was decided in 1979, after the shock of the *Holocaust* TV series, to abolish the statute of limitations for crimes against humanity.)

The scale of the Nuremberg trials was bigger, and the defendants were grander, but the impact on most Germans of the Auschwitz and Majdanek trials (the latter held in Düsseldorf from 1975 until 1981) was far greater. This was partly a matter of timing. In 1945 most Germans were hungry and defensive. By 1964 a new generation had grown up in relative prosperity. And it was partly the nature of the crimes. Trying the vanquished for conventional war crimes was never convincing, since the victors could be accused of the same. *Tu quoque* could be invoked, in private if not in the Nuremberg court, when memories of Dresden and Soviet atrocities were still fresh. But Auschwitz had no equivalent. That was part of another war, or, better, it was not really a war at all; it was mass murder pure and simple, not for reasons of strategy or tactics, but of ideology alone.

One of the ironies of modern history is that these crimes— which were not the main business of the Nuremberg court (or, it must be said, of the Allied war effort) and of which the majority of Germans after the war claimed ignorance—became the main focus of (West) German historical remembrance, in courts, in schools, in memorials. As the military campaigns, the crimes against peace, recede into history, the Final Solution continues to haunt the present more than ever. Whether you are a conservative who wants Germany to be a "normal" nation or a liberal/leftist engaging in the "labor of mourning," the key event of World War II is Auschwitz, not the Blitzkrieg, not Dresden, not even the war on the eastern front. This was the one history lesson of Nuremberg that stuck. As Hellmut Becker said, despite his skepticism about Nuremberg: "It was most important that the German population realized that crimes against humanity had taken place and that during the trials it became clear how they had taken place."

I believe this is right. But the lesson might not have been so convincing had the trials not been taken on by German courts. When a British court tried the *Kommandant* and guards of Bergen-Belsen in 1945, the effect was by no means the same. Stephen Spender ran into a friend in Germany at the time who told him about a visit to "a charming and sympathetic German family, mostly of young people. They all said the Belsen trials were propaganda and that the alleged crimes of Kramer, etc., were humanly impossible . . . The majority of Germans believed that the trials were a put-up job and that they were only being prolonged because the accused had so much to be said on their side . . ."

But even the great death camp trials in Germany did not dispel all doubts about the adequacy of trials as history lessons. Trials, by their very nature, limit criminal responsibility to specific individuals; in the case of Nuremberg, to the leaders. In his famous essay on German guilt, *Die Schuldfrage (The Question of German Guilt*), written in 1946, Karl Jaspers distinguished four categories of guilt: criminal guilt, for breaking the law; political guilt, for being part of a criminal political system; moral guilt, for personal acts of criminal behavior; and metaphysical guilt, for failing in one's responsibility to maintain the standards of civilized humanity. Obviously these categories overlap. But Jaspers made it clear that an entire people could not be held responsible for a crime legally, morally, or metaphysically. (Political responsibility was another matter.) The great advantage, in his view, of a war crimes trial was its limitation. By allowing the accused to defend themselves with arguments, by laying down the rules of due process, the victors limited their own powers. And: "For us Germans this trial has the advantage that it distinguishes between the particular crimes of the leaders and that it does not condemn the Germans collectively."

Jaspers did not mention the problem of selecting the right defendants; some of the men on trial in Nuremberg probably should not have been there (Schacht, Fritzsche), while others certainly should have (Alfried Krupp), but that is another matter. In any event, the trial distanced the German people even further from their former leaders. It was a comfortable distance, and few people had any desire to bridge it. This might be why the Nazi leaders are hardly ever featured in German plays, films, or novels. Famous or infamous historical figures are never easy to integrate into works of fiction, to be sure. The known facts intrude; history is too heavy. But this does not explain why there are not many biographies of the Nazi leaders either. Historians have backed away from them. The standard biographies of Hitler were written by two journalists, Joachim Fest and Werner Maser. Biographies of Göring and Himmler are virtually all by foreigners. This fear of biography, in fictional or documentary form, is due possibly to an idea common in the 1960s and 1970s—that structures and institutions, not human beings, explain the past. But it must also have something to do with the fear of identification; what Germans call *Berührungsangst*, literally the fear of making contact.

If this was true of the leaders, what, then, about the lesser-known doctors, administrators, gas chamber operators, and other small thugs who carried out their orders? Is identification with them any easier? Peter Weiss, in his play about the Auschwitz trial, identifies them in an interesting way. The former victims who speak as witnesses at the trial are anonymous, but their torturers have names: Boger, whose specialty was to suspend his victims from a kind of swing and beat them to death; or Dr. Capesius, the death camp's pharmacist, who had forgotten all about the fact that his inventory contained Zyklon B; or Dr. Lucas, the good Catholic, who claimed to have deliberately shirked his duties on the railway ramp. It was certainly not Weiss's intention to make the audience identify with these characters. The point was, rather, that Auschwitz was an extreme symbol of industrial exploitation, of capitalism gone mad. The victims were as anonymous as the proletarian masses churned up by insatiable machines. The process went on, even as the Third Reich dissolved into the German Federal Republic. The last words of the play are spoken by Mulka, the adjutant of the camp:

> "We only did our duty, all of us,
> even when it was often hard
> and if we should despair
> today
> now that our nation once again has
> worked its way up to a leading position
> we should busy ourselves with other things
> than with accusations whose time
> surely has passed long ago."

This was not an uncommon attitude in Germany at the time. Indeed, it was pretty mainstream. Serious conservative intellectuals, such as Hermann Lübbe, argued that too many accusations would have blocked West Germany's way to becoming a stable, prosperous society. Not that Lübbe was an apologist for the Third Reich. Far from it: the legitimacy of the Federal Republic, in his opinion, lay in its complete rejection of the Nazi state. The problem was how to turn millions of former Nazi supporters into loyal citizens in a liberal democracy. This, Lübbe argued, could not be achieved without a certain discretion about the past. Nevertheless, the Bogers, the Mulkas, and the Dr. Capesiuses were accused, albeit twenty years after the war. And their reaction was often one of indignation. "Why me?" they would say. "I just did my duty. I just followed orders like every decent German. Why must I be punished?"

The defendants in the Majdanek trial said this over and over in a German television documentary. Why me? Why indeed. But one line in the film stuck in my mind. It was spoken by "Bloody Brigitta," a particularly vicious female guard. "You know," she explained to the interviewer, "these former prisoners all complain how hard it was. Of course it was cruel inside the camp. But you have to realize one thing: if you offered these people one finger, they'd take your whole hand." These were the words of a stupid school matron, a customs inspector, a petty ticket puncher suddenly given absolute power over thousands of slaves.

And yet, despite the shabby mediocrity of these people and the banality of their statements, it proved almost impossible to identify with them. The grossness of their crimes and the scale of their murderousness gave the trials a horrific atmosphere, with new revelations appearing in the newspapers every day. Martin Walser wrote in the year of the Auschwitz trial that Boger became a prince of darkness, a gruesome celebrity identified in the press as "the beast" or "the monster." Dante's name was constantly invoked in lazy accounts of the death camps. The unimaginable was compressed in catchy headlines: "Women driven into fire alive," or "the torture swing of Auschwitz." Walser wrote: "The more ghastly the slogans about Auschwitz, the more pronounced our distance to it becomes."

A trial can only be concerned with individual crimes. The "monsters" and "butchers" on trial in Frankfurt and Düsseldorf had committed terrible crimes. So did many people who were never held to account. But, said Walser, "that these criminals were so like all of us at any point between 1918 and 1945 that we were interchangeable, and that particular circumstances caused them to take a different course, which resulted in this trial, these matters could not be properly discussed in the courtroom." The terrible acts of individuals are lifted from their historical context. History is reduced to criminal pathology and legal argument. What is left is horror and fascination. Which is not to say that the trials were wrong. But they will not do as history lessons, nor do they bring us closer to that elusive thing that Walser seeks, a German identity.

Not so far from the court where Schwammberger was tried, virtually on the outskirts of Stuttgart, lies the old Swabian town of Ludwigsburg. The dukes of Württemberg had their residence there. Schiller was born there (his house is now a branch of the Wienerwald restaurant chain, next door to McDonald's hamburgers). And in the eighteenth century, the duke's financial adviser, Jew Süss, caricatured in Nazi propaganda as the archetypal evil Jew, was hanged there. Outside the gates of the ducal palace is a sign that reads: "This city presents a cheerful and delightful face. Its lively, liberal atmosphere is still in evidence today, provided one is ready to take the time to visit more than just its parks and palaces."

I was there to visit the Zentrale Stelle der Landesjustizverwaltungen zur Aufklärung von NS Verbrechen, literally Central Office of the State Judicial Administrations for the Clearing-up of National Socialist Crimes. It was housed in a former women's jail. Next door was a large seventeenth-century fortress, which served as a prison (the oldest in Germany) until 1990. It is now a penal museum. The young man who let me in smiled politely and listed the treasures of the house: a guillotine, used until the late 1940s, thumbscrews, uniforms, ropes and belts with which prisoners had hanged themselves, a restored death cell, an executioner's ax, colorful prints of torture scenes, and the menu of Jew Süss's last meal: meat soup, braised veal, beans, and white bread.

The taxi driver who took me from the station to the Central Office for the Clearing-up of Nazi Crimes—Nazi crimes, note, not war crimes—was not pleased with this mission. At first he pretended not to know the place. Then he told me at length why he thought the office should be abolished: it was high time we forgot about all that old Nazi stuff, as though there weren't more important things to deal with, what with reunification and all that, as if the Communists hadn't been just as bad, and so on.

This kind of thing, I was told by Alfred Streim, who heads the institution, used to be much more common. When it was decided to open the center in 1958, the people of Ludwigsburg had protested, firebombs had been thrown, and it had been difficult to find a venue. But now, said Streim, with the younger generation, things were better.

With its huge quantity of documents, filed under personal and place names, the central office is, as it were, the bureaucratic memory of the Nazi past. Whenever there is a case to be made against former Nazis, this is where the prosecutors turn for their documentary evidence. When I was shown around the premises by one of Streim's colleagues, people came up with such requests as "Schmidt, Dachau, 1943." Often my guide, a lawyer, like Streim, would know the answer from memory. If not, he would open one of the steel filing cabinets, filled with papers neatly tagged "Auschwitz" or "Buchenwald" or "Dachau," and swiftly pull out the required information.

Streim was not a cheerful man. His skin looked as gray as his Bavarian-style horn-buttoned suit. He was a schoolboy when he was bombed out of his home in Hamburg. He was evacuated to Czechoslovakia, and then had to walk back to Hamburg at the end of the war. He said that young people today could not possibly understand the pressures his generation was under. Hitler Youth, bombings, censorship, and the rest. Streim's father was a Nazi, employed by the railways: "He always said it wasn't true about the Jews." Streim would argue with him, but his father denied the truth, even after the war. "My father's generation was very naive," Streim said. "He only changed his mind when I showed him the documents."

The central office has collected more than 1,400,000 documents: witness testimonics, case histories, Gestapo documents, court records, etc. In 1986 the United Nations supplied documents on 30,000 people. Further information came from Poland, the Soviet Union, France, Romania, Hungary, Holland, indeed from everywhere in Europe. There was but one exception: the German Democratic Republic. Only the East German State Security Police, or Stasi, kept all its information to itself.

The GDR had its own ways of using courts of law to deal with the Nazi past. They were in many respects the opposite of West German ways. The targets tended to be the very people that West German justice had ignored. Thorough purges took place in the judiciary, the bureaucracy, and industry. About 200,000 people—four-fifths of the Nazi judges and prosecutors—lost their jobs. War crimes trials were held too; until 1947 by the Soviets, after that in German courts.

The trials were swift. Instead of limiting the powers of the state (or the victors) by allowing the accused to defend themselves, the Communist courts did the reverse. In the notorious Waldheimer trials, in 1950, the appointed judges and prosecutors were informed that since the guilt of the defendants was obvious, there would be no need for witnesses, defense lawyers, or documentary evidence. It was also one of the last Nazi trials to be held in the GDR. There were two more before 1957, and none after that. All in all, about 30,000 people had been tried and 500 executed. In the Federal Republic the number was about 91,000, and none were executed, as the death penalty was abolished by the 1949 constitution.

The antifascist German people's republic did a better job

than the Federal Republic in weeding out Nazis in high places. But the smaller Nazis were left alone as long as they were obedient Communists. East German methods were both ruthless and expedient, and the official conclusion to the process was that the GDR no longer had to bear the burden of guilt. As state propaganda ceaselessly pointed out, the guilty were all in the West. There the fascists still sat as judges and ran the industries that produced the economic boom, the *Wirtschaftswunder*. Shortly after the Israeli Prime Minister, David Ben-Gurion, announced the arrest of Eichmann in 1960, the East German press revealed that Hans Globke, a state secretary in Adenauer's government, had helped to write the Nuremberg race laws of 1935. "Globke is the Eichmann of Bonn" was the headline in *Neues Deutschland*, the national newspaper of the GDR.

This peculiar state of innocence in the GDR produced peculiar problems after the Communist state ceased to exist. There was, for example, the case of Gustav Just, a politician of the Social Democratic Party, whose career had taken off after unification. At seventy he had become senior president of the Brandenburg state assembly and chairman of the parliamentary constitutional committee. But not long after he achieved this eminence, his career took an unpleasant spill: in March 1992 a newspaper revealed that Just had shot six Ukrainian Jews in 1941, after having volunteered as a soldier. His first response was that he had simply followed orders. His second response, after much pressure, was to resign.

Just was only one of many, and not a very significant one at that. What was interesting about his case was that he had been prosecuted once already in the GDR, in 1957, for counterrevolutionary activities, and sentenced to four years in jail. He had edited a mildly critical weekly paper. His was a show trial meant to scare off other intellectuals who diverged from the Stalinist line. During the trial, the judge actually read out parts of Just's wartime diary, which described the shootings in the Ukraine. But nothing was made of this. According to Just, he was threatened with a war crimes trial if he should displease the authorities again. "The Stasi," he said, "were experts on war crimes."

One might think that the experience of show trials and political corruption of historical memory would have made the eastern Germans chary of political trials and purges after 1990. But this was not the case. There was considerable enthusiasm in the former GDR for putting Communist leaders on trial and for rigorous purges of Stasi agents and informers. The eastern German equivalent to the central office in Ludwigsburg is an institution in Berlin run by a Protestant pastor named Joachim Gauck. His office is the depository and dispensary of documentary information on all Stasi activities. Dispensary is probably the right word, since Gauck sees his work in rather medical terms: he is the dispenser of moral hygiene; his files are the medicine which should cure a rotten society. Although some of his critics, mostly on the old left, in both former Germanys, called him a grand inquisitor, few doubted the pastor's good intentions. His arguments for trials were moral, judicial, and historical. He set out his views in a book entitled *The Stasi Documents*. Echoes of an earlier past rang through almost every page.

"We can safely predict," Gauck wrote, "that individual trials might go on for a long time, as was the case with trials against Nazi criminals in the old Federal Republic, and for some crimes time might even run out. But we cannot allow a general amnesty for Stasi agents, if only for the sake of their victims. And it is certain that such an event would shatter people's faith in the rule of law."

So much for the legal lesson. On history he had this to say: "The West Germans already know better than the former GDR citizens how bitter it is to leave it to the next generation to face up to an evil past. They have already burnt their fingers once, so they can't be expected to allow this German negligence to become a bad tradition. In his famous speech on May 8, 1985, the fortieth anniversary of the end of the war, Richard von

Weiszäcker spoke of the importance of remembrance in the process of shaping the present as well as the future. The way we now face up to our own past offers an excellent opportunity to counter the prejudice that Germans generally turn away from their past and are 'unable to mourn.' "

The reference to the inability to mourn shows how deeply the lessons of Alexander and Margarethe Mitscherlich had sunk in. We must do it right this time. We cannot allow the second past to haunt us like the first one. It is an argument, or, more accurately perhaps, a sentiment that appealed to many West Germans too. Maybe one should say especially to West Germans, for it is they—or at least some of them—who felt guilty about tolerating Nazis in their midst. And although newspaper columnists, clerics, academics, and German opinion makers in general continued to point out distinctions between the two undigested pasts, the difference between Nazi Germany and Stasi Germany had a tendency to get blurred. Not just that, but a certain air of capitalist triumphalism among the Wessies provoked once again the accusation of victors' justice; only this time it wasn't Western and Soviet Allies, but western Germans who were in the victor's seat.

It was a situation full of irony: the Germany of the guilty, the people who felt *betroffen* by their own "inability to mourn," the nation that staged the Auschwitz and Majdanek trials, *that* Germany was now said to stand in judgment over the other Germany—the Germany of the old antifascists, the Germany that had suffered under two dictatorships, the Germany of uniformed marches, goose-stepping drills, and a secret police network, vast beyond even the Gestapo's dreams. And as the last Nazi war criminal was sentenced in Stuttgart, thousands of Stasi men and Communist thugs were waiting to play their parts in the second round of juridical history lessons.

TOKYO

The law court in Nuremberg looks solid—indestructible almost—in a city that lacks solidity. The restored medievalism of the old town center gives the city a stagey atmosphere, as though Nuremberg were a mere backdrop to a historical fancy. The other solid building in Nuremberg is Albert Speer's only remaining work, the stadium on the Zeppelin Field, where the annual Nazi Party rallies were held. It was too massive to blow up—the men's lavatories are as big as average cinema halls— but it has not been maintained. Thick weeds sprout from the crumbling stone grandstands.

I asked an old man selling souvenirs (beer mugs, flags, knives) where the court building was. "You mean the place where they hanged our officers?" Yes, I said, that was the place. He gave me directions, but I lost my way. So I had to ask again at my hotel. The young woman behind the reception desk had no idea. Her supervisor, a bleached blonde in her fifties, came over to ask what I wanted. I repeated my question. Her lips curled. "What do you want to go there for?" she snapped. "There is nothing interesting to see. Why don't you visit our Old City . . ." I said something about history. She turned away. "Foreigners," she muttered.

The building is, as I said, solid, Wilhelmine, designed to impress. It is as pompous in its way as Speer's stadium. Former judges stand on their stone pedestals like stern gods overlooking the Fürtherstrasse. Above the main entrance is a large frieze showing the various symbols of authority: tablets engraved with Roman numerals denoting the Ten Commandments, an open law book flanked by branches, and an ax projecting from a bundle of birch rods, the Roman insignia of penal power, later adopted by the fascists.

Although the Japanese, too, went in for Wilhelmine grandeur (perhaps more in the colonies than in Japan itself), there is nothing in Tokyo like the Nuremberg law court. There were more than 2,000 war crimes trials held by Allied tribunals in

Japan, Southeast Asia, and other Asian and Pacific locales. But the building where the International Military Tribunal of the Far East sat in judgment of the 28 Japanese wartime leaders from 1946 until the end of 1948, the so-called Class A defendants, was a former military academy, which had served as the Japanese Army headquarters at the end of the war. The auditorium had been hastily transformed into a wood-paneled courtroom, lit by blinding klieg lights, which reminded Joseph Keenan, the chief prosecutor, of a Hollywood film studio. Later, the building was demolished to make way for a new town hall.

There was, however, another, more poignant building associated with the trial: Sugamo prison. Here it was, in the "death house," that six generals and one civilian were hanged in the middle of a December night in 1948, after being sentenced by the Allied judges of the Tokyo tribunal. Sugamo prison, built in imitation of nineteenth-century European jails, was torn down in the 1970s. On its site—against the advice of astrologers and geomancers, who deemed it inauspicious—rose one of the highest skyscrapers in Asia—a glossy white building called Sunshine 60, which is part of Sunshine City, a massive complex of leisure centers, offices, and shopping arcades.

I don't want to read too much significance into these architectural differences. No doubt the Japanese were glad to be rid of Sugamo prison, just as the receptionist at my Nuremberg hotel would prefer that there be no more law court, or Zeppelin Field, to be visited. But I do not think there ever was a building in Japan quite like the Nuremberg court. The court with all its paraphernalia never was—unlike, say, the railway station or the government ministry—a central institution of the modern Japanese state. The law was not a means to protect the people from arbitrary rule; it was, rather, a way for the state to exercise more control over the people. Even today, there are relatively few lawyers in Japan. It is almost a form of subversion to defend a person who stands accused in court. So the idea of holding political and military leaders legally accountable for their actions was even stranger in Japan than it was in Germany. And yet, the shadows thrown by the Tokyo trial have been longer and darker in Japan than those of the Nuremberg trial in Germany. Nationalist revisionists talk about "the Tokyo Trial View of History," as though the conclusions of the tribunal had been nothing but rabid anti-Japanese propaganda. The tribunal has been called a lynch mob, and Japanese leftists are blamed for undermining the morale of generations of Japanese by passing on the Tokyo Trial View of History in school textbooks and liberal publications. The Tokyo Trial View, in brief, is that Japan was guilty since 1931 of plotting and waging an aggressive war in Asia. But the revisionists argue that the war was in fact a tragic and indeed noble struggle for national survival and the liberation of Asia from Western colonialism. As long as the British and the Americans continued to be oppressors in Asia, wrote a revisionist historian named Hasegawa Michiko, who was born in 1945, "confrontation with Japan was inevitable. We did not fight for Japan alone. Our aim was to fight a Greater East Asia War. For this reason the war between Japan and China and Japan's oppression of Korea were all the more profoundly regrettable. They were inexpressibly tragic events."

Revisionist worries about generations of Japanese being brainwashed by the Tokyo trial are, to say the least, exaggerated. Japanese school textbooks are the product of so many compromises that they hardly reflect any opinion at all. As with all controversial matters in Japan, the more painful, the less said. In a standard history textbook for middle school students, published in the 1980s, mention of the Tokyo trial takes up less than half a page. All it says is that the trial took place and "was criticized for being a one-sided trial by victors over the vanquished."

West German textbooks describe the Nuremberg trial in far more detail. And they make a clear distinction between the retroactive law on crimes against peace and the other new law, on crimes against humanity. The former "revealed the main problem of the prosecutors, and of the International Court itself: crimes against peace presupposed an international ban on offensive war, which did not exist." The point is made that by refusing to take their own conduct during the war into account, the Allied judges created double standards. But it goes on to say that the law on crimes against humanity, though retroactive, "contributed to the further development of international law." This difference between (West) German and Japanese textbooks is not just a matter of detail; it shows a gap in perception. To the Japanese, crimes against humanity are not associated with an equivalent to the Holocaust, but with military excesses that occur in any war. And given the shock of Hiroshima and Nagasaki, Japanese found it easier, in the case of war crimes, to turn around and say "you too."

When Hellmut Becker said that few Germans wished to criticize the procedures of the Nuremberg trial because the criminality of the defendants was so plain to see, he was talking about crimes against humanity—more precisely, about the Holocaust. And it was crimes of the Holocaust that German courts judged after Nuremberg.

There never were any Japanese war crimes trials, nor is there a Japanese Ludwigsburg. This is partly because there was no exact equivalent of the Holocaust. Even though the behavior of Japanese troops was often barbarous, and the psychological consequences of State Shinto and emperor worship were frequently as hysterical as Nazism, Japanese atrocities were part of a military campaign, not a planned genocide of a people that included the country's own citizens. And besides, those aspects of the war that were most revolting and furthest removed from actual combat, such as the medical experiments on human guinea pigs (known as "logs") carried out by Unit 731 in Manchuria, were passed over during the Tokyo trial. The knowledge compiled by the doctors of Unit 731—of freezing experiments, injection of deadly diseases, vivisections, among other things— was considered so valuable by the Americans in 1945 that the doctors responsible were allowed to go free in exchange for their data. Some of the doctors rose to high positions in the postwar medical establishment. Dr. Yoshimura Hisato used his expertise on extreme temperature conditions to advise a Japanese expedition to the South Pole. And Dr. Kitano Masaji, who had performed many experimental operations, became head of Green Cross, Japan's largest blood-processing facility.

The story of Unit 731 was not utterly unknown in Japan, for a book had appeared based on the Soviet trial of some of the Unit's staff, and a documentary had been broadcast on Japanese television in 1976. But the first time most Japanese knew about it was in 1982, when the mystery writer Morimura Seiichi published the first book of his trilogy on the subject, entitled *The Devil's Gluttony*. Although Morimura's research was thorough, the title reflected the tone of his book, which did not help to attract scholarly attention. The books were a commercial success, however, and Morimura's work inspired others to research the subject. He also invited menacing attention from the extreme right wing.

Some Japanese have suggested that they should have conducted their own war crimes trials. The historian Hata Ikuhiko thought the Japanese leaders should have been tried according to existing Japanese laws, either in military or in civil courts. The Japanese judges, he believed, might well have been more severe than the Allied tribunal in Tokyo. And the consequences would have been healthier. If found guilty, the spirits of the defendants would not have ended up being enshrined at Yasukuni. The Tokyo trial, he said, "purified the 'crimes' of the accused and turned them into martyrs. If they had been tried in domestic courts, there is a good chance the real criminals would have been flushed out."

Fair enough, but on what grounds would Japanese courts have prosecuted their own former leaders? Hata's answer: "For starting a war which they knew they would lose." Hata used the example of General Galtieri and his colleagues in Argentina after losing the Falklands War. In short, they would have been tried for losing the war, and the intense suffering they inflicted on their own people. This is as though German courts in 1918 had put General Hindenburg or General Ludendorff on trial.

It is an arresting idea, but it shows yet again the fundamental difference between the Japanese war, in memory and, I should say, in fact, and the German experience. The Germans fought a war too, but the one for which they tried their own people, the Bogers and the Schwammbergers, was a war they could not lose, unless defeat meant that some of the enemies survived.

As with virtually everything connected with the wartime past, the Japanese left has a different view of the Tokyo trial than the revisionist right. It is comparable to the way the German left looks upon Nuremberg. This was perfectly, if somewhat long-windedly, expressed in Kobayashi Masaki's documentary film *Tokyo Trial*, released in 1983. Kobayashi is anything but an apologist for the Japanese war. His most famous film, *The Human Condition*, released in 1959, took a highly critical view of the war. The film's main character was a peaceful young man named Kaji, who was compelled, like Kobayashi himself, to witness the horror of war as a private soldier in China.

Tokyo Trial, which lasts for four and a half hours, begins with the bombing of Hiroshima and Nagasaki and ends with the famous shot of the naked Vietnamese girl running in terror from a napalm bomb attack. Nothing in the film suggests that Kobayashi was against the trial in principle or disagreed with its conclusions. But scenes of the trial are interrupted by images of the nuclear test on the Bikini atoll. And footage of Japanese massacres in Nanking—rarely enough seen in Japan—is immediately followed by yet another shot of the mushroom cloud over Hiroshima. Just as German leftists did in the case of Nuremberg, Kobayashi used the trial to turn the tables against the judges. But not necessarily to mitigate Japanese guilt. Rather, it was his intention to show how the victors had betrayed the pacifism they themselves had imposed on Japan.

There are other views in Japan, somewhere in between revisionist apologetics and the *tu quoque* principle. Yet nobody in Japan remembers the Tokyo trial without ambivalence. This has less to do with the lack of a legal tradition, or with nationalist bloody-mindedness, than with the nature of the trial itself. In

1970, one of the most distinguished Japanese playwrights, Kinoshita Junji, wrote a play which turned the Tokyo trial into a melancholy farce. The best-known Japanese book about the trial, published in 1974, and later the subject of a television drama, was a sympathetic account of the one civilian who was hanged in Sugamo: *War Criminal: The Life and Death of Hirota Koki*, by Shiroyama Saburo.

Neither Kinoshita nor Shiroyama was a right-wing revisionist. Nor was Yoshimoto Takaaki, philosopher of the 1960s New Left. Yet he wrote in 1986 that "from our point of view as contemporaries and witnesses, the trial was partly plotted from the very start. It was an absurd ritual before slaughtering the sacrificial lamb." This, from all accounts, was the way it looked to most Japanese, even if they had little sympathy for most of the "lambs." In 1948, after three years of American occupation censorship and boosterism, people listened to the radio broadcast of the verdicts with a sad but fatalist shrug: this is what you can expect when you lose the war.

But Yoshimoto went on to say something no revisionist would ever mention: "I also remember my fresh sense of wonder at this first encounter with the European idea of law, which was so different from the summary justice in our Asiatic courts. Instead of getting your head chopped off without a proper trial, the accused were able to defend themselves, and the careful judgment appeared to follow a public procedure."

Yoshimoto's memory was both fair and devastating, for it pointed straight at the reason for the trial's failure. The rigging of a political trial—the "absurd ritual"—undermined the value of that European idea of law. The great thing about the trial, in the words of Joseph Keenan, was that "individuals are being brought to the bar of justice for the first time in history to answer personally for offenses that they have committed while acting in official capacities as chiefs of state"—an unfortunate slip of the tongue, for there was just one chief of state, the emperor, and he was absent from the proceedings. The only model for the Tokyo trial was Nuremberg. And the trial was not always conducted fairly: evidence for the defense was sometimes barred, and prosecution witnesses were favored. But, as in Nuremberg, there was the other, more overt aim of the trial: teaching the Japanese, and by extension the world, a history lesson. Frederick Mignone, one of the prosecutors, said a trifle histrionically that "in Japan and in the Orient in general, the trial. is one of the most important phases of the occupation. It has received wide coverage in the Japanese press and revealed for the first time to millions of Japanese the scheming, duplicity, and insatiable desire for power of her entrenched militaristic leaders, writing a much-needed history of events which otherwise would not have been written."

It was indeed much-needed, since so little was known. The political scientist Ishida Takeshi, a student at the time, would "never forget the shock of hearing about the massacres perpetrated by the Imperial Army in China immediately after the occupation of Nanking." Some of the information even surprised the defendants. General Itagaki Seishiro, a particularly ruthless figure, who was in command of prison camps in Southeast Asia and whose troops had massacred countless Chinese civilians, wrote in his diary: "I am learning of matters I had not known and recalling things I had forgotten." After it was over, the *Nippon Times* pointed out the flaws of the trial, but added that "the Japanese people must ponder over why it is that there has been such a discrepancy between what they thought and what the rest of the world accepted almost as common knowledge. This is at the root of the tragedy which Japan brought upon herself."

The discrepancy is still there today. But in hindsight, one can only conclude that instead of helping the Japanese to understand and accept their past, the trial left them with an attitude of cynicism and resentment. Political trials produce politicized histories. This is what the revisionists mean when they talk about the Tokyo Trial View of History. And they are right, even if their own conclusions are not. For to condemn the trial is not necessarily to deny Japanese guilt, which is the theme of Kinoshita's brilliant play.

Between God and Man is composed of two parts. Part I, entitled *The Judgment*, is about the Tokyo trial, using actual transcripts. It has great fun with scenes of Allied confusion when such delicate matters as the Hiroshima bomb, or the belated Soviet war declaration (two days after the bomb), are introduced. Political embarrassment is covered up in absurd legalese. The conventional reading of this part of the play would be to see it as yet another attempt to water down Japanese guilt by saying *tu quoque*. And by stressing, as Kinoshita does, the hypocrisy of the court, he seems to be denying the conclusions of the trial. But there are other possible interpretations. The Japanese defendants are not heard, but can be seen, sitting in the audience. So in effect it is not just these 28 men, but the (Japanese) audience that is sitting in the dock. Clearly, there is more to the play than an indictment of trial procedures. The audience is not let off the hook so lightly.

Part II, entitled *A Romance of the South Seas*, is a typical story, no doubt with a firm base in reality, of a man being hanged for crimes committed by others. The story of the crimes is told by a music-hall singer. The farcical trial, which parodies grotesquely the Tokyo trial, with jabbering monkeys as witnesses, is re-created in a dream sequence. As soon as this nightmare is over, everybody wants to forget that it ever took place. Only the music-hall singer is unwilling to forget. And she is also the only one to refuse to complain about the unfairness of the trial: "If it all depended on the simple fact that the trial was a farce, who could make any sense out of it?"

Kinoshita's play, which appeared to be an apology for Japanese crimes, in fact goes deeper into the question of guilt and retribution than the two German plays about war crimes trials. And, ironically, it also shows a greater influence of Christianity (Kinoshita had once been a Christian) than the works of the two Europeans. Peter Weiss and Rolf Schneider wrote about the politics of Nazi crimes. Weiss tried to show what produces torturers like Boger. Neither doubted the validity of the trials. But Kinoshita's point was a different one. His play shows that war crimes trials are not up to dealing with collective responsibility and truth. The language is simply wrong. Even the artificial banter of the music hall is more appropriate. Yet it is not enough to cry "victors' justice," for that won't help people come to terms with their past. It is just another evasion. And the question of whether the 28 men in Tokyo, or the thousands of war criminals of lesser rank, were guilty or not is not the real issue either. It is we, in the audience, who have to be judges of our own guilt.

The Tokyo trial was modeled after Nuremberg, as though the Japanese wars in Asia had been more or less the same as Hitler's war, but even the judges recognized that the Japanese defendants were not simply Oriental Nazis. The president of the Tokyo tribunal, Sir William Webb, thought "the crimes of the German accused were far more heinous, varied and extensive than those of the Japanese accused." Put in another way, nearly all the defendants at Nuremberg, convicted of crimes against peace, were also found guilty of crimes against humanity. But half the Japanese defendants received life sentences for political crimes only.

Frank Tavenner, one of the attorneys for the prosecution, said: "These men were not the hoodlums who were the powerful part of the group which stood before the tribunal at Nuremberg, dregs of a criminal environment, thoroughly schooled in the ways of crime and knowing no other methods but those of crime. These men were supposed to be the elite of the nation, the honest and trusted leaders to whom the fate of the nation had been confidently entrusted . . ."

But the question of responsibility is always a tricky affair in Japan, where formal responsibility is easier to identify than actual guilt. Not only were there many men, such as the hero of Kinoshita's play, who took the blame for what their superiors had done—a common practice in Japan, in criminal gangs as well as in politics or business corporations—but the men at the top were often not at all in control of their unscrupulous subordinates. It is hardly a surprise, then, that hastily convened tribunals all over Asia, made up of men who had no knowledge of Japanese ways, were hardly up to the task of sorting out who in the Japanese chain of command had been responsible for what. As a result, many people were wrongly accused of the wrong things for the wrong reasons. This is why there was such sympathy in Japan for the men branded by foreigners as war criminals, particularly the so-called Class B and Class C criminals, the men who followed orders, or gave them at a lower level: field commanders, camp guards, and so on.

In 1953, a campaign demanding the release of all Japanese war criminals received more than fifteen million signatures. A dispatch from the West German embassy in Tokyo to the Federal Ministry of Justice in Bonn reported: "The Japanese people are of the opinion that the actual goal of the war crimes tribunals was never realized, since the judgments were reached by the victors alone and had the character of revenge. The [Japanese] war criminal is not conscious of having committed a crime, for he regards his deeds as acts of war, committed out of patriotism."

The year 1953 was also a rich period for movies, such as *Taiheyo no Washi* (*Eagle of the Pacific*), that painted wartime leaders as martyrs or peace-loving heroes. The eagle in the Pacific was Admiral Yamamoto Isoroku, the planner and executor of the attack on Pearl Harbor, who was indeed in many ways a moderate and admirable figure. Less moderate, though certainly the victim of kangaroo-court justice, was General Yamashita Tomoyuki. He, too, was the subject of a hero-worshipping picture, *Yamashita Tomoyuki*. Terrible atrocities were committed under his command in the Philippines. The sacking of Manila in 1945 was about as brutal as the Nanking Massacre. So to depict him in the movie

as a peaceful gentleman, while portraying the American prosecutor in Manila as one of the main villains, might seem an odd
way to view the past.

But it was not entirely wrong, for the trial *was* rigged. Yamashita had no doubt been a tough soldier, but in this case he
had been so far removed from the troops who ran amok in
Manila that he could hardly have known what was going on.
Yet the American prosecutor openly talked about his desire to
hang "Japs." And General MacArthur wanted his revenge for
having lost the Philippines, so he speeded up the trial, and
decided to have Yamashita hanged, even before two dissenting
opinions had arrived from the Supreme Court. The dissenting
judges called it a "judicial lynching without due process of law."
Yamashita's death sentence was announced on the anniversary
of Pearl Harbor. With this kind of precedent, few Japanese,
even those who found it convenient to blame all their troubles
on "the militarists," had the stomach to carry on with war crimes
trials of their own.

The political theorist Maruyama Masao called the prewar Japanese government a "system of irresponsibilities." He identified
three types of political personalities: the portable Shrine, the
Official, and the Outlaw. The Shrine ranks highest. It is the
supreme symbol of authority, shouldered (like a shrine on fes-
tival days) by the Officials. The Shrine is the icon, but those who
carry it, the Officials, are the ones with actual power. But the
Officials—bureaucrats, politicians, admirals and generals—are
often manipulated by the lowest-ranking Outlaws, the military
mavericks, the hotheaded officers in the field, the mad nationalists, and other agents of violence. One result of this system of
irresponsibilities is that political cause and effect disappear from
view. History will seem like an endless string of faits accomplis,
periods of oppressive stillness interrupted by violent storms
whose source is always mysterious: foreign demons, nature, or,
in the words of Hayashi Fusao, the father of Japanese revisionism, "the coldheartedness of history."

The Class A war criminals in the dock in Tokyo were Officials, as well as Shrines. They were Officials, shouldering the highest Shrine of all, the emperor himself; but they, in turn, were held aloft by men further down in the hierarchy and manipulated by Outlaws. Political responsibility moves like a perpetuum mobile, round and round, up and down, without stopping at any point. When the system spins out of control, as it did during the 1930s, events are forced by violent Outlaws, reacted to by nervous Officials, and justified by the sacred status of the Shrines. Here we come to the nub of the problem, which the Tokyo trial refused to deal with, the role of the Shrine in whose name every single war crime was committed, Emperor Hirohito, now known posthumously as the Showa emperor.

In the summer of 1990, after visiting Nanking, I met Saeki Yuko, an attractive woman in her early forties, who wrote traditional Japanese poetry. Her poems, in the tanka style, are minimalist laments about a family in disgrace:

My father was drunk, like a pomegranate
the day after grandfather's execution.

All of us together, one family
with tightened throats since the time of father's father.

Mrs. Saeki was the granddaughter of General Doihara Kenji, also known as "Lawrence of Manchuria." Doihara was hanged at Sugamo prison in 1948 for crimes against humanity, crimes against peace, and conventional war crimes. He was a colorful figure and, though of high rank, a typical Outlaw, involved in terrorism, drug trafficking, and the running of concentration camps. As commander of the Kwantung Army in Manchuria, he was one of the men who pushed along the war in China.

Mrs. Saeki's father buckled under the strain of being Doihara's son; he couldn't hold a job, drank too much, and died young. Mrs. Saeki herself was bullied at her primary school (though not at her elite high school). She had hoped that the emperor would come to her rescue, since she had been taught that he was "the father of us all." But her parents told her she could not expect the emperor's help anymore, because Japan had lost the war. "We have to live on our own now," her mother said. Nonetheless his portrait hung on the wall of the family house until she went to high school in the 1950s. Only then was it replaced—by a poster of James Dean.

Mrs. Saeki felt she was part of a tragic family. As a result of what had happened, she also felt bitter about the fickleness of authority. She had always had very mixed feelings about the emperor. The emperor, she said, allowed the question of guilt to be evaded at the Tokyo trial: "The defendents were his children. There wasn't much sympathy among the Japanese people for the Class A war criminals, such as my grandfather, it is true, but the Class B and Class C war criminals were seen as victims. They had only carried out the emperor's orders." Mrs. Saeki felt less angry now that the emperor was dead.

She was not proud of being Doihara's granddaughter. Indeed, she had disliked the idea as a child. But her teenaged son had a different perspective. He was fascinated by his great-grandfather and everything to do with the war. Mrs. Saeki said he was intelligent but very nationalistic. He rejected the Tokyo Trial View. When he watched Kobayashi's *Tokyo Trial* with his friends, he boasted of being Doihara's great-grandson. That, said Mrs. Saeki, is when she realized how much times had changed.

Emperor Hirohito was not Hitler; Hitler was no mere Shrine. But the lethal consequences of the emperor-worshipping system of irresponsibilities did emerge during the Tokyo trial. The savagery of Japanese troops was legitimized, if not driven, by an ideology that did not include a Final Solution but was as racialist as Hitler's National Socialism. The Japanese were the Asian *Herrenvolk*, descended from the gods. The historian Ienaga Saburo tells a story about a Japanese schoolchild in the 1930s who was squeamish about having to dissect a live frog. The teacher rapped him hard on the head with his knuckles and said: "Why are you crying about one lousy frog? When you

grow up you'll have to kill a hundred, two hundred Chinks."
A veteran of the war in China said in a television interview
that he was able to kill Chinese without qualms only because
he didn't regard them as human. There was even religious merit
in the killing, for it was part of a "holy war." Captain Francis
P. Scott, the chaplain at Sugamo prison, questioned Japanese
camp commandants about their reasons for mistreating POWs.
This is how he summed up their answers: "They had a belief
that any enemy of the emperor could not be right, so the more
brutally they treated their prisoners, the more loyal to their
emperor they were being."

Emperor Hirohito, the shadowy figure who changed after the
war from navy uniforms to gray suits, was not personally comparable to Hitler, but his psychological role was remarkably
similar. The Mitscherlichs described Hitler as "an object on
which Germans depended, to which they transferred responsibility, and he was thus an internal object. As such, he represented and revived the ideas of omnipotence that we all cherish
about ourselves from infancy. The same was true of the Japanese imperial institution, no matter who sat on the throne, a
ruthless war criminal or a gentle marine biologist.

It was precisely this symbol of authority, however, this holiest
Shrine, that General MacArthur chose to preserve after 1945.
This, by the way, was just what Japan had demanded as a condition of surrender. But this was turned down by the Allies,
who then forced Japan to surrender unconditionally by destroying Hiroshima and Nagasaki. The fear after 1945 was that without the emperor Japan would be impossible to govern. In fact,
MacArthur behaved like a traditional Japanese strongman (and
was admired for doing so by many Japanese), using the imperial
symbol to enhance his own power. As a result, he hurt the
chances of a working Japanese democracy and seriously dis-
torted history. For to keep the emperor in place (he could at
least have been made to resign), Hirohito's past had to be freed
from any blemish; the symbol had to be, so to speak, cleansed
from what had been done in its name.

This might or might not have made Japan easier to rule, but it also caused a great deal of ill feeling. In 1987, Hara Kazuo made an extraordinary documentary film about a veteran of the Imperial Japanese Army named Okuzaki Kenzo. It was entitled *The Emperor's Army Marches On*. Okuzaki had béen a private soldier in New Guinea. At the end of the war, after Okuzaki had already returned to Japan, two young soldiers in his platoon were shot by their own commander in vague circumstances. Okuzaki grew obsessed with this; he *had* to find out what happened. So he decided to track down all the survivors.

Okuzaki was an eccentric figure, to say the least. He had spent time in jail for shooting pinballs at the emperor and distributing pamphlets with pornographic cartoons of the emperor. He drove around Japan in a van festooned with banners and slogans demanding the emperor's apology for having sent millions of young men to their deaths. His search for the truth was, as he put it, his way of "consoling the spirits of those who sacrificed their lives for the emperor."

Okuzaki was neither a Christian nor a member of any Buddhist or Shinto sect. He believed in something he called the "Okuzaki religion," a combination of natural law and anarchism. The literary model that comes to mind was not Japanese but German, Kleist's Michael Kohlhaas, the horse trader from Brandenburg whose zeal for justice resulted in murder and mayhem.

All the while, Hara's handheld camera follows Okuzaki on his quest, producing jerky, gritty images. You never know what will happen next. The action is forever on the edge of chaos. In one scene, Okuzaki kicks a sickly old comrade who refuses to tell the truth. In another he wrestles a former officer to the ground. When the police try to interfere, Okuzaki tells them to mind their own business. His aversion to authority, any authority, is clear from the start. The police, he says, are just like soldiers in the war; all they can do is follow orders. But slowly, in spite of endless lies and evasions, a very unpleasant story begins to emerge. The two young men were not executed for desertion, as people had thought. The platoon commander had ordered them to be killed so they could be eaten. Cannibalizing Japanese soldiers was not normal practice. Natives or enemy soldiers were preferred. But these were not always available, and the two privates were not popular with their commander. The commander himself never admitted this, of course. The truth had to be pieced together from the accounts of others.

But finding out the truth was not enough. Okuzaki wanted his old commander to admit it. The lying enraged him. The commander, a plump old man, lived in a large house. Life had treated him well. Okuzaki grabbed him roughly and screamed that he should come clean and take responsibility for what he had done. The man said he didn't see it that way. One had to realize what it was like in those days. He had only done his duty, as a Japanese soldier. Okuzaki shouted: "That's all you have to say! I think the highest symbol of human irresponsibility is the emperor, followed by loyal officers, like you . . ." In the end Okuzaki tried to shoot him. He failed. He shot the commander's son instead. This was God's justice, he said, as he was sentenced to life in jail.

Emperor Hirohito not only escaped prosecution at the Tokyo trial; he could not even be called as a witness. A deal was struck to keep the supreme Shrine out of the whole business. Aristides George Lazarus, the defense counsel of one of the generals on trial, was asked to arrange that "the military defendants, and their witnesses, would go out of their way during their testimony to include the fact that Hirohito was only a benign presence when military actions or programs were discussed at meetings that, by protocol, he had to attend." No doubt the other counsel were given similar instructions.

Only once during the trial did the game plan threaten to go wrong. During chief prosecutor Keenan's cross-examination of Tojo Hideki, the general agreed that there was "no Japanese subject who would dare act against the emperor's will." This was not at all in the scenario so carefully prepared by MacArthur. And Keenan was forced to prevail upon another defendant in the trial, Marquis Kido, keeper of the privy seal and the emperor's closest adviser during much of the war, to try to get Tojo to correct his statement. Tojo, ever a loyal subject, did so a week later. He said that "because of the advice given by the High Command the emperor consented, though reluctantly, to the war." His "love and desire for peace remained the same right up to the very moment when hostilities commenced, and even during the war his feelings remained the same."

The point here is not that most Japanese would have liked to see the emperor hang, or even stand trial. But the question of the emperor's guilt was of far more than just historical interest. For the imperial institution had been used until the end of the war to quash free speech and political accountability. Without examining his part in the war, the "system of irresponsibilities" could not be properly exposed, which made it likely that, in one form or another, it would continue.

Early critics of the imperial institution realized this. In 1946, the left-wing filmmaker Kamei Fumio made a film entitled *The Japanese Tragedy*, which was highly critical of the emperor's wartime role. At first the American censors could see nothing wrong with this collage of newsreels, photographs, and newspaper reports. But after a private screening, the Prime Minister, Yoshida Shigeru, complained to General Charles Willoughby, head of the Military Intelligence Section, that the film was subversive. Willoughby agreed and the movie was banned. In 1984, Kamei attended a screening of *The Japanese Tragedy* with the film historian Hirano Kyoko. She was told that it was around the time this film was banned that the Japanese people stopped actively discussing the war responsibility of Emperor Hirohito. This suited more people than just the Japanese and American authorities. As long as the emperor lived, Japanese would have trouble being honest about the past. For he had been formally responsible for everything, and by holding him responsible for nothing, everybody was absolved, except, of course, for a number of military and civilian scapegoats, Officers and Outlaws, who fell "victim to victors' justice."

TEXTBOOK RESISTANCE

GERMANY

IN *American Hijiki*, Nosaka Akiyuki describes what it was like to be a Japanese schoolboy in 1945. During the war it was useless learning English. "Yes" and "no" were the only words you needed to know, the history teacher said. "Yes or no?" is what General Yamashita shouted at General Percival in 1941, when he demanded the unconditional surrender of the British in Singapore. But now that the war was over, it was time to learn how to say "thank you" and "excuse me."

General Percival, the history teacher used to say, was the archetypical white man: tall, but weak in the knees. When it came to a fight, any Japanese could best the white man, for the Japanese had strong thighs. This was because the white man was soft and sat in chairs, whereas the Japanese exercised their muscles by sitting on the floor. But when the war was over, the history—suddenly renamed "social studies"—teacher said: " 'Look at the Americans. Their average height is five feet, ten inches. For us, it's only five feet three. This difference of seven inches figures in everything, and I believe that's why we lost the War. A basic difference in physical strength is invariably manifested in national strength.' " The boys were not quite sure why the teacher had made this point, "but he was so good at it you never knew how seriously to take him. Maybe this was just his way of covering up the embarrassment he felt at suddenly having to preach Democratic Japan after Holy Japan from textbooks filled with the censors' black blottings."

As a result, nobody believed a word teachers said anymore. One day it was the divine race fighting the Anglo-American demons to the last man, woman, and child, the next it was thank you, excuse me, and *demokurashi*.

I thought of Nosaka's novella when I set off to meet two history teachers at a high school on the outskirts of East Berlin. It was only two years after the antifascist republic of workers, soldiers, and farmers, bound in fraternal solidarity to the U.S.S.R., had been joined with the capitalist Federal Republic of Germany, allied to the U.S.A. History, as the underpinning of so much politics, had to be stood on its head. How did teachers explain this? How did any of *their* pupils still believe them?

Mrs. Lein and Mrs. Nass looked to be in their forties. Mrs. Nass, the headmistress, had been in the Communist Party. Mrs. Lein had not, which is why she could never have become headmistress. Both women had intelligent no-nonsense faces, hair pulled back sensibly from their pale foreheads. Both wore sensible, no-nonsense clothes: sturdy shoes, thick sweaters. The school building suffered the effects of long neglect. The dung-colored walls showed watery cracks. We met in a cold room that smelled of cabbage.

I told them about Nosaka's story. They shrugged and looked at one another. Mrs. Nass, as the senior teacher, spoke first. In 1945, she said, there had been no such problems in their part of Germany. Ninety percent of the teachers in the Soviet zone had been fired. And those who stayed after 1949 were sure to have been antifascists. As for 1990, there had been relatively few problems at their school, for—and here they both nodded vigorously—it had been quite a democratic school.

Of course, she went on, one could not mention certain aspects of history. The massacre of Polish officers in Katyn was a topic that was best avoided, as was the Molotov-Ribbentrop pact. "We didn't know about these things," said Mrs. Nass. "We said nothing that was incorrect, you must realize. We just skipped certain subjects."

Judging from old GDR schoolbooks, this was not strictly true. The Molotov-Ribbentrop pact of August 1939, which enabled Nazi Germany and the Soviet Union to carve up Poland, was mentioned, but it was given a particular explanation. I looked it up in the history textbook given to me by Mrs. Lein herself. There it was, on page 145: "The nonaggression pact between the U.S.S.R. and Germany: . . . The plans to solve the inner contradiction of the imperialist system at the expense of the Soviet Union had failed. The U.S.S.R. thwarted the aim of building a mighty anti-Soviet coalition and set the limits to German aggression in Eastern Europe. The pact assured the Soviet Union two years of peace, during which it could build up its defenses." The Soviet invasion of Poland was not intended to rob Polish land, but "to protect the lives and freedom of the peoples of the Ukraine and Byelorussia from the fascists."

The young readers of this text were asked to address two questions, printed in the margins: "What was the meaning of the German-Soviet nonaggression pact?" and "Why is it still disparaged today by imperialist ideologues?" It had been the task of Mrs. Lein and Mrs. Nass to teach the politically correct answers.

"Of course," said Mrs. Nass, "we have to tell the children that we simply didn't know some of the things we teach them nowadays. They accept this. They understand. Even before, they knew we didn't believe everything we had to tell them. This is Berlin, we all watched Western television. We all knew that. We just didn't talk about it." I thought of all the people in East Germany watching *Holocaust*, without being able to discuss it, because they were not supposed to have seen it in the first place.

"There was no question of guilt here," said Mrs. Lein. "I had to tell my pupils to behave themselves discreetly on school trips to Poland and C.S.S.R. [Czechoslovakia]. I had to explain that to those people we were still the ones who started the war.

You see, all this business about fraternal solidarity was rubbish. They still hated us. But my pupils found this hard to understand. They just didn't know. One of them went around Warsaw wearing Bermuda shorts in the German colors. He was beaten up."

What about now? I asked. Were the pupils receptive to a different interpretation of history now? Both women rolled their eyes.

"They've become very passive," said Mrs. Lein. "They never ask us any questions anymore," said Mrs. Nass. "They are not critical. They just watch videos." Yes, said Mrs. Lein, "and the older children, they just shrug their shoulders and wonder why they should bother about anything. 'What's it all for?' they say."

And the new school textbooks from the West. What did Mrs. Lein and Mrs. Nass think of those?

"Well," said Mrs. Nass, "they look better, but the contents, well . . ."

"Not at all good," said Mrs. Lein. "Very superficial."

I asked them to be more specific.

"There is not enough analysis about the war, why it happened, and so on. There is a lot of stuff about the Jews—but it's all about superficial events, no framework, no background . . ."

I wondered what background they expected. Did they miss the Marxist explanations about monopoly capital being at the root of Hitler's fascism?

"Oh," said both women at once, "but we still believe *that*. People who profit from it wage wars. That is obvious. We still teach our pupils *that*. But you know what the problem is: our pupils are very sensitive to the distinctions between old GDR sources and new FRG ones. The problem is, we have to leave it up to them to make up their minds."

The main thrust of East German histories of World War II can be summarized in two short passages, both from Mrs. Lein's textbook. One refers to the 1935 Communist Party conference in Brussels: "Because the Hitler regime was a dictatorship consisting of the most reactionary and aggressive elements of the grand bourgeoisie, it was objectively in contradiction with the interests of the majority of all classes. The struggle against the Hitler dictatorship therefore had to have an antifascist, democratic order as its aim. All democratic and peace-loving forces had an interest in such a goal. The program for this wide alliance was proposed by the German Communist Party."

The second refers to the first postwar German Communist Party program: "Even as the armies of the anti-Hitler coalition approached the German borders from east and west, the Communists in the resistance, in the concentration camps, or in exile were preparing for the foundation of a democratic, peace-loving Germany, as soon as the fascist regime was toppled."

How could the pupils of Mrs. Lein and Mrs. Nass have felt guilty? They had been born in this democratic, peace-loving Germany. They were the children of the resistance. Their elders had struggled against the Hitler regime (never Germany, or even Nazi Germany; the good Germany had continued to exist, underground, in exile, among Communists). The story of the Third Reich is not presented as a tragic aberration in the long and troubled flow of German history. Nor is it presented as a logical outcome of the darker strains of German idealism: indeed, some of the most chauvinistic German idealists, such as Johann Gottlieb Fichte, the author of *Addresses to the German Nation*, or Friedrich Jahn, the father of German calisthenics, were revered figures in the Democratic Republic. Instead, it is shown as a story of continuity, following the unbroken laws of history. The "Hitler regime" was simply the last and most violent stage of bourgeois capitalism. As an East Berlin comedian once observed: the past belongs to the West, the future belongs to us.

The selection of illustrations in GDR textbooks supports this thesis. There are portraits of Communist resistance heroes, such as Erich Honecker, who ruled the GDR for almost two decades, and Heinz Kapelle, who cried out: "Long live the Communist

Party!" before his execution in 1941. There is a photograph of Soya Kosmodemyanskaya, the Russian partisan, who shouted: "Comrades, carry on the struggle without fear!" before she was hanged near Moscow. And there are pictures of Hitler himself, surrounded by captains of industry, to show what the resistance was up against. There are few pictures of the war itself, except for one or two photographs of Soviet soldiers fighting on the eastern front. There are some pictures of concentration camps: almost all taken in Buchenwald, where many Communists were incarcerated. But one picture shows a Soviet soldier shaking hands with a concentration camp inmate in striped camp garb. This could not have been at Buchenwald, since the Americans got there first.

Atrocities and genocide are less in evidence in these texts than the heroism of Soviet liberators and Communist rebels. The children of the GDR were not asked to atone for or reflect on the crimes committed by their parents or grandparents. Auschwitz was not meant to be part of their identity. They were taught to identify with heroes.

As Mrs. Lein and Mrs. Nass were saying, West German schoolbooks show a rather different picture of the past. It is a picture that must have been shocking to those who "just didn't know." Textbooks in the Federal Republic contain few photographs of resistance heroes, but many of the Holocaust. Virtually every book carries the famous photograph of SS officers on the railway ramp at Birkenau, standing tall in their polished boots, as they choose their victims for immediate killing. Nazi documents are quoted in detail. We find the disciplinary rules of a typical concentration camp, and the racial laws of 1935, and speeches by Goebbels or Göring, as well as the bureaucratic pedantry of Heydrich's report on the *Kristallnacht* of 1938.

Bernd Wetzka, the high school teacher who brought his class to the Schwammberger trial, told me that about sixty hours of Nazi history per year was the recommended norm in West German schools. Wetzka teaches history in a tiny Swabian town, with cobbled streets, a medieval castle, and rows of seventeenth-century houses. He directed me to the Jewish cemetery to see the graves of two brothers. One died in France, as a German officer in the Great War. The other, younger brother died twenty-five years later in Theresienstadt, the "model" concentration camp.

I had tea with Wetzka and his girlfriend, a German teacher. She was in her early thirties, about ten years younger than he. They both said their pupils showed a great deal of interest in the Nazi period. More than in the history of the GDR? "Absolutely," said Wetzka, "for we don't really feel that the GDR —the Stasi and all that—was part of our own history, while the Third Reich certainly was."

Wetzka's parents were conventional people. That is to say, they had been small-time Nazis. His father served in the Waffen SS on the eastern front, and his mother was a keen Hitler Maiden. His father still kept his Iron Cross with the swastika attached. So Wetzka found it hard to talk to his parents about the past. Nor did his teachers tell him much. Those who had been children during the war felt no need to talk. The ones who had been adults didn't want to. There was one teacher, though, an older man with a war wound, whom Wetzka particularly disliked. His manner was harsh and authoritarian. But when the children asked him about the Third Reich one day, he suddenly broke down and cried. "We were all guilty," he said. "We saw the slogans on the walls saying death to the Jews, and we stood by and did nothing. We were all guilty."

Schoolbooks in the Federal Republic are not written by scholars selected by the central government, as was the case in the GDR. The books differ from state to state. Publishers submit their texts for approval to the state governments, who appoint committees of schoolteachers (recommended by parents and pupils) to vet them. In principle, the books are vetted on constitutional, not on ideological grounds. They are passed as long as they accord with the constitution and the laws on education.

One of the laws on education stipulates that educational materials "should not hinder students in making up their own minds." Judging from a typical history textbook for high school students in Bavaria, this is taken seriously. The questions asked in every chapter are not so much tests of political correctness as incentives for pupils to think for themselves. There is, for example, a quotation from the jurist Carl Schmitt, written in 1933, in which he defines the legal status of the Nazi Party. The party, he argued, was neither a private organization nor the state itself; it stood alone, and could not be subject to the scrutiny of law courts. This is followed by a speech, in 1937, by the chief of an SS academy, who tells his pupils that they are to be the aristocracy of a new type of Hellenistic city-state, accountable only to Hitler's will. After reading these quotations, the students are asked to "discuss the problem of how an individual is to behave in a state based on false norms."

The effectiveness of such class discussions depends a great deal on the teachers. Wetzka was not entirely sure how to approach the Third Reich, how to give it meaning, beyond teaching the facts. His girlfriend favored the postmodern approach. She would ask her pupils to read Hitler's speeches and then deconstruct them, to analyze how his audiences had been manipulated. Wetzka, being a generation older, struggled with the *Sonderweg* theory, the idea that German history had progressed on a unique, fatally flawed track. He found it "hard to say whether Nazism was typically German. Maybe it is better to teach children how quickly things can go wrong when a particular group is despised by the majority."

Perhaps this is what the two teachers in East Berlin meant by the lack of a "framework." In fact, however, there is a framework in West German textbooks, which is different from Communist state propaganda and yet in one important respect not unlike the old East German books. A handbook for Gymnasium teachers in Baden-Württemberg explains what is to be achieved by teaching children about the "National Socialist dictatorship": "The pupils should learn about Hitler's foreign policy, and how the dictatorship was established. They should also find out about the inhumanity of the Nazi system of persecution and mass murder. By coming to grips with the totalitarian character of the 'Third Reich,' the pupils must recognize how the liberal-democratic order of our state guarantees our basic rights." The handbook highly recommends visits to concentration camps.

The aim is to foster what Jürgen Habermas calls constitutional patriotism (*Verfassungspatriotismus*): "Constitutional patriotism is the only patriotism which does not alienate us from the West. Alas, a loyalty to universalist constitutionalist principles, rooted in conviction, could be established in the cultural German nation [*Kulturnation*] only after—and by virtue of—Auschwitz."

One might call it the social science approach to history. Schoolchildren are no longer asked to identify with flags, songs, heroes, or a carefully constructed sense of historical continuity, but with an idea, the liberal democratic order. It differs from the socialist order of East Germany in form and in substance, since the socialist state did not believe in basic individual rights, but rather in sacrifice for a collective ideal, inculcated with all the paraphernalia of the old regime: flags, torchlight parades, great leaders, militarized youth organizations, and so on. The worship of Communist resistance leaders was also worship of the state they supposedly built, and in some cases ruled. Constitutional patriotism, as conceived by Habermas and West German textbook authors, was expressly not meant to make a cult of the state. And since, in Habermas's view, liberal patriotism came "by virtue of" Auschwitz, it meant a break with the past, with the *Kulturnation*.

What it lacks is the symbolism of national identity. It is criticized for being dry, abstract, shallow. "We are in danger of becoming a nation without history," said the president of the Federal Republic, Walter Scheel, in 1975. Ten years later, the historian Michael Stürmer fretted over the spiritual vacuum and loss of national orientation in West Germany. This was one of the issues of the "historians' debate," which began in 1986, with the publication of an article in the *Frankfurter Allgemeine Zeitung* by the conservative historian Ernst Nolte. It was entitled *The Past That Will Not Go Away*. Nolte, Stürmer, and other conservatives argued that Auschwitz should not be allowed to drive a wedge into the continuity of German history. For history must provide a nation with identity—spiritual, political, aesthetic. Germans must be able to identify with national heroes, even, in the opinion of one famous historian, Andreas Hillgruber, with the common German soldier in 1944, defending the German homeland against the Communist hordes. Habermas accused the conservatives of reviving reactionary historicism to propagate anti-Communist German nationalism.

But in fact West German textbooks did provide an identity of a kind, both national and regional. As in the East German books, it was based on the notion of resistance; an identity, that is, erected in opposition to the Nazi state. The case is made that Germany between 1933 and 1945 was not entirely absorbed by the Nazi movement, "even though the Allies would not recognize this during the war." Every textbook includes detailed descriptions of the various resistance groups, including Communists, priests, pastors, students (the White Rose), social democrats, and finally, of course, Count Schenk von Stauffenberg and his mostly aristocratic army colleagues, who just failed to kill Hitler in July 1944. Hitler wreaked a terrible revenge and thousands of Germans were murdered. The plotters were hanged in a dark chamber at Plötzensee prison, which is still kept as a lugubrious shrine. Just before his execution, Stauffenberg is said to have cried: "Long live holy Germany!" Hitler watched a film of the hanging, over and over, in the comfort of his Bavarian mountain retreat.

Since Stauffenberg, although undoubtedly a heroic figure, was part of a "bourgeois-military" conspiracy, which had no intention of building a socialist state, East German textbooks had to make it clear that he was not one of us, so to speak, without actually condemning him. And so we learn that his circle included men with "progressive political ideas," who had contacts in the Communist Party. But in West Germany, too, his reputation has not been entirely without controversy. "Long live holy Germany!" was not a slogan that appealed to the left.

And however much one might have detested Hitler and his satraps, an assassination attempt still smacked of treason in right-wing eyes. Although a street was named after Stauffenberg in Berlin in 1955, it was only in 1967 that the Berlin Senate decided to build a memorial and documentation center in the former military headquarters where Stauffenberg planned his coup.

Religion played a role in the German resistance, and the Bavarian textbook makes the most of this. Hitler's politics, the authors observe, stood in contrast to Stauffenberg's religious humanism. But this being Bavaria, special attention is paid to the Catholic Church. One learns, for example, that most Bavarians, being Catholic, did not vote for the Nazi Party in 1932. And the bravery of individual priests, such as Augustin Rosch, a Munich Jesuit, is singled out. This is all perfectly proper, but it did not mean that the Nazis were unpopular in Bavaria. It just showed that Catholics voted the way their priests told them to—for the Catholic conservatives, who were, in any case, forced to disband after 1933.

But these specifically regional interests make way in the end for a strong political message, or framework, if one prefers: "The representatives of Communist, socialist, bourgeois, religious, military, and aristocratic circles in Germany paid for their rebellion against Hitler with their freedom and their lives. But this alliance of rebels against the Nazi dictatorship provided a starting point for the development of a constitutional and social order in postwar Germany . . . The resistance movements forged a link to the German freedom movements and made it easier to anchor human values and the principles of rule of law, democracy, the welfare state, and federalism in the constitution of the Federal Republic of Germany."

Both Germanys, then, in their textbook versions of history, were built upon the legacy of resistance. It is an appealing idea, and if identification with historical figures is to be encouraged, it is surely better to identify with Count von Stauffenberg than with, say, Heinrich Himmler. (Such heroes of the East as Ernst

Thälmann and Erich Honecker were less attractive role models, though still better than Himmler.)

But the consequences were not entirely benign. Enforced worship of heroes in the East was part of totalitarian propaganda and a gross distortion of history. When the heroes crumbled to dust, and the propaganda lost its force, hundreds, maybe thousands of disillusioned youngsters rebelled by reviving the heroes and symbols of the earlier dictatorship. They cried "*Sieg Heil!*" in the streets and worshipped the Nazi leaders, as though they were hankering after a more heroic age, whose glory had been suppressed by the elders who had failed them.

In the West the official legacy of resistance left many of "Hitler's children" with the idea that any resistance against the state not only was justified by the past but was a moral imperative. The Red Army Faction, no matter how grotesque their methods or aims, could count on some sympathy among the generation of '68, if only because it dared to do what the majority of Germans had failed to do when it really mattered, some thirty years before.

And yet the cooler heads of that same generation also understood that liberal democracy in Germany had to rest on an openly critical attitude toward the Nazi past. It was time to break with the discretion, the silence, the evasions that were thought to have been necessary to turn millions of former Nazis into republican citizens. If that break was sometimes too abrupt, too abrasive, too self-righteous, it also freshened the atmosphere with debate and intellectual challenge. Instead of turning away from politics in disgust or snobbish disdain, as had been the custom of previous generations of German intellectuals, many of "Hitler's children" took part in it. And when they saw things going wrong—not always without a touch of hysteria—they at least stood up to be counted. When thugs sporting Nazi regalia became a serious menace in 1992, setting fire to asylum homes and murdering foreigners, millions of Germans came out to protest. More than half the population of Munich took part in candlelight parades, to demonstrate its opposition to violent xenophobia. Symbolically, at least, Germans had learned the value of dissent.

JAPAN

Ienaga Saburo is a Japanese history professor and former high school teacher. He wrote a widely used history textbook for high school students in 1952. But four years later his troubles began. The Ministry of Education decided that Ienaga's text was too "one sided," that is, too negative about the Japanese war in Asia. He was frequently told to rewrite his manuscript. But in 1964, he had had enough, and in the following year he sued the government for acting unconstitutionally. This was followed by two more lawsuits, in 1967 and 1984. In the 1980s he was told to delete passages about, among other things, the Nanking Massacre, rape by Japanese soldiers, and Japanese medical experiments in Manchuria. Censoring textbooks, Ienaga claimed, was against the postwar constitution, which guaranteed freedom of expression. He was still fighting his case, after appeals and counterappeals, in the Tokyo High Court in 1992, when he was seventy-nine years old.

The first thing I noticed about Ienaga was his frailty. He walked with some difficulty and tired easily. His pale bald head sat, egglike, on a small, brittle frame. His glasses looked too large in relation to the rest of him. I wondered where he found the energy and the motivation to carry on his struggle for twenty-seven years. Sitting in his study in a suburb of Tokyo, he answered my question by talking about his war:

"I taught history then at a high school in Niigata. The Ministry of Education ordered teachers of middle schools and junior high schools to teach the imperial myths, about the divine ancestry of the Japanese race, and so on."

He produced a textbook of the time. Ancient Japanese gods and mythical emperors were described as carriers of unique Japanese virtues. Myth was presented as history. Ienaga sighed as he leafed through the brittle pages, and said that he never wanted Japanese children to have to read such books again.

"The schoolroom was a place of apostasy, where we had to stamp on our own principles. I am ashamed that I didn't resist teaching the view of history propagated by the state. I shall always be ashamed of it. Mind you, I was not a propagandist for the war, but I did nothing to stop it either."

He had spoken of his sense of shame in court when he first pleaded his case in 1965: "I only thought of my own conscience, but I committed the sin of standing by as my ancestral land was being destroyed. Millions of my countrymen died in that war, and I was lucky enough to survive. I feel deeply guilty about having been a passive witness to my country's ruin . . . I am just a humble citizen now, but even if I cannot do much, I wish to make up for my sin of not offering any resistance before. This is why I am filing this suit today."

It is a refrain running through all his writings and speeches: the lack of resistance in Japan. He said it again after his last appearance in court in November 1992. He spoke to his supporters, who had gathered in a large rented hall not far from the High Court building: "The great difference between Nazi Germany and its Axis partner Japan was that many Germans resisted and lost their lives. In Japan, hardly anyone resisted. We were a nation of conformists. That's why the most important thing now is not whether we win or lose this case, but our resolve to fight on." When it was time for him to go, his supporters stood up and cheered as he shuffled slowly down the hall, his narrow shoulders bent, as though burdened by a heavy weight, his eyes blinking behind his owlish glasses.

He lost his case, of course, on all counts. The verdict was announced on March 16, 1993. Ienaga had expected it, but even he was taken aback by the shabbiness of the decision. He gave a spirited press conference, saying he could not contain his anger and that the verdict had brought shame upon Japan. I rang him up a month later, hoping to see him again, but he was too exhausted, he said. Would he fight on? "Of course, of course. The textbook trial is my reason to live." He observed that the provincial press had been much more supportive than the metropolitan papers, whose editorials had been lukewarm. "The farther away you get from Tokyo," he said, "the more freedom you have to be critical of the government." The Ienaga case is not the only instance where this has been true.

It had all seemed so promising when the war was over. Immediately after the Japanese surrender, there were no new text- books, so the old ones were used with the militaristic passages blotted out with ink. But in 1946 a new book was published, entitled *The Course of Our Country*. It was the first history textbook since 1881 that began with a description of the Stone Age instead of national myths about ancient gods and their imperial descendants. A year later, the Fundamental Law of Education was passed, which limited government control over educational materials. The aim of education was "to bring up a people that loves truth and peace" and to build "a democratic and cultural state" in "accordance with the constitution of Japan." Schools would be free to choose their own textbooks, which would be prepared and published privately. Ethics was abolished as a subject, and history became part of the social studies course.

It amounted to a revolution. At least since the Imperial Rescript on Education of 1890, Japanese education had been an exercise in imperial propaganda. The Prime Minister at the time, Yamagata Aritomo, said that "education, just like the military, ought to possess an imperial mandate." He also said that in national crises, all Japanese should be taught to offer themselves "courageously" to the state, and "thus guard and maintain the prosperity of Our Imperial Throne."

Even geography lessons were harnessed to the imperial cause. In a wartime geography textbook, "the shape of Japan" is described as "not without significance. We appear to be standing in the vanguard of Asia, advancing bravely into the Pacific. At the same time we appear ready to defend the Asian continent from outside attack."

Ethical studies were given extreme importance. This is how such national virtues as self-sacrifice, military discipline, ancestor worship, and the imperial cult were bred. And as was true in most countries in the first half of the century, military heroes were held up as the cardinal models to follow. *Kimigayo*, a prayer for the everlasting imperial reign, was sung as the national anthem, and the Rising Sun flag hoisted all over Asia. It was the duty of all Japanese to spring to attention at the very mention of the divine emperor. Every Japanese school had a shrine with the emperor's portrait. A speck of dust on the picture and careless hanging were reasons for severe punishment.

All this was officially abolished in 1947 and 1948, when the Imperial Rescript on Education was invalidated by both houses in the Diet. Constitutionalism, pacifism ("truth and peace"), democracy, and social studies had arrived instead. When Ienaga wrote his first textbook, it was published without any official interference. But around that time, a year after the start of the Korean War, things began to change. A government committee for educational reform issued a report that said, among other things: "By basing our system on that of a foreign country where conditions differ, and by pursuing only ideals, we have incorporated many undesirable elements into our system."

To counter these elements, educational boards no longer would be elected but would be appointed by local governments. And the Ministry of Education once again assumed responsibility for preparing and publishing school textbooks. This pitted the government against the leftist Japan Teachers' Union in a long struggle that pushed both institutions toward extreme positions. The union suspected the government of militarist revivalism, while the government regarded the leftist teachers, including Ienaga, as dangerous idealists at best and traitors at worst. As a result of this endless tug-of-war, Japanese history textbooks failed to satisfy either side. Leftists and liberals criticize them to this day for being dishonest, evasive, and nationalistic. Conservatives and nationalists see too many "alien" traces of leftist ideology. Neither side is entirely wrong: the compromised textbooks are evasive, and Marxists have dominated historical scholarship since the war.

Ienaga never disguised his politics. In his 1962 history textbook, he used as an illustration a photograph of a maimed Japanese Army veteran, with the stump of one arm in a leather cast and a money box around his neck. The caption carried a message: "This tragic sight eloquently conveys to us the poignant meaning of the phrase from the preface to the constitution which reads: '. . . [we] resolve that we shall never again be visited with the horrors of war through government action.' " It perfectly summed up Ienaga's and the Teachers' Union's "constitutional patriotism" and their pacifist disposition. War, any war, was bad, but especially a war fought by "imperialist" powers on the Asian continent. Ienaga's explanation for Japan's failure to destroy the Chinese Communists was "the democratic power of the Red armies." The Japanese war in China was "a struggle of political values: the democracy of China versus the militaristic absolutism of Japan." Twenty years later, this was precisely his analysis of the Vietnam War too.

Ienaga's leftist pacifism and pro-Chinese bias were just the kinds of things Japanese conservatives sought to banish from the textbooks. The Ministry of Education wanted both the photograph of the maimed soldier and the caption to be deleted, since they conveyed "an excessively negative impression of war."

Ienaga had also included photographs of students going to war and young girls working in arms factories, with the caption: "The destruction of people's lives." Yet the ministry took a more positive view of these pictures. They were "good photos that show the bright faces of students devoting themselves to their country."

I looked at a high school textbook published in 1984. It was used in schools all over Japan. There were no pictures of maimed soldiers or Japanese atrocities. There was a photograph of Hiroshima in ruins, of the *Arizona* sinking in Pearl Harbor, of contemporary newspaper headlines, of Japanese evacuees from the bombings, and of citizens practicing fire drills. The caption of this last picture was in keeping with the spirit of the ministry: "The neighborhood association helps out during a fire drill. The women, dressed in baggy trousers and head scarves, are diligently practicing how to pass water buckets."

References to Unit 731, which carried out the fatal medical experiments on thousands of prisoners in Manchuria, were deleted in Ienaga's books, because there had been "no credible scholarly research" on the subject. (Research was indeed difficult, since most of the information was in American or Soviet hands.) But enough evidence had emerged by the 1980s to prove that Ienaga had been right to include it. He was confident in 1992 that Japanese textbooks would deal with Unit 731 in future editions.

Ienaga had also mentioned in his 1962 textbook that "many of the Japanese officers and soldiers violated Chinese women" during the China campaign. The ministry decided to have this deleted too. "The violation of women," the ministry claimed, "is something that has happened on every battlefield in every era of human history. This is not an issue that needs to be taken up with respect to the Japanese Army in particular."

In fact, rape by the Imperial Army was so pervasive that some of the generals began to worry about the consequences—the outrages provoked Chinese resistance. So it was decided to set up military brothels ("sexual comfort facilities") near the front lines, stocked with Chinese, Korean, Southeast Asian, and some European women, taken from villages, towns, and POW camps all over the Japanese empire. Most of these "comfort women" died, of disease, murder, or enemy fire. Ienaga mentioned them in his book *The Pacific War*, but they did not appear in any Japanese textbooks. Again, evidence has emerged to prove Ienaga's case, and future history books will have to include them.

The evidence came out in an interesting way. Until the late 1980s, South Koreans needed special government permission to travel abroad. And since the South Korean government had agreed, in 1965, to settle Japan's war responsibility by accepting a lump sum, individual Koreans were not able to claim compensation. The history of the comfort women was embarrassing in any event, for it brought shame on the families of the survivors, and there had been a great deal of Korean collaboration. This, needless to say, was kept out of Korean textbooks. But in the more liberal climate of the late 1980s, South Koreans were able to travel to Japan, and with the encouragement of feminist groups, a number of former comfort women decided to press their claims. The Japanese government, however, denied any responsibility. It argued that wartime prostitution had been a private enterprise and that no evidence existed of any official involvement.

And there the matter would have rested had not the historian Yoshimi Yoshiaki watched these denials on television. He remembered some documents he had seen while doing research in the Self-Defense Agency library. So he went back to the library and in a few days he found what he was after: official orders for the construction of "sexual comfort facilities," signed by the high command of the Imperial Japanese Army. The story of the comfort women was widely reported in the Japanese press. The Japanese Prime Minister was forced to apologize to the Korean people. And when a BBC reporter asked the chief Japanese government spokesman why it had taken the government so long to admit the truth, the spokesman said that government researchers had not known about the documents. When the reporter politely expressed his surprise about this, since it had taken a lone scholar only a few days to find them, there followed a great moment of television: for a full minute, the spokesman remained silent, biting his lip, avoiding the reporter's gaze. Finally he said it was "a very unfair question."

Ienaga used the term "aggression" to describe Japan's war in China. The examiner appointed by the ministry made the following suggestion: "Aggression is a term that contains negative ethical connotations. In the education of the citizens of the next generation it is not desirable to use a term with such negative implications to describe the acts of our own country. Therefore an expression such as 'military advance' should be used." The suggestion was duly taken up. The Chinese government protested against this wording on various politically opportune occasions, which only helped to sharpen the political divisions in Japan. The history of aggression blocked the Japanese from using military force, which is why the right denied it, why the left kept on bringing it up, and why the mainstream conservatives preferred not to talk about it at all. As long as the LDP remained in power, the right, some of whose older members were themselves tainted by the war, had to be appeased. In 1989 a Communist member of the Japanese parliament asked the Prime Minister, Takeshita Noboru, whether Japan had been guilty of aggression in World War II. Takeshita answered that this "should be left up to future historians to judge."

In 1970 Ienaga actually won his case. The judge of the Tokyo District Court, Sugimoto Ryokichi, ruled that the screening of textbooks by the ministry should not go beyond the correction of typographical and factual errors. Censorship of substantial matters was deemed unconstitutional, and so it was decided in Ienaga's case. After the verdict, the judge told the press that the position of teachers should be respected and their freedom protected. Right-wing extremists issued death threats to the judge, the defense lawyers, and Ienaga himself. Ienaga's house was surrounded day and night by thugs who kept him awake by shouting slogans and banging pots and pans like battle drums. The atmosphere at the Tokyo District Court was so tense that Ienaga and his counsel had to enter the building under police protection through a secret door.

After the ministry appealed the verdict, Ienaga did not win his case again, or at least not so categorically. In 1974, another judge agreed that the screening process had been "excessive," but not unconstitutional. In the 1980s, yet another bench pronounced all the screening suggestions perfectly in order. One of Ienaga's longest-serving defense lawyers, Oyama Hiroshi, called the early 1970s the "Golden Age of Japanese justice." I asked him what had changed. He said it was a fairly simple matter: "Judges who go against the government are not chosen to sit in the higher courts. So if you don't care about having a successful career, you pass fair judgments." Judge Sugimoto's career did not prosper.

However, much to everyone's surprise, the Tokyo High Court ruled on October 20, 1993, that the Ministry of Education had exceeded its bounds by censoring Iena a's textbook on several counts, including his description of the Nanking Massacre. The election defeat of the LDP might have contributed to this new mood. But a more likely reason was the mass of new evidence of Japanese atrocities furnished by young Japanese historians.

When Japanese right-wing nationalists claim that their leftist opponents in the teaching profession are influenced by "foreign" ideas, they are, of course, right. Which is not to say that nativist ideas are pure, but they appear to have a stronger claim on tradition. Just as German conservatives once denounced the constitution of the Weimar Republic as un-German, "Jewish," not worthy of support, Japanese rightists condemn the postwar Japanese constitution, and the educational system that supports it, as alien and thus unsuitable. One notable scholar of comparative culture, Irie Takanori, actually drew the parallel between the Weimar Republic and postwar Japan. The Japanese constitution, he said, was written by Jews who had "an antipathy toward the state."

German constitutional patriotism and the postwar constitution itself were the creations of German jurists and thinkers, who could, if necessary, call upon the spirit of the European Enlightenment, Goethe's humanism, and the German resistance against Hitler to give themselves a sense of continuity. The Japanese had a harder time, since it was the American occupation, more than the Japanese themselves, that instigated constitutional and educational change. And as Ienaga said, there was no tradition of resistance to fall back on. Instead, there was Marxism, which had an intellectual history in Japan as well as in the West and which provided a ready antidote to nationalist myths.

The textbook for high school students published in 1984 tells the whole melancholy story of Japanese wartime resistance— or rather the lack of it—in the space of one page: "In 1933, the leaders of the Japanese Communist Party publicly renounced their political creed. This had a widespread influence on socialists, most of whom followed suit. Even the very few people who adhered to socialism, such as Suzuki Mosaburo of the Japanese Proletarian Party, were put under such pressure that they discontinued their activities in 1937."

The complicated case of Professor Minobe Tatsukichi is briefly touched upon. Minobe was a constitutional jurist who in 1935 devised the theory of the emperor as an "organ of state." The state, in his opinion, was sovereign and the emperor was its supreme organ. He was immediately criticized as an enemy of the national polity, for the sovereignty of the emperor was absolute.

The textbook goes on to say: "As a result of this controversy over Minobe's theory, not only Marxism but also liberalism was denounced as a form of antinational thinking. And soon the ideas for domestic reform planned by the radical army factions dominated the mass media. This could be seen in cultural affairs as well. In tune with official cultural policy, militaristic and reactionary trends grew stronger and the uncritical emulation of Western civilization was reconsidered. There was an increasing tendency to reevaluate traditional Japanese culture."

That, so far as resistance is concerned, is it. But far from using the few that did resist—Minobe, for example—as role models, there is a marked ambivalence in these phrases. To be sure, militarism and suppression of thought are to be condemned, but "uncritical emulation" of Western civilization cannot be a good thing either. And what is so wrong about a reevaluation of "traditional Japanese culture"? To "reconsider" and a "tendency to reevaluate" are, in any case, odd words to describe straight government censorship.

So even though nobody openly supports a militarist revival, many Japanese nationalists feel the need to defend traditional Japanese culture against uncritical emulation of the West. In political terms this means a defense of Japanese sovereignty, including its right to wage war, against the influence of Marxism and pacifism. In terms of propaganda, the "culture" under siege is a vague concept of the family state whose ancient values are passed on through the supposedly unbroken imperial line. Since the postwar order was not set up by Japanese who inherited the mantle of resistance against the *ancien régime*, feelings about the past are bound to be more ambivalent than is the case in Germany, East or West. In effect, the defense of Japanese identity often *is* a defense of the old regime, not just against the Japanese left but also against foreigners, in East and West, who criticize Japan for what it did and for the way it chooses to remember.

This is why Fujio Masayuki, a former Education Minister, once told me that "there were no shameful episodes in modern Japanese history." He was sacked by his Prime Minister in 1986 for upsetting relations with South Korea, after stating that the Koreans had been partly to blame for their own annexation by Japan in 1910. The Tokyo trials, he said in an interview, had been a "racial revenge," meant "to rob Japan of her power." Fujio said these things because he wanted to "restore the Japanese spirit through history and tradition."

Fujio was neither eccentric nor the first to voice such thoughts after the war. In 1974, Prime Minister Tanaka Kakuei, who was soon to be indicted in a corruption scandal, worried about the lack of moral development in Japanese education. He suggested that the old Imperial Rescript on Education be revived, since "much of it expresses universal moral principles." But in 1957 the Ministry of Education had come to the crux of the matter. In its report on Ienaga Saburo's first textbook, it said that in his "zeal to make people reflect on the past, he has strayed a long way from the proper aims of teaching Japanese history, which are to acknowledge the historical achievements of our ancestors, to raise our awareness of being Japanese, and to foster a rich feeling of love for our people."

In 1991, the old imperial hymn, *Kimigayo*, and the Rising Sun flag, despite some vehement protest from leftists and liberals, were officially declared to be the national symbols of Japan. This decision came not through legislation but in the form of a guideline issued by the Ministry of Education in approving the revised textbooks, which included, for the first time since the war, favorable passages about Japanese military heroes. And at least one school, the Nichidai Matsue High School, had unofficially revived the Imperial Rescript. Its headmaster, Okazaki Isao, insisted that the Rescript be read out loud every morning, since it was "the best text to make you Japanese with a true Japanese spirit."

In the autumn of 1992 I waited outside the Tokyo High Court, together with about 250 people. Space inside the courtroom was limited, so we had to draw lots to see who could attend Ienaga Saburo's last appearance in court. Many were members of an organization of Ienaga supporters. Some had come all the way from Hokkaido and Okinawa. There were men, women, old people, students, teachers, office workers, and housewives. The mood was remarkably cheerful, despite the gloomy prospects for Ienaga's case. Pamphlets were handed out to publicize meetings to discuss human rights, or freedom of speech, or compensation for former comfort women and other victims of Japanese militarism. There were cheers for the people who had come from farthest away, and more cheers for people who had stood as witnesses in former Ienaga trials.

But the biggest cheer, like a great rush of feeling, was for Ienaga himself, as he entered the building ahead of his lawyers. He doffed his hat in salute and blinked behind his glasses, looking both fragile and stubborn.

The courtroom was sober, without visual symbols of power, secular or religious. The judges wore simple black togas, in the continental European style. The walls behind them were of pale-colored marble. The lawyers' rhetoric was delivered in a sober, even artless manner. There was one woman among Ienaga's defense counsel. The ministry's team had none.

I listened to Oyama Hiroshi, who had pleaded Ienaga's case from the very beginning, in 1965. He spoke clearly and well, about the steady reversion to prewar methods of education, about the low standards of human rights in Japan, and about Japan's poor record, in comparison to Germany, in facing the darker pages of its past. He quoted Montesquieu on the spirit of law. And he pointed out that the constitution was there to protect people from a state monopoly on the truth. This, he said, was why writers of textbooks had to be free to express their ideas. For without freedom of thought there could be no democracy.

The judges and some of the counsel for the ministry sat back with their eyes closed, in deep concentration, or fast asleep. Perhaps they were bored, because they had heard it all before. Perhaps they thought it was a pointless exercise, since they knew already how the case would end. But it was not a pointless exercise. For Ienaga Saburo had kept alive a vital debate for twenty-seven years. One cussed schoolteacher and several hundred supporters at the courthouse might not seem much, but it was enough to show that, this time, someone was fighting back.

MEMORIALS, MUSEUMS, AND MONUMENTS

STANDING AT THE southwest corner of the Marienkirche in Wittenberg, the church where Martin Luther used to preach, you can just make out a curious sculpture jutting out from the church wall, like a gargoyle, about thirty feet from the ground. It is of a sow suckling three piglets. Her hind leg is lifted by a little man wearing a pointed hat. The hat identifies the man as a Jew of the fifteenth century. Above this scene of Jew and pigs—the sow, I was told, representing "Satan's synagogue"— is the Hebrew name for God. The ornament is called a *Judensau*, Jew's pig. Many of these used to adorn German churches, as tokens of Jewish humiliation. A few still remain, though the tourist guides tend not to mention them.

I would not have noticed the *Judensau* in this prettily rundown East German town, officially known as Luther City Wittenberg, if a notice board inside the church had not alerted me to the fact. The notice had been put up in 1988, after the church was renovated. During the renovation, which began in 1983, young members of the Lutheran congregation had decided something needed to be done about the *Judensau*; it could not just sit there unnoticed. So money was collected to commission a monument to remind people of the sculpture's significance. It was to be a *Mahnmal*, a "monument of warning." This still being the GDR, however, where antisemitism was not officially

202

recognized as a problem, no city official turned up for the unveiling.

The monument of warning is located on the pavement directly under the *Judensau*. It is made of bronze. Four square plates, rather like an oddly shaped manhole, are lifted slightly from below by probing bronze fingers. On the side is a poetic text that reads: "Under the sign of the cross, God's own name, so sacred that Jews cannot pronounce it in front of Christians, was used as a form of abuse, and six million Jews died." The bronze fingers suggest the victims of antisemitism rising from a mass grave. They also suggest something more abstract, more in keeping perhaps with a monument of warning: shameful memories which cannot be repressed, which claw their way into our conscience, like a constantly recurring nightmare. The *Mahnmal* of Wittenberg is one of thousands of warning monuments in Germany, but it is the only one I have seen which refers less to a particular event than to memory itself.

Before World War II there were no warning monuments in Germany. Instead there were war memorials, to fallen soldiers, dying, like marble Christs, for the fatherland. The bonds of national community were strengthened through their sacrifice. War, in Great War monuments, is a mystical experience, a Calvary of valor, sacrifice, and regeneration. Great Gothic memorial fortresses were built in the German Reich to pluck honor from defeat. Nothing like this emerged after World War II. Instead, the Germans built monuments not to glorify but to warn; *Denkmal* became *Mahnmal*.

Like a monumental rosary, spread mostly over western Germany, the monuments testify to a fretting over memory, a neurotic fear of amnesia, an obsession with casting the past in stone. It was not always like this. In the late 1940s and 1950s, the compulsion to forget was stronger. Reminders of the past—not just Hitler's past—were destroyed, blown up, removed. Sites of concentration camps were used for some time to house German prisoners, by Soviets and Western Allies alike, but as soon as was possible they were either razed or abandoned. What physically remained of the Third Reich was left out of apathy or force majeure, as in the case of Speer's indestructible Nuremberg stadium, or for political reasons, as was usually the case in East Germany. The warning monuments and memorial places (*Gedenkstätte*) are mostly products of the reaction, which set in during the 1960s, propelled by the postwar generation, as eager to warn and remember as their parents were to forget.

Warning monuments come in many different forms. Former concentration camps have become *Gedenkstätte* which combine the functions of museum, tourist attraction, and memorial. Some, such as Ravensbrück in the East, are more or less intact, and some, such as Bergen-Belsen in the West, are no more than sites.

The Wannsee Villa, outside Berlin, where Reinhard Heydrich discussed the logistics of the Final Solution with fellow bureaucrats over an after-breakfast cognac on January 20, 1942, was opened as a *Gedenkstätte* on the fiftieth anniversary of the occasion. The opening was celebrated in the afternoon with a conference about memory and the Holocaust, followed by a champagne reception.

The museum in the *Gedenkstätte Haus der Wannsee-Konferenz* does not show much that is new. The pictures on the wall are less about the Nazi bureaucrats who planned the Final Solution than about the victims, photographed with eager thoroughness by their tormentors. There they all are again, frozen in their misery: the boy in the Warsaw ghetto holding up his hands, the terrified eyes peeping through the door of a sealed cattle car, the selection on the ramp, the rabbis playing piggyback, etc., etc. I leafed through the visitors' book and read the professions of national shame: "It is embarrassing, sad, and humbling to have to call oneself a German." "How could this happen among a largely Christian people?" "After this visit I am ashamed to be a German."

There is a warning monument in the center of West Berlin, facing some of the busiest department stores. Hundreds of thousands walk past every day, with shopping bags full, seeing it, but not seeing it. It is a sign listing the main concentration camps and telling us never to forget. There are other such signs scattered around the city.

One artist, Jochen Gerz, born in 1940, came up with the idea of making an invisible warning monument. He was critical of conventional memorials and monuments, which beautify the past by casting history in bronze, as it were, thus turning personal, meaningful remembrance into a communal ceremony. This, he argued, was just another way of suppressing the past. The representation of history replaces memory itself, especially after the witnesses are gone; it hinders personal reflection. The question is: How do you visualize memory? Gerz's answer is: You don't.

What he did instead was to trace the continuity of Jewish life and culture by finding out the names of Jewish cemeteries in Germany. Then, as a variation of the Jewish custom of leaving stones on visited graves, Gerz and his pupils dug up paving stones in a street in Saarbrücken, outside the castle which used to contain a Gestapo prison. Every stone was inscribed with the name of a Jewish cemetery and the date of its discovery by Gerz, and restored to its place in the street, making sure the inscription was underneath. Gerz's team dug up 1,926 stones, and inscribed and replaced them in this manner. A sign indicates the place of the "Invisible Warning Monument."

In an essay entitled "The Past Must Not Be Normalized," Jürgen Habermas, as is his wont, criticized the desire among German conservatives to unburden Germany from its recent past by making it seem less singular, more normal, more in the mainstream of history than is warranted. He quoted the following description (by Helmut Dubiel) of this attitude: "People relate to the national past as they do to a nuclear power station for whose radioactive waste no final destination has been found." Reading this, I was reminded of Walter Benjamin's description of history as an accumulation of rubble. But even as some (perhaps many, perhaps even most) Germans wish to have the radioactive rubble buried, others try their hardest to retrieve every stone, every cinder, to be preserved in monuments and museums.

The site of the former Gestapo headquarters in Berlin, for example, consists of nothing but stones. Himmler chose some of the grandest addresses in Berlin for his operations. The Gestapo was in the former School of Industrial Arts and Crafts on the Prinz-Albrecht-Strasse, and the Security Service, under Heydrich, was in the Prinz-Albrecht-Palais on the Wilhelmstrasse. The latter was a fine baroque palace, renovated by Friedrich Schinkel in the early nineteenth century. These two buildings formed the hub of the entire network of concentration camps and secret police organizations; here the procedures of mass murder were worked out. The Gestapo also built a "house prison" in the cellars of the art school.

Like the rest of Berlin, both buildings were damaged in the bombings. They were not beyond repair, however, but as was the fate of many reminders of the old days, the palace was demolished in 1949, and the old arts and crafts academy was blown up in stages between 1953 and 1964. There was not even a *Mahnmal* to commemorate the place. Nothing remained but a mountain of rubble which was never properly cleared away.

In 1983 the Berlin government decided to do something about it. A competition was held to see if some suitable artistic concept for this historical site might emerge. Concepts emerged, but nothing happened. Six years later, the government appointed a commission to look into the possibility of a museum, or perhaps a documentation center, or maybe a *Mahnmal*. Again nothing happened officially, but meanwhile a group called Active Museum of Fascism and Resistance in Berlin had built a makeshift museum on top of the ruins of what was assumed to have been the Gestapo prison. In fact, they were the broken walls of a washroom. But ghoulish legends grew easily from these sites. A hotel across the street, once the billet for middle-ranking SS officers, was torn down. I was told by a local resident, speaking in a low confiding voice, that some of the hotel's furniture had come from the Gestapo's torture rooms.

The foundations of the house prison had indeed been dug up some years before, but they had been sealed by the state Ministry of Archaeology. The ministry was engaged in a bureaucratic wrangle with the authorities in charge of historical buildings. The heritage authorities wanted to turn the entire site into a "Pompeii of the SS"—to borrow the phrase from Alfred Kerndʼl, Berlin's chief archaeologist since 1968. Kerndʼl had plans to build a memorial around the jail, with some modest plantings to indicate the outlines of the cells.

By the middle of 1992, still nothing had happened. The makeshift museum, called Topography of Terror, was still there. Kerndʼl worried about the state of the cell foundations, and outside the museum children climbed the rubble on mountain bikes. New ideas for the site were offered. A politician suggested that a slab of the old Berlin Wall might be positioned behind the ruins, with some appropriate text, like "End of two dictatorships." But finally, by the end of the year, the senator for cultural affairs made a decision. The Topography of Terror would be expanded and an "international center" built, for seminars, meetings, and conferences on the Nazi past.

In the meantime another archaeological dispute had erupted. In June 1990, Berliners were about to celebrate the fall of the Berlin Wall by staging a rock concert by Pink Floyd on the site of Hitler's old chancellery. This spot, near the Brandenburg Gate, had been wasteland, lying like a sandy mine-filled moat along the eastern side of the Berlin Wall. Escapees had been shot there and rabbits ran wild. Not long before the Wall came down, gray housing blocks were built on top of Hitler's bunker. Before the concert, workmen dug into the rubble, looking for unexploded mines, and struck the roof of a bunker—part of the concrete labyrinth built to house Hitler and his retainers at the end of the war. Alfred Kerndʼl—asserting that "everything under the ground is my territory"—rushed to the scene on his bicycle and found something remarkable. For inside the bunker nothing had changed since 1945. Somehow, the Red Army had forgotten to blow it up, even though the odd black smudge left by flame throwers showed they had been there.

There were bunk beds for the SS guards, and on the wooden table, empty bottles, knives and forks, and porcelain bowls had gathered decades of dust. An amateur painter had left frescoes on the walls of tall SS men in tight trousers and shiny black boots, shielding blond German children playing under German oak trees, and blond bosomy women holding hands on checkered tablecloths with blond soldiers drinking beer. With the customary taste of rock impresarios, the promoter of the Pink Floyd concert contrived to have himself photographed in front of the painting before Kernd'l sealed the door. The concert was duly held. Pink Floyd sang about sitting in a bunker behind a wall waiting for the worms to come. And the quarrel about the bunker began.

Conservatives were embarrassed by yet another unwelcome reminder of the past and wanted to destroy it. Some liberals and members of the Jewish community worried that it would become a neo-Nazi shrine and wanted to be rid of it as well. But Kernd'l insisted it should be preserved as an important relic of history.

Kernd'l has an office in the Charlottenburg Palace. You can see the Nefertiti jewels as you enter the building. His manner is brusque and he speaks in a thick Berlin accent, a rarity in the western part of town. He also uses the phrase "typically German" a great deal, always with contempt. It is "typically German" to want to bury the past. The Japanese, he said, push their history away, but so do the Germans. What happened to Spandau prison just one month after Hess died? "Bang, blown to bits, another bit of our history gone. Typically German!"

I asked him what the chances were of preserving the bunker. Not much chance, he said. "They only want history to be displayed in museums." But why, I asked, did he feel that the bunker was worth preserving? "It is a sad thing," he said, "that all that is left on a spot where royal mistresses had palaces, and

Bismarck used to live, a spot which romantic poets once described as paradise, that all that is left there is a bunker for SS
men. But it needs to be preserved. You see, the Germans have
so little identity. Why destroy what little we have got?"

Identity: I thought about all the German towns I had visited,
each with its own *Heimatmuseum*, each hanging on for dear life
to the artifacts of its folklore, its local history, as though to ward
off the ravages of change. Napoleon built museums to glorify
his reign and boast of his conquests. The great museums of
Victorian England celebrated progress and imperial reach. The
German *Heimatmuseum* shows who the local people are, or once
were, or more precisely, who they think they are, or once were.
But there is one thing that many European history museums
have had in common, at least since the French Revolution: the
aim of showing that the here and now, our customs, our taste,
and even the way our societies are governed, are the logical,
inevitable outcome of the past. This aim can be politicized, to
give legitimacy to a revolution, a nation, a particular form of
government. This is inevitably the case when the government
ideology rests on a belief in the unshakable laws of history.

There is a spot on top of a green hill outside Weimar where
Goethe used to sit with his friend Eckermann. They would lean
back against an oak tree, savor the green velvety folds of the
Thuringian countryside, and discuss literature and life. Eckermann noted down the master's words: "Here one feels great'
and free."

In 1937, when the forest was cleared to build a concentration
camp, Goethe's oak was protected by a special act, decreed by
the Nazi regime. It was known as the Nature Protection Act. A
fence was built around the oak, and thus it survived until the
last year of the war, when one side caught fire during an American bomb attack. The Nazis decided to have it felled. An inmate
of the camp, who made death masks in the medical block, used

some of the wood to carve a human face, which can still be seen in the museum of the Buchenwald National Warning and Memorial Place (*Nationale Mahn- und Gedenkstätte Buchenwald*).

The exact spot of Goethe's oak was pointed out to me in the winter of 1991, on my second visit to the camp. My guide was a tall, thin man whose ingratiating manners suggested nervousness. "Here you can see," he said, indicating the setting of the former camp in one swooping gesture, "the typical German mentality." (The guide was himself a German.) "The Goethe oak—culture and romanticism; the crematorium—barbarism; the zoo—sentimentality."

I had not heard about the zoo before. Created to amuse the SS guards, it was located just outside the barbed-wire fence, near the main gate (the animals, needless to say, were treated far better than the inmates of the camp). Otherwise, my guide's sketch of the German "mentality" was a cliché.

But it was a cliché not often heard there until recently, for Buchenwald was the "Red Olympus," the holiest shrine of the German Democratic Republic. Many important Communists were imprisoned in Buchenwald; Ernst Thälmann, the chairman of the prewar German Communist Party, was murdered there. And an alleged last-minute uprising led by Communist prisoners in April 1945 had entered Communist lore as one of the great historic events. That the German mentality was now being blamed for what had happened in Buchenwald fifty years ago was a sign of how much had changed in East Germany during the last two years.

On my first visit to Buchenwald, a year earlier, everything was still normal—that is to say, orthodox. Like most visitors from the West, I was struck and somewhat horrified by the grandiose monuments erected on the site of the mass graves. Along the Street of Nations were eighteen huge stone pylons, crowned by great chalices, representing the countries where the Nazis had rounded up their victims. There was the soaring, forty-five-meter bell tower, whose bell, my guidebook said, would "echo through the land." Inside the bell tower a bronze plate covered the soil taken from various concentration camps. Outside stood the groups of giant prisoners breaking their bonds and raising their stone fists. There were friezes of heroic figures punishing their tormentors, or better still, in the words of the Buchenwald Oath, taken on the day of liberation in April 1945, "tearing out the Nazi evil by its roots."

I saw the cell where Ernst Thälmann, the Stalinist hero, was killed. There was a plaque about the "great son of the German people and leader of the German working class, murdered by fascism," an eternal flame, and wreaths from fraternal parties and trade union organizations.

But the myth of Buchenwald, like similar myths all over the Soviet empire, had the usual hole in the middle. There was hardly any mention that there had been many Jews among the sixty-five thousand men, women, and children who died in the camp. Buchenwald was not a death camp, like Auschwitz or Treblinka, specifically designed to annihilate the Jews. Prisoners at Buchenwald were worked to death, or they died of disease, hunger, torture, and executions. All prisoners were treated horribly, but according to most accounts, the Jews were treated worst of all. Yet I found only one small plaque to commemorate the "special camp" where ten thousand German Jews had languished in terrible conditions, after being arrested during the *Kristallnacht* in 1938. About the transports from Auschwitz of tens of thousands of Jews, many of whose skeletal remains had to be literally scraped from the cattle cars, not a word.

In Communist dogma, the war against the Jews did not really exist. World War II had been a class war, waged by fascists and plutocrats against the People. Jews, like Gypsies, were not essentially different from the other victims of fascism. As my guidebook, printed in 1988, put it: "Destruction of Marxism, revenge for the lost war, and brutal terror against all resisters, these were the stated aims of German fascism from the very start. What was really at stake was the interests of monopoly capital, lavishly used to promote the Nazi movement."

The Buchenwald museum did, however, offer a display of

women's hair and children's shoes, and a human heart, pierced
by a bullet, generously provided by the "memorial place Auschwitz." And the guidebook contained two photographs of the
selection ramp at Birkenau. But the only caption above these
pictures was a quotation from Ernst Thälmann, stating that "the
bourgeoisie is serious about its aim to annihilate the party and
the entire avant-garde of the working class."

Like all former concentration camp sites, Buchenwald attracts
the usual combination of tourists (one of the SS barracks was
turned into a hotel), survivors, and ghouls. I was accosted in
the parking lot, just outside the notorious iron gate, decorated
with the motto *"Jedem das Seine"* ("To each his own"), by an
American veteran who told me he visited the camp at least once
a year. He claimed to have been with General Patton's leath-
ernecks, who liberated the camp on April 11, 1945. "The ovens
were still warm," he drawled, "the ovens were still warm."

This version of events hardly fit the orthodox view in the
GDR. The myth of Buchenwald held that the inmates, led by
members of Communist cells in the camp, liberated themselves
in an armed rebellion. There was indeed a resistance organization in the camp, whose members had captured some weapons. But whether these weapons were ever used is open to
question. Several surviving witnesses, living in the West, claimed
that the camp was freed—without bloodshed—by the U.S.
Army. As Patton's tanks surrounded the camp, the SS guards
either fled or surrendered.

But it was an important story, for it served as the founding
myth of the German Democratic Republic. Every East German
schoolchild had to read the novel *Naked Among Wolves*, by Bruno
Apitz, the man who carved a face mask out of Goethe's oak. It
is a clumsy novel of the socialist realist school, in which the men
of the Communist resistance committee contrive, at great risk
to themselves, to save a little Jewish boy, while plotting the final
uprising. The book revolves around the question of collective
versus individual interests. Is the fate of the community worth
jeopardizing in the interests of one boy? The question is ago-

nized over but never quite resolved. In the end, both boy and community are saved. In the final, climactic scene, the heroes press through the main camp gate and "drag along on the crests of their liberating waves the unstoppable stream of humanity." And so began, in the words of the Buchenwald Oath (sworn on the parade ground that very same day), the struggle "toward a new world of peace and freedom." The nature of this world soon became clear. When Otto Grotewohl, the first Prime Minister of the German Democratic Republic, addressed 80,000 people at a rally in the former Buchenwald camp in 1958, he declared that the oath had already come true in the socialist German state. And to pay tribute to this achievement, hundreds of thousands of schoolchildren, workers, socialist youths, soldiers, farmers, and foreign comrades flocked every year to the "Red Olympus" to lay wreaths, listen to speeches, march in torchlight parades, and generally demonstrate their resolve to continue on the road to the Communist millennium.

But by 1991, when I visited Buchenwald for the second time, things had begun to change. The grandiose monuments were still there, of course. So was the documentary film shown in the movie theater, which contained footage of Otto Grotewohl and Walter Ulbricht and Frau Thälmann marching along the Street of Nations. But I was also handed a new pamphlet in the museum, which announced, with excruciating delicacy, that it had been decided in the spring of 1990 to "institute some changes, as far as technically feasible, to overcome a certain one-sidedness in the presentation."

These words did little to convey the controversy involved in rewriting the myths of the German Democratic Republic. Rewriting myths on a historical site, a "warning and memorial place" so loaded with symbolism, is difficult. Old myths had to be challenged without replacing them with new ones. The shrine of Buchenwald offered particular problems, since one or two skeletons had come tumbling from its cupboards.

In 1983 builders came across a mass of human bones, dumped into a common grave in the woods outside the perimeter of the

Nazi camp. The East German government immediately ordered the grave, and the matter, closed. But after 1989, more bones were discovered, and what could not even be mentioned for forty years was now openly discussed: Buchenwald, as well as other concentration camps in East Germany, such as Sachsen-hausen and Ravensbrück, had remained fully operative until 1950. As soon as the Soviet army arrived in Weimar, Buchen-wald had been pressed into service again, this time to punish former Nazis, class enemies, and counterrevolutionaries, in-cluding Social Democrats who refused to let the Communists take over their party. There is no evidence that the Soviets subjected their prisoners to the Nazi regime of murder by hard labor. Still, one third of the 30,000 prisoners interned in Soviet Buchenwald died, mostly of hunger and disease.

I met Robert Zeiler, one of the survivors, in West Berlin. His story, which he has told for years—to students, journalists, sur-vivors' associations—is a kind of epic myth in itself. Zeiler's father was an "Aryan" orchestra conductor; his mother was Jewish. When Zeiler was eleven, the first racial laws were passed; shortly afterward his parents were divorced. As a *Mischling* (half-caste), Zeiler was able to protect his mother for some years by living under her roof. His sister was less lucky. She was sent to Ravensbrück for sheltering her Jewish fiancé.

By 1943, the Nazis had decided that no Jew was to be spared, and Zeiler's mother was picked up and sent to Theresienstadt. Soon after, Zeiler, at the age of twenty, was arrested too, for harboring Jews—that is to say, his own mother. He was sent to Buchenwald. Before long he weighed only ninety pounds. It was hard to imagine, seeing him today, a roly-poly man in a jogging suit.

After being liberated from the camp, Zeiler went to Czecho-slovakia in an American jeep to find his mother, who had sur-vived. Together they drove back to Berlin, stopping for the night in Potsdam. While his mother was resting, Zeiler set off in his jeep for Berlin, to see what was left of their house. But he was stopped on the way by the Soviet secret police, who accused him of being an American spy. When he claimed to have been a Jewish victim of the Nazis, he was told he was a liar, since all Jews were dead. After some months of being shunted from one camp to another, Zeiler found himself in Buchenwald once again. He was to stay there for three more years. The Soviet guards, he recalled, had not behaved particularly badly, not as badly as the young Communist block leaders in the Nazi camp. They were mostly homesick young men who liked singing sentimental songs. The worst thing about the Soviet camp, Zeiler said, was the boredom.

I asked Zeiler what people thought of his story when he finally got home. He studied the tea cloth on his table, embroidered with a picture of the Hiroshima Peace Dome. He had told his story to many people, he said, Germans as well as occupation authorities. Then he fell silent. I studied his room, filled with knickknacks and his father's musical mementos. Again I asked him how people had responded to his story. He said that nobody had shown any interest at the time. Everyone was still preoccupied by the Nazis. Some West Germans had begun to complain about the treatment of German prisoners by the Allies—in Dachau, for example. But in the German Democratic Republic, the subject of Soviet camps simply did not exist.

Dr. Irmgard Seidel was still the deputy director of the Buchenwald memorial place during my second visit to the camp. Her office was in one of the former SS barracks—a large building, with long corridors, built by the Buchenwald prisoners. It smelled of wax and washing detergent. On the wall next to the door of Dr. Seidel's office was a drawing of an SS man, whip in hand, standing in front of a torture victim hanging by his wrists from a pole. The caption said: "Lord, forgive him, for he knows not what he does."

"I had no idea about this Soviet camp," said Dr. Seidel when I asked her about it. "December 1989 was the first time I heard about it. You know, what happened here between 1945 and 1950 was a taboo. It could not possibly be discussed."

Dr. Seidel's manner was not exactly impolite, but it was testy and betrayed a sense of pique. A former party member, she now lived in a new Germany unified by a conservative government. The tables had truly been turned: a committee of concerned Weimar citizens was agitating to have her removed from her job. Dr. Seidel's boss had already been purged, only to be replaced by a West German historian, who was swiftly replaced in turn, when his connections with the West German Communist Party became known.

Dr. Seidel was eager to show me documents proving her bona fides, and in particular her independence from Communist propaganda. She was conscious of the way the socialist state had ignored the Holocaust. But this didn't mean she accepted the view of some of her conservative opponents, who claimed that the Soviets had been worse than the Nazis. To prove that she had the right kind of backing, she produced a letter from a society of Holocaust survivors in New York. It was a protest against any attempt to equate the victims of the Soviet secret police, the NKVD, with the Nazi victims. The letter also mentioned the bravery of German political prisoners "whose sacrifices laid the foundation for the moral rebirth of Germany . . ."

"Of course," said Dr. Seidel, "we have neglected the Jewish victims, but this we intend to change. Our Jewish friends know this and support me fully." Perhaps they do, and maybe Dr. Seidel had reason to feel maligned. But I didn't quite believe her protestations. She must have known something about the postwar history of the camp. In a booklet printed in Weimar in 1988, and freely available at the camp museum bookshop, there was mention of the kind cooperation of the Soviet authorities in turning Buchenwald into a memorial place. This was made possible, it said, in 1950, when "the internment camp for Nazi functionaries was cleared in four weeks."

But what is to be done, now that the truth—or at least some of the truth—is out? German conservatives are quick to point out the similarities between Soviet and Nazi crimes. It is time, wrote a contributor to the *Frankfurter Allgemeine Zeitung*, to dust off the totalitarianism theory once more, the idea, that is, that right-wing and left-wing tyrannies "may not be identical, but should be assessed in the same way. What better place for this theory to prove its worth than Buchenwald?" The Christian Democratic Party in Weimar wanted to turn the camp into "a memorial place for the victims of all dictatorships"—as though the Third Reich were just another dictatorship.

Buchenwald, then, became the handy focus of a view which had gained currency, particularly in right-wing circles, since the collapse of the German Democratic Republic: the view that the Communist state had been a kind of continuation of the Third Reich. In a way, it was argued, the GDR had been worse than Nazi Germany: it lasted for more than forty years, whereas Hitler was around for only twelve. It was an attractive theory, since it reduced the Third Reich to more local, less horrific proportions. It also slipped rather easily into the conclusion that started the historians' debate in 1986, the conclusion that Nazism was merely a defensive reaction to Soviet tyranny. Ernst Nolte, the conservative historian who proposed this theory, argued that Hitler had tried to defend Europe from Stalin's "Asiatic barbarism." The historians' debate came only one year after Chancellor Helmut Kohl's invitation to Ronald Reagan to stand hand in hand with him at the military cemetery of Bitburg, only hours after they visited the Gedenkstätte of Bergen-Belsen. In a great moment of reconciliation, Kohl thought, it would be churlish, indeed it would be missing the point entirely, to distinguish between the graves of SS men and other victims of war. The time had come to forget about distinctions. To paraphrase Ernst Nolte, it was time for the past to go away.

Victim against victim, grave against grave. Since 1988, a row about just such distinctions had been brewing in Berlin. The senator for cultural affairs had given permission for a Holocaust memorial to be built on the site of Hitler's chancellery. The original idea was to dedicate the monument to the memory of the murdered Jews of Europe. But the central committee for Gypsy affairs protested and demanded that it should remember all the victims of racial persecution. This, the planners countered, would render the whole thing meaningless. The dispute became bitter, even grotesque. Arguments arose as to whether the persecution of one-quarter Jews was worse than that of one-eighth Gypsies. Soon members of both sides were talking like pedantic Nazi race theorists.

History is all about distinctions. Which is why a committee of eminent historians was appointed in 1990 to sort out the historical disputes at Buchenwald. Should all the victims of the Nazis and the Soviets be remembered together? If not, how should they be separated? Must the GDR monuments be dismantled? What about the museum? And so on. It was a delicate mission, since most of the members of the committee were from western Germany. And Ossies did not always take kindly to Wessies meddling in their historical myths. Former Communists objected when too much emphasis was put on Soviet crimes, whereas others felt the committee did not go far enough. One of the western German historians, Dr. Eberhard Jäckel, told me it was "a frightfully embarrassing situation between us and the people of the former GDR, for they put us in the position of the victorious Allies in 1945." In the event, the committee recommended some minor changes. The plaque in Ernst Thälmann's old cell was changed to a simpler one, reading: "Chairman of the German Communist Party, imprisoned, murdered here." And a small museum on Soviet Buchenwald, distinct from the larger one dealing with the Nazi period, was planned.

But the question remains whether a history museum can be combined with a memorial place, or a *Mahnmal*, without distorting its purpose. A memorial is a religious or quasi-religious monument where remembrance of the past is a collective ritual. People pray at monuments, they light torches, they lay wreaths. But a museum is a secular institution, which ought, in a liberal society, to strive for independent scholarship. In a dictatorship, where everything—politics, scholarship, memorializing—is reduced to public ritual, there is no contradiction; in a liberal democracy there is.

Until 1992, forty-seven years after the end of the war, there was only one war museum in Japan, and a very odd museum it was too. There was the Peace Museum in Hiroshima, of course, but that was only about Hiroshima. And there was a small museum in southern Kyushu, on the site of a former air base, with memorabilia of a kamikaze squadron. But only the museum of the Yasukuni Shrine in Tokyo dealt with the history of the entire war.

The shrine itself is controversial. It is a Shinto shrine dedicated to the worship of the spirits of those who laid down their lives for the emperor since the Meiji Restoration of 1868. A leaflet handed out at the museum said these patriots died for the "nation," but this unquestioned equation of emperor and nation is typical of the place; indeed, it is its raison d'être. Several million spirits are enshrined at Yasukuni, including those of generals and politicians hanged as Class A war criminals after the Tokyo trial. Conservative politicians who visit the shrine each year to commemorate the Japanese war dead have claimed Yasukuni is no different from the war cemetery of Arlington, Virginia, or the Cenotaph in London. But it is.

The "restoration" of the emperor as a political figurehead of the new government that had toppled the Tokugawa shogunate in the 1860s did not come without bloodshed. It was to the spirits of those who had fought on the imperial side against the shogun that the Meiji emperor dedicated the shrine. So in a way Yasukuni is a revolutionary or, better, a Bonapartist shrine. The Restoration was started by samurai, and until 1945 the armed forces, accountable only to the emperor, were often at the heart of the Japanese order. The first thing you see as you approach the huge gate of the shrine is a bronze statue of Omura Masujiro, military strategist and founder of the Imperial Japanese Army. He was assassinated by political rivals in 1869, the year the Yasukuni Shrine was opened.

Although every Japanese regime in recorded history made sure it was blessed, voluntarily or not, by the emperor of the day, the militaristic imperial cult (sometimes called State Shinto) was a Meiji invention, indeed a Japanese variation of modern nationalism. The head shrine of this cult was Yasukuni. Wars were fought "for the emperor," orders were obeyed "for the emperor," and enshrinement as a deity would follow death "for the emperor."

After the war, to separate state from church, the American occupation authorities insisted the Japanese abolish Shinto as a state religion. Shinto shrines, including Yasukuni, would henceforth be private enterprises. Most Japanese, glad to be rid of military oppression, welcomed the move. But by 1951, former military officers had formed right-wing groups and demanded the release of all war criminals and the rehabilitation of the Yasukuni Shrine. And it has been on the right-wing agenda ever since. Nationalist intellectuals still write angry books about the loss of "national identity," and various pressure groups are eager to restore some of the prewar values. In an essay about Yasukuni, the critic Eto Jun argued that the Japanese, unlike any other people, "live with the dead." Thus, he concluded, worship at Yasukuni was vital to the continuity of the Japanese nation.

The Japan Association of Families of the War Dead, which has more than a million members, most of whom vote for the conservative Liberal Democratic Party, is an important pressure group. And right-wing politicians, who wish to rewrite the constitution to reinstate the divine status of the emperor, and restore the sovereign right to wage war, naturally insist that Yasukuni be an official place of worship. And so each year the combination of right-wing agitation and personal conviction has prompted Japanese politicians, including Prime Ministers, to visit the shrine.

To minimize controversy they would visit "as private individuals," even though their collective worship was a public event recorded for the evening news. In 1985, however, Nakasone Yasuhiro was the first to worship in his official capacity, signing the visitors' book as Prime Minister. His offering to the shrine, an expensive sprig from a sacred tree, was reimbursed from the public purse. Christians, leftists, pacifists, and the governments of South Korea and China protested. A member of a Japanese Buddhist group sued the Prime Minister for causing "spiritual damage in using our taxes." But Nakasone insisted he was only there to pray for peace. Yasukuni's official pamphlet says the same thing—it is a shrine dedicated to peace. *Yasukuni* means "to bring peace to the nation."

It is a peculiar concept of peace. The cherry blossom trees in front of the shrine bear white tags with the names of Imperial Army regiments and famous battleships. Behind the shrine is a stone monument in the shape of a globe, in memory of the Kempeitai, the Japanese equivalent of the SS. Nearby is a long concrete slab pocked with holes, containing different-colored rocks from the battlefields of Leyte, Guadalcanal, Guam, and Wake Island. There is also a "Mother's Monument": a white marble sculpture resembling a deep throat with water gushing through. It is, so the inscription informs, "the image of mother in the minds of men who were dying of thirst."

Along the gravel path leading to the main shrine, several blue-and-khaki trucks were parked, festooned with nationalist slogans. A wartime military march boomed from loudspeakers mounted on top. The trucks belonged to some of the extreme right-wing organizations that wished to restore the prewar order, what they called, before Hirohito's death, the Showa Restoration (Showa being the name of Hirohito's reign). Uniformed young men with shaven skulls barked in unison and bowed in the direction of the Imperial Palace.

In front of the museum is a well-maintained display of vintage machine guns, a World War II tank, a howitzer, a torpedo, and the first railway engine to pass along the Burma Railroad. This is what the museum pamphlet describes as "sacred ground."

And the weapons on exhibit had been "used with love and care" by "the deities of the shrine." Their "sacred relics" are shown in the museum.

There, in the first room, the visitor is confronted by a large oil painting, in a heavy gilt frame, of Emperor Hirohito visiting the Yasukuni Shrine in the 1930s. He is dressed in military uniform and flanked by bowing priests in white robes. A sacred sword is shown too, forged by priests attached to the shrine. And there are various items left by soldiers who fought in the wars against China and Russia, just before and after the turn of the century.

Other relics on display are a "human torpedo"—a steel sausage with enough room for one man, who would sacrifice his life by steering its explosive charge into an enemy ship. There are battle flags, signed by soldiers in their own blood, the names now barely more than faded brown smudges. There is a replica of a "cherry blossom" plane, used in kamikaze attacks. Letters from soldiers to their mothers or wives are preserved in glass cases. The torn, bloody shirt of a soldier who died in the Philippines is exhibited among the stained battle flags, as well as a cracked picture of his mother which he had with him when he died.

There are more oil paintings, all in the same pompous nineteenth-century manner as the picture of the emperor at Yasukuni—paintings of Japanese troops at the Great Wall of China fraternizing with grateful Mongolians and paintings of human torpedoes or cherry blossom planes engaged in their fatal missions. There is a large model, resembling a miniature garden, depicting the hopeless battles in Burma and the Philippines, with little plastic suicide tanks rolling off felt cliffs. Much attention is paid to the hard plight of Japanese soldiers captured by the Soviets after the war and imprisoned in Siberian camps. And at the end of the exhibition is a glass case displaying, among other items, a Burmese flag presented to Japan by General Ne Win, the Burmese military dictator, who was trained in Japan before the war. It was given, so the text informs, by "one who owes the liberation of his country to Japan." And President Sukarno of Indonesia left a stuffed bird of paradise as a token of his gratitude.

The texts between the exhibits, explaining the background of the war, are straight wartime propaganda. The annexation of Manchuria in 1931 was a necessary move to protect the Asian continent from Soviet Communism and Chinese rapaciousness. The war in China was inevitable, because Chinese rebels were being spurred into anti-Japanese activities by the British and the Americans. The war with America was a matter of national survival. And the suffering of Japanese POWs, as well as millions of others, at the hands of Communist regimes proved that Japan had been on the right side all along. In short, to quote from a history booklet sold at the museum bookshop, "the Greater East Asian War was not a 'war of invasion,' but just the opposite: it was a holy war to liberate the world from Communism."

It is easy to conclude from all this that the Yasukuni war museum glorifies militarism. In fact, it is more complicated than that. What it glorifies in a quasi-religious manner is not belligerence or hatred, but self-sacrifice. The tone of the museum and indeed the entire shrine is summed up by a large bronze plaque put up by the Association to Honor the Special Attack Forces (kamikazes). It was unveiled in 1985, on the anniversary of the attack on Pearl Harbor. Engraved in stylish characters are the words of Takeda Tsuneyoshi, president of the association: "Some six thousand men died in suicide attacks that were incomparable in their tragic bravery and struck terror in the hearts of our foes. The entire nation shed tears of gratitude for their unstinting loyalty and selfless sacrifice."

In a small room next to the main shrine, I spoke to a young priest whose crisp white robe denoted the purity of his office. He was no more than thirty years old. His father had been a Shinto priest before him. After exchanging name cards and pleasantries, I asked him what he thought of the Pacific War. First, he said, it was a big mistake to call World War II the Pacific War; it was the Great East Asian War. It was also a mistake to think that the Great East Asian War was a war of invasion. "We had no choice. It was purely a matter of national survival. Besides, the idea was to liberate Asia. The Asian people are still grateful . . ."

He must have noted signs of impatience, because he stopped and asked me what I specifically wanted to know. So I asked him about the purpose of the museum. Here he gave a perfectly honest and plausible account. It was not meant to be an educational museum, he said. As long as survivors of the war were alive, it would not be a proper museum. It was a place to preserve the relics of people enshrined at Yasukuni. But, given time, he said, it certainly should become a proper war museum.

I asked him how that should be done. How would the material be selected and explained? Would historians be appointed for the task?

He had to think about this, but not for very long. "The thing is," he said, "as soon as you bring historians in, you run into problems, you get distortions. As a shrine, we must think of the feelings of the spirits and their families. We must keep them happy. That is why historians would cause problems. Take the so-called war of invasion, which was actually a war of survival. We wouldn't want the families to feel that we are worshipping the spirits of men who fought a war of invasion."

If one disregards, for a moment, the differences in style between Shinto and Christianity, the Yasukuni Shrine, with its "relics," its "sacred ground," its bronze paeans to noble sacrifice, is not so very different from many European memorials after World War I. By and large, World War II memorials in Europe and the United States (though not the Soviet Union) no longer glorify the sacrifice of the fallen soldier. The sacrificial cult and the romantic elevation of war to a higher spiritual plane no longer seemed appropriate after Auschwitz. The Christian knight, bearing the cross of king and country, was not resurrected. But in Japan, where the war was still truly a war (not a Holocaust), and the symbolism still redolent of religious exultation, such shrines as Yasukuni still carry the torch of nineteenth-century nationalism. Hence the image of the nation owing its restoration to the sacrifice of fallen soldiers.

A wooden sign outside the Peace Museum for Kamikaze Pilots, near Chiran on the southern tip of Kyushu, is the perfect example of what I mean: "We"—the Japanese, that is—"are grateful to receive life through their noble self-sacrifice . . . We are grateful our country is on the way to prosperity. And we are grateful Japan is at peace today . . . We believe that [the kamikaze pilots] wished for restoration of peace and prosperity."

Quite possibly they did want peace. But as I walked toward the museum, through the garden of a small shrine dedicated to Kannon, the goddess of mercy, it was not immediately clear to me how they contributed to it. The shrine offered no answer. Amid the stone lanterns, donated by veterans' associations to soothe the spirits of the dead, stood a silver suicide plane, used by the kamikaze pilots, who were also known as the "cherry blossoms"—beautiful and short-lived.

Shrine and museum were built on the site of a former kamikaze air base, used for suicide missions to Okinawa. The nearest city is Kagoshima, set along a lovely bay so much like Pearl Harbor that the Japanese Navy used it for practice runs in 1941. Upon entering the museum, I was handed a leaflet which told me that the museum "was founded to preserve the true facts of World War II on record and to contribute to true peace on earth." Much of the museum—a dull modern building put up in 1985 with government money—is built around the relics of the cherry blossoms. These include sashes, embroidered by a thousand female hands to give strength to the pilots who wore them. There are also torn uniforms and bits of blown-up planes dredged from the ocean bed. But the most important relics are the letters and diaries the pilots left behind. Many are almost unbearably moving.

It was customary to write a farewell letter to one's loved ones. The letters contain the hackneyed sentiments one would expect: patriotic phrases about the glory of dying for the emperor and his sacred land, pride in doing a soldier's duty, and so on. But these were conventions, written because they were required, like the pathetic apologies to parents for failing to repay one's filial debt. Many letters also include, in more or less similar phrases, a request to parents and siblings not to cry or be sad, but to raise a cup of sake and rejoice in the manner of the soldier's honorable death.

Laughter is the essence. It is stressed not just in the letters but also in the photographs of the young men displayed on the walls. It is also a feature of contemporary press accounts. Boyish laughter in the face of certain death was as conventional and as highly praised as the patriotic sentiments. One of the photographs in the museum shows a merry group of pilots ready for takeoff. One of the pilots, a mere boy, is saying goodbye to his pet dog. The caption reads: "There is great beauty in the laughing faces of these men just before facing certain death."

This type of youthful bravado was not peculiar to the Japanese, of course. British bomber crews laughed a lot too. Very young men have a weakness for the romance of glorious death. But it is disturbing to see how it is held up as a thing of beauty in the Peace Museum today. For the patriotic slogans and the youthful laughter cannot disguise the tragedy of wasted lives. On the contrary, they add a ghastly poignancy, for underneath the merriment is a feeling of despair and barely contained hysteria.

This is how an eighteen-year-old ended his final letter to his parents: "What a weakling I was not to cry out for you, Mother, with all my heart, even though I wanted to. Mother! Please forgive me. You must have felt so lonely. But now I will shout it as loudly as I can: Mother! Mother! Mother!"

Or this, from a boy named Shigeru, age unknown: "It is time to go now. The cherry blossoms boarding the sacred planes are in full bloom. I shall join them and bloom splendidly myself. Father, Mother, everyone, please don't worry about me. Take care. I just wish you all a happy life in this world . . ."

The letters, as well as the photographs, have a pronounced effect on the visitors. The men fall silent, and swiftly walk on to inspect the model airplanes. The older women sob and dab their eyes with little folded handkerchiefs. "So young," they say, "so young." Schoolchildren, only a few years younger than the cherry blossoms, file past the displays. Some laugh, some gossip, some say nothing.

The tragedy is not just that the suicide pilots died young. Soldiers (and civilians) do that in wars everywhere. What is so awful about the memory of their deaths is the cloying sentimentality that was meant to justify their self-immolation. There is no reason to suppose they didn't believe in the patriotic gush about cherry blossoms and sacrifice, no matter how conventional it was at the time. Which was exactly the point: they were made to rejoice in their own death. It was the exploitation of their youthful idealism that made it such a wicked enterprise. And this point is still completely missed at the Peace Museum today.

For the phony ideals and the saccharine poetics are still part of the atmosphere of the place. The street lined with cherry blossoms leading to the museum; the blurbs about "beauty in the laughing faces"; the stuff in the museum guide about this being "a hall of tears"; the ghastly oil painting, three meters by four, of a dead pilot being lifted to heaven from his burning plane by six white-robed angels; and most important of all, the denial that the suicide missions were an utter waste of life which only prolonged the war. Instead, the death of thousands is imbued with bogus significance: the young men died for peace and prosperity, their sacrifice was a noble example of patriotism.

Mr. Matsumoto, a local civil servant in charge of the museum, stood in front of the green, white, and red suicide plane inside the main hall, and spoke to about three hundred schoolchildren, sitting on the floor in their navy blue and black uniforms. Matsumoto spoke in the lilting twang of a storyteller in old magic lantern shows. He asked the children where they were from. They gave him the name of their hometown. "This, then, is your senior," he said, as he reached for a picture of a pilot from their town. And holding up the pictures of dead men smiling at the camera, he told the stories of their fates; noble stories of sacrifice, of bravery, of pure, selfless sentiments and beautiful ideals. He concluded his account by saying that some people might criticize him for idealizing the war or promoting militarism. But nothing could be less true, he said. War is bad, very bad. We must never go to war again.

But why, I asked him later, in his office, why should children conclude that war was so bad if its protagonists were so heroic and their ideals so pure? "Because the pilots of the Special Attack Forces sincerely believed in peace."

I knew it was pointless to argue. Matsumoto and the founders of the museum were not bloodthirsty men, nor were they apologists for the war. But their faith in the ideals upon which war propaganda has always been based—sacrifice, sincerity, the sacred cause—was too deep to shake.

Gauging change is always an imprecise business, for it goes on all the time, mostly without anybody noticing. But as far as memories of the war are concerned, the early 1990s were a time of significant change in Japan; or at least it looked that way. Since the late 1980s army veterans had started to relate their memories in public. In 1991, the former comfort women from South Korea, as well as some surviving slave workers from China, arrived to claim compensation. And two new war museums, stressing Japanese aggression, were opened in Osaka and Kyoto. All in all, it felt as though a few windows had opened, letting in a gust of fresh air. Emperor Hirohito's death in 1989 was one explanation, and Richard von Weizsäcker's speech to the Bundestag in 1985 was often given as another. The speech—"Anyone who closes his eyes to the past is blind to the present. Whoever refuses to remember the inhumanity is prone to risks of new infection"—was translated into Japanese and widely read. It was quoted to me by many Japanese as an example they should follow.

But there was another, more political reason, too, for the new stress on Japanese aggression. Prompted by the Gulf War, a serious debate began on the future role of Japanese armed forces. A new bill (the PKO Bill) was passed to enable Japan to send troops abroad for the first time since 1945, as part of United Nations peacekeeping forces. This was not as dramatic as it sounded, for they could only bear side arms and could not engage in any combat. But it was dramatic enough for many Japanese pacifists, who saw this as yet another sign of a militarist revival. The activist in Hiroshima who pressed for an "Aggressors' Corner" at the Peace Museum thought so. As did Oda Makoto, the writer and former political activist. And vigorous pacifism was very much behind the two new war museums: the Osaka International Peace Center and the Kyoto Museum for World Peace. Neither was funded by the national government. The Osaka museum was established by the Osaka prefectural and municipal governments, and the museum in Kyoto is part of Ritsumeikan University.

The new museums were secular institutions without obligations to anyone's sacred spirit; there were no "relics," no "sacred grounds," and certainly no paeans to sacrifice. And yet, pacifism is not without its own air of religiosity. In the entrance hall of the Kyoto Museum for World Peace were two large murals by the cartoonist Tezuka Osamu. Both showed cranes in full flight—one flying in terror from the dark and cruel past, the other making its way toward the radiant future. The artist has contrived, in the words of the brochure, to "sing a hymn to the cosmos, brimming with life, and to Providence, which allows all living creatures to live their lives to the full."

And the final exhibition room of the Osaka International Peace Center, on the third floor of the handsome modern building, showed the dangers that still confront us: nuclear, ecological, social. Ethereal music, of the kind one associates with New Age cults, filled the air, as people from all over the world expressed their views on peace on video disks. One American woman argued that wars were masculine, and only the healing powers of women would bring peace, because women weave and nurture.

Otherwise, the conception of the two museums was as simple as it was clear: to change the image of wartime Japan from that of a victim to that of an aggressor. Japanese suffering was not neglected; one section of the Osaka museum showed in great detail how Osaka was destroyed by incendiary bombs, and how it felt to be on the receiving end, particularly from the point of view of a child. One colorful drawing by a child at the time showed people fleeing across a bridge in terror, as bombs explode and the severed head of a baby jets through the air, trailing blood. But unlike at the Hiroshima museum, care was taken to show that this happened as the result of a war that Japan had started.

The room filled with artifacts, documents, and photographs of the "Fifteen-Year War" made that quite clear. Nothing was glossed over; the Nanking Massacre, the chemical warfare unit, and the comfort women were all there. But not a great deal was explained, except in the simplest terms. The idea, evidently, was not to go deeply into the nature of wartime propaganda— State Shinto was barely mentioned—but to impress youthful visitors (mostly middle school students, I was told, since high school students are too busy with exams) with the cruelty of war.

The museum in Kyoto was more illuminating, since it paid more attention to the regimentation of daily life, the suppression of free speech, and nationalist propaganda. It was more political, and in its brief summary of the postwar period it drew the usual leftist conclusions. An illustrated booklet for schoolchildren explained, for example, that the Vietnam War was a "war of invasion" by the United States. But "the Vietnamese people, thirsting for freedom and independence, struggled hard and were victorious."

The point, however, was not to foster anti-Americanism so much as to demonstrate that all wars are bad. In the words of the Osaka International Peace Center's brochure: "We live in a free and prosperous Japan, but the dark clouds of war are still hovering over us. The Fifteen-Year War taught us many things.

The most important thing is that there is no such thing as a good war."

In a leaflet written by one of the founders of the Osaka museum, Professor Katsube Hajime, the political background of this pacifism was made more specific. It was entitled *The Role of Japan*. Katsube discussed the U.S.-Japan Security Treaty and the PKO Bill. In his view, the government was deliberately distorting or suppressing Japan's wartime history to justify Japan's revival as a military power. He wants Japan to break off "the current hegemonic global partnership with the United States and become a member of the democratic zone of peace . . ." And "if it is to choose this alternative, Japan must admit its war crimes in the Fifteen-Year War and compensate war victims."

Professor Katsube is a man of integrity. It seems he always was. He spent two years in prison during the war, from 1943 till the end, for casting doubt on the war effort in a private research group. He pointed out that, like all political prisoners, he had been liberated from jail not by his own government but by the American Army. This experience left him scarred, and he has expected the worst of any Japanese government ever since. He was dressed in the casual manner of elderly progressives: a gray sports shirt, a string tie, and slacks. He explained the symbol of the Osaka International Peace Center, a green dot in a purple band. The green dot, he said, was Osaka, spreading its message of peace. The purple ring was the rest of the world.

After a tour of the museum, one of the curators showed me the way to the roof terrace. From there we gazed at the large park surrounding Osaka Castle, where the Imperial Army used to practice drills and maneuvers. And I reflected on the Japanese war museums I had seen, in Osaka, in Kyoto, on the former kamikaze base in Kyushu, in Hiroshima, and at Yasukuni Shrine. Yes, there had been change in Japan since the war, yet the basic arguments had remained the same. On the one side was a vision of Japan that had learned from its crimes and would never fight in another war again. On the other was a Japan that should be free once more to be a "normal" military power. As long as one side used historical sins to support its vision of peace, the other would deny them.

Dieter Schulte was one of the most bitter men I met in Germany. For seven years he had been the curator of the history museum in Potsdam, the city of palaces and barracks, located in the former GDR. He was fired from his job after unification. His successor, a medievalist from West Berlin, appointed to revamp the museum, described him as a "stiff party man." She also told me that the secret police, the Stasi, had occupied an office above his.

We met in the Kino Café, a dingy modern place in the wing of a dilapidated palace. Schulte was a dapper man, dressed in pressed blue jeans, a patterned sweater, and soft slip-on shoes. His white hair was perfectly groomed. His nails bore the sheen of a recent manicure. His eyes strayed around the room as he spoke, and he pursed his lips when silent.

It had not been easy, he said, to let go of the museum, for it had been so much a part of his life. And he was not happy with the way things were changing. He talked about the historical significance of Potsdam. Every regime since the days of Frederick the Great had used Potsdam to project its image, he explained. Potsdam was a center of right-wing politics in the 1920s. Hitler's top generals were stationed there during the war, including the plotters of the failed coup in 1944. Yet none of this was given sufficient attention in the museum, he said. The most important function of a museum, he believed, was to "show the laws of history."

His successor, Frau Bierschenk, had shown me parts of the old museum, including the rooms with exhibits on World War II, which had not yet been changed. They had been closed to the public since unification. There was already a moldy smell inside, like that of ripe mushrooms. The new curator switched on the lights and lifted a white sheet off a glass cabinet to reveal the "symbols of the new regime," meaning the old regime, before the birth of a Communist Germany. There they were, in a straight row: a World War I spiked helmet, a plutocrat's top hat, and an SA man's brown cap. It was as logical as that, the laws of history, as neat as a progression of dominoes. Elsewhere in the room I learned how fascism was the logical outcome of "the contradictions in the Weimar Republic between democracy and imperialism."

I asked Schulte, who had written these explanations, whether he still believed them. He pursed his lips, looked over my shoulder, and said, almost in a whisper: "Those were written almost seven years ago. Scientific knowledge has progressed since then . . ."

In what way had he changed his mind? "I still believe that socialism must be the basis for tracing relations, contexts. History cannot be just a mosaic of details. A museum showing nothing but objects would not be a museum."

Then he suddenly changed tack and spoke of his difficulties under the Communist regime, how every exhibit had to be approved by the censors before you could get access to the simplest things, such as paper to print on.

Did he feel that Germany was freer now? "No, we are never free, never!" Even relatively speaking? "No, you see, just as we had to compromise before to get paper or money, you won't get anything done now if it doesn't fit in with the capitalist system. It has to be sexy, and so on. Well, maybe it is true that the history museum will be more entertaining . . ."

I did not like Schulte much. He was an apparatchik, like so many before him. He even spoke like the petty officials who suddenly found their world had collapsed in 1945. Asked about the Stasi above his office, he said he had known nothing: "I was never told. I didn't know. How could one have known? I knew nothing, nothing."

But he had a point about museums. A museum, especially a history museum, cannot just show random objects. Objects must

be organized according to ideas. Without stories history is un-
intelligible. Which is not to say there is no truth and all stories
are propaganda. But to catch the truth there must be conflict,
debate, interpretation, and reinterpretation—in short, a discourse without end. The problem is how to show this in a
museum.

One possible way was demonstrated in East Berlin. Before
the collapse of the GDR, every housing project, every school,
every factory, and every military base had a so-called *Traditionskabinett*, a tradition room. These were miniature museums showing the same potted history of the German workers' movement,
the Communist antifascist resistance, the Red Army liberating
Germany east of the Elbe, and the founding of the German
Democratic Republic. Here, in its purest form, was the historic
"tradition" that lent legitimacy to the Communist state. Like the
ubiquitous busts of Lenin, most of these places were demolished
after 1990. Yet one, in the corner of an East Berlin park, was
left entirely intact. Its subject was no longer history, however,
but propaganda. Tags were pasted around the exhibits explaining and criticizing what was shown, deconstructing, as it were,
the myths left by the old regime.

It was not quite the same thing, yet I was reminded of the
famous warning monument in Hamburg, sculpted by Alfred
Hrdlička. Hrdlička's monument of grotesquely mangled corpses
and emaciated prisoners was a critique of an older monument
next to it—a hideous block, like a massive bunker, erected in
1936 in honor of the Second Hanseatic Infantry Regiment 76.
Rows of identical soldiers, carved in relief, march around the
block. Above their helmets is a quotation, in Gothic letters, from
a poem by Heinrich Lersch, written in 1914: "Germany must
live, even if we have to die" (*"Deutschland muss leben, und wenn
wir sterben müssen"*). Instead of tearing it down, as happened
with virtually all Nazi memorials, Hrdlička's stone corpses were
chosen as a more appropriate response. Here was a *Mahnmal*
used as argument.

Such examples are rare, though, and they do not offer a

practical solution to the problems of history museums or memorials. It was certainly not what Chancellor Kohl had in mind when he suggested, in 1983, that the Federal Republic should have its own museum of German history. Work on the museum was to begin in 1987, to celebrate Berlin's 750th anniversary.

Helmut Kohl, inspired by his advisers, such as the conservative scholar Michael Stürmer, was interested in history. Like other conservatives, he worried about the lack of a historical identity in the Federal Republic. Richard von Weizsäcker, mayor of Berlin when the museum plan was hatched, observed that the East Germans at least had a more coherent sense of the past—East Berlin also had a German history museum, a kind of oversized *Traditionskabinett* in the splendid baroque Arsenal. Michael Stürmer wrote that "the search for our lost history" was "morally legitimate and politically necessary, for at issue is the inner continuity of the German republic and the predictability of its foreign policy." And the Christian Democrat member of parliament Alfred Dregger was concerned that without enough knowledge of "the entire history of Germany" young Germans would not fully support "the democratic state." "The entire history" (*die ganze Geschichte*) was a code phrase; what he meant to say—and did say on some occasions—was that too much attention was being paid to the history of the Nazi period. In short, German conservatives above a certain age worried that citizens of the Federal Republic of Germany, one half of a split nation, would not feel sufficiently German. History—that is, "the entire history"—would help them do so.

So when Kohl made another speech in parliament, in 1985, about the museum project, he spoke about the need to know "where we came from, where we are today, as Germans, and where we will be going." But he also spoke about relations with East Germany, the *Deutschlandpolitik*, which dealt with the "core of our national identity and our national as well as European destiny."

A committee of historians and museum experts was duly appointed and a debate followed. Politicians and intellectuals of the left were unhappy about the whole idea. They distrusted the motives behind the conservative government's plans. They deeply distrusted the conservative idea of national identity. Indeed, they felt identity was really none of the government's business. The Social Democrat politician Freimut Duve argued this case in 1986: "History does not belong to the government. Nor does it belong to politics. In a democracy the government neither can nor should be building museums in the manner of feudal lords in the olden days." And so it went, to and fro, on and on. Until 1990, when the whole issue became redundant: the two Germanys had become "Germany" once again.

The nearest thing to an official German history museum today is the Deutsches Historisches Museum in Berlin. It is in the Arsenal in East Berlin, where the Communist German history museum used to be. Attempts at revising the Communist museum had already been made in 1989, just after the Wall was breached. A sign at the door explained that "we realize now that this museum, which reflects a historical view that justifies an increasingly bureaucratic-authoritarian society, prohibits a lively and active relationship with the past and the present . . . Everything must be revised and seen in a new light. We appreciate any help you can give to show history in a truly desirable manner."

There was a note of desperation in these words, a hint that the east Germans, with the best will in the world, could not hack it alone. As a result, west Germans were brought in, the inside of the Arsenal was gutted, and a new museum installed. The new German history museum does not have a permanent collection; instead, historical themes and topics are brought up in temporary exhibitions. "These are designed," according to the curator, Christoph Stölzl, "to make people think."

Stölzl is an elegant liberal from Munich, well groomed in the *style anglais*, silk bow ties, tweed suits: an aesthete, as well as an experienced administrator, with the smooth talk of an advertising man. Stölzl was born just at the end of the war. Yet he does not share the moralistic preoccupation with guilt that torments so many intellectuals of the '68 generation. He started our conversation with the remark that "you cannot mourn psychologically for something you didn't do." He was referring, of course, to the old issue of being a German after Auschwitz. "All you can do," he said, "is something symbolic, ceremonial. It would be a fine thing to have an Auschwitz Day every year and donate money to Amnesty International. That would be more productive than all this soul-searching. But it is typical of German idealism to long for the impossible and neglect to do the possible."

I had come to see Stölzl to ask him about his museum, and here he was talking about memorials. Yet he did try to make distinctions between the two: "I believe in dealing with the past symbolically and artistically, but there are many people in Germany who think that discourse should replace ritual. The problem is they turn discussion into a pseudo-religious activity, instead of a political one."

In a museum, the combination of aesthetics and political discourse can work, even though some will always complain that art was sacrificed to discourse, or vice versa. In a memorial, ceremony and analysis simply don't mix. Stölzl might stand accused of emphasizing the art in what is after all a history museum. He worries about form. In memorials it is perhaps all he worries about. And even he gets museums and memorials confused—though perhaps in some cases this is inevitable.

Stölzl was critical of the Holocaust museum in the Wannsee Villa, for example, because it chose the wrong form. It showed the Jews of the Holocaust, as he put it, "in a perpetuum mobile of victimhood." He objected to the photographs of death camps and ghettos. Realism, to him, was not the point. He wanted the forms of memory to be uplifting. He preferred the presentation of the dead in Catholic cemeteries, where the dead are remembered alive, so to speak, in photographs attached to their tombstones. "This," said Stölzl, "is more like the resurrection. It seems better to me to remember the dead as human beings, not as skeletons or corpses in an industrial murder machine."

The problem with the Wannsee Villa, however, is the ambiguity as to whether it is a museum or a memorial. Presumably it is both, which is the core of the problem. You can remember the Holocaust through art, through ceremony, or through analysis and discourse, but you cannot do all this at the same time, or in the same place. I put it to Stölzl that the ritual, artistic approach to history is a Catholic one, while the demand for moral discourse is more in the Protestant tradition. He agreed that this was possible. Later I thought this generalization might be expanded even further, since the problems of memorial museums in Germany and Japan were essentially the same. Memory can be religious or secular. Both are valid. But the two should not be confused. Germany has hardly been more successful than Japan in avoiding this confusion. The religious mind still stalks both lands in just about equal measure.

PART FOUR

A NORMAL COUNTRY

BONN, NOVEMBER 10, 1988, fifty years after the *Kristallnacht*.
Philipp Jenninger, president of the Bundestag, insisted on commemorating the anniversary himself, with a speech to the West
German parliament. He wanted no one else to speak, not even
Heinz Galinski, the head of the Jewish community. If he had
let Galinski speak—so he told me later, in Vienna—he would
have had to let the Catholic primate speak too, and what about
the Protestants? No, there would have been no end to it, and
the Bundestag was not their stage. In any case, he, Dr. Philipp
Jenninger, the president, was adamant that the heirs of the
aggressors, not the victims, should speak and remember that
day.

So up he got and spoke, or rather read, in the official drone
of a bureaucrat reading a protocol. I quote:

> . . . We have gathered today in the German Bundestag to
> commemorate the pogroms of November 9 and 10, 1938,
> because it is not the victims, but we, in whose midst the
> crimes took place, who must remember and account for
> them. We Germans must be clear about our understanding
> of our history and the lessons we can draw for the way
> we constitute our politics in the present and in the fu-
> ture . . .

The victims—the Jews all over the world—know precisely what November 1938 meant in the course of their suffering. Do we know it as well? . . .

The [German] population was largely passive; as they had been in previous years, toward anti-Jewish actions and measures. Not many took an active part in the excesses, but nobody rebelled either. There was no resistance to speak of . . .

Looking back, ladies and gentlemen, it is clear that a real revolution took place in Germany between 1933 and 1938—a revolution which turned a state ruled by law into a criminal state, into an instrument of destruction of precisely those legal and ethical norms and foundations whose preservation and defense is what the state—by definition —should be about . . .

So far as the lot of German and European Jews was concerned, Hitler's successes were even more fateful than his crimes and misdeeds. Even seen from the distance of time and with the knowledge of what followed, the years between 1933 and 1938 are mesmerizing, insofar as the march of Hitler's political triumph in those first years are virtually without historical parallel . . .

For the Germans who saw the Weimar Republic mostly as a sequence of foreign policy humiliations, all this must have seemed like a miracle. And above and beyond that, people were given jobs instead of being out of work, and mass misery turned into something like prosperity for most . . .

As for the Jews, well, hadn't they been too big for their boots? So it was phrased at the time. Shouldn't they learn at last to be more humble? Hadn't they deserved to be taken down a peg? Above all, didn't the propaganda— apart from wild exaggerations which couldn't be taken seriously—basically accord with one's own assumptions and convictions? And when things went too far, as in November 1938, one could always say, in the words of a contemporary: "Why should we care? Look away if it horrifies you. It's not our problem."

Ladies and gentlemen, there was antisemitism in Germany, as well as in many other countries, long before Hitler . . .

It is true that the National Socialists took great pains to conceal the truth of their mass murder. It is also true, however, that everyone knew about the Nuremberg [racial] laws, that all could see what happened fifty years ago today, and that the deportations happened in full public view . . .

Many Germans allowed themselves to be blinded and seduced by National Socialism. Many, being indifferent, made it possible for the crimes to be committed. Many became criminals themselves. The question of guilt and its repression is one that every person must answer for himself.

What we must all resist is the questioning of historical truth, the setting off of one category of victims against another, the denial of facts. Anyone who wishes to reduce our guilt, who says that it wasn't all bad—or not really as bad as all that—is trying to defend the indefensible.

To illustrate his points, Jenninger quoted an eyewitness account of a mass execution of Jews in 1942. Every detail—the twitching bodies of bleeding infants, the naked mothers, the young executioners, smoking between shots—was recounted, relentlessly, in a flat voice, without feeling. He quoted Himmler, admonishing his SS men not to flinch at the sight of a hundred or even five hundred or even a thousand corpses lying in a heap. Jenninger quoted the jargon of the time: Jews as "vermin" and so on. He quoted Nietzsche and Dostoevski. But it was all to no avail. The damage was done. The speech was a disaster.

Soon after the beginning, most of the delegates from the Green Party had left the hall in protest, and by the end 40 percent of the Social Democrats had left. Members of Jenninger's own Christian Democratic Party, according to a news report, "had shrunk in shame." Ida Ehre, the elderly Jewish actress who had read Paul Celan's "Death Fugue" to great effect just before Jenninger's speech, hid her face in her hands. Jenninger left the hall alone, streaks of sweat streaming down his ashen brow. Not even his closest political friends shook his hand. Jenninger had wanted to teach a history lesson. It had been received at best as a tactless exercise in missing the point, at worst as a crude attempt to let Germans off the hook.

"Shameful!" cried a Christian Democrat as soon as it was over. "A black day," said a Free Democrat. "A catastrophe," said a Social Democrat. "*Betroffen*," said another. The foreign press was unanimous in its rage: "Antisemitism in the German Parliament" was the top story of an Italian daily. The headline in a Dutch paper said: "Hitler Worship Causes Mayhem in the Bundestag." *The Times* of London called it "a national disaster for West Germany." Two days later Jenninger resigned. A year or so later he was appointed, somewhat oddly, to be ambassador in Vienna.

Reading Jenninger's speech, as he might have put it, from the distance of time, it is hard to understand why it caused such hysteria. He may not have chosen his words with sufficient care. He might have been clumsy in his quotations. But to look only at the words is not enough. To understand the outrage, one must picture the setting, or rather the staging of the affair.

Jenninger admitted to me in his office in Vienna—modern, functional, without personal touches—that he had made one big mistake. He should not have followed Ida Ehre's reading of Paul Celan's poem. "It was so moving," he said. Yes? "Well, it was not the ideal preparation for a sober historical speech." No, I said, I suppose it wasn't.

> Black milk of daybreak
> we drink you at night
> we drink you at midday
> Death is a master from Germany . . .

It is impossible not to be moved. In the words of the *Frankfurter Allgemeine Zeitung*: "The forceful voice trembled. You could hear her drawing breath, the paper crackled in her hands. No one in the hall could fail to be moved by the power and the sorrow of her language. Then Jenninger stepped to the lectern and began in a businesslike manner: 'Ladies and gentlemen . . .'"

Jenninger is not a prepossessing figure, not the sort of man who could easily move an audience. He is a short, chunky Rhinelander, a self-made man of peasant stock, a type you could find at any beer-hall table in Germany. He has a rasping laugh and his suit looks too tight. None of this helped his performance that day. He *looked* bumbling, tactless, insensitive.

Not once, complained a Social Democrat, did he use the word *Trauer*. The word can be translated as "sorrow" or as "mourning." It was the tone of Jenninger's speech that bothered many. It was not *betroffen* enough. Willy Brandt, a master of moral gestures, the West German Chancellor who fell on his knees in the former Warsaw ghetto to apologize for what the Nazis had done, called it "a dark day in postwar German history." Jenninger "failed, not because he is a bad fellow, but because he was out of his depth."

Jenninger's talk was compared to Richard von Weizsäcker's celebrated speech in the same Bundestag three years before. *His* speech was drenched in *Trauer*. He spoke of the need to remember "so purely, so honestly, that it becomes part of one's inner life." Jenninger's performance was even compared to a speech given the day before by his friend Helmut Kohl, not usually known for his grace or tact. But at the Westend Synagogue in Frankfurt, even Kohl had risen to the occasion, and had spoken about the Holocaust as "a reason for profound shame." Jenninger's failure, so almost everyone thought, had been to misjudge the occasion, which called for a memorial, not a "sober historical speech."

And yet Jenninger was not speaking in a synagogue as a German Gentile to Jews; he was talking in the worldly Bundestag, the great hall of German politics, as a Gentile German to other Germans. Recalling that painful day, in his Viennese office, he began to shout: "We had to speak out! But not in the usual way. It was not enough to say we were ashamed and would not let it happen again. I wanted to hold a mirror up to the Germans!"

I felt a certain sympathy for Jenninger. Interestingly enough, so did many people speaking from the point of view of the victims. Michael Fürst, a member of the central committee of the Jewish community in Germany, saw no reason for Jenninger to resign. After all, he said, Jenninger had spoken the truth. And Robert Kempner, prosecutor at the Nuremberg trials, thought Jenninger's speech was "even very good."

So why were the Germans so upset? Why did so many insist on misinterpreting Jenninger's quotations? Why did they think that he, Jenninger—and not just the people he cited—regarded Hitler as a mesmerizing statesman and Jews as "vermin"? Perhaps neither the setting of his speech nor the words entirely explain the debacle. It also had something to do with the climate of suspicion in Germany. Greens, liberals, and leftists suspected conservatives of using every opportunity to whitewash the war, and conservatives suspected Greens, liberals, and leftists of rubbing German noses in Auschwitz. The climate of suspicion was at its most feverish on the fiftieth anniversary of the *Kristallnacht*. For it happened near the end of a decade marked by conservative attempts to revise history, to escape from the burden of guilt. It was six years after Alfred Dregger, right-wing Christian Democrat, called for all Germans "to come out of Hitler's shadow—we must become normal."

It was four years after Helmut Kohl's visit to Israel, when he spoke of "the mercy of being born too late"—too late to have actively killed Jews, that is. He, too, used the word "normal," as in "normal relations" between Germany and Israel. It was three years after Bitburg. And two years after Ernst Nolte unleashed the "historians' debate" by proposing that the Holocaust was a defensive imitation of Stalin's "Asiatic barbarism"; not at all unique, in other words, but a horridly normal event in the horrid history of man.

Jenninger, in his stumbling, mumbling way, had walked straight into this postwar German battle zone. Entrenched on one side were those who wanted Germany to be normal, graced by late birth, not guilty; and on the other were those who had made Auschwitz part of their identity. In the event, Jenninger was shot down by both sides, for talking about too much guilt and not appearing guilty enough.

Like Helmut Kohl, Jenninger was graced by a birth that was too late for him to have been an active Nazi. He was born in 1932, a year before Hitler came to power. His father, a printer, had been against the Nazis, Jenninger recalled. Jenninger had older brothers, all of whom served in the army. Two of them didn't want to go: one was immediately killed in Italy, the other in Russia.

Jenninger is only slightly younger than Günter Grass (born in 1927). Theirs is an odd generation, too late to be Nazis, early enough to be educated as Nazis: Jungvolk, Hitler Youth, and so on. It has rendered many people of that age mute about the past. (It was their children who talked.) "Late birth" has given them perhaps the most complicated perspective on the past of all generations: too young to be responsible, yet tainted by guilt. Those, like Grass, who have talked and written about the war, have often done so incessantly, almost obsessively, and frequently, as in Grass's *Tin Drum*, from a child's point of view. Their burden is to explain their parents. It is the hardest thing of all to do, for to explain your parents, you have to try to imagine the world as they saw it. This implies identification, if only in the mind, and identification can so easily turn into justification. Which is why most people of Jenninger's age have preferred to say nothing at all.

One of the criticisms of Jenninger's speech—from a Free Democrat politician—was that he tried "to explain the inexplicable." It is a common accusation. Primo Levi wrote (about the Holocaust, not about Jenninger): "Perhaps one cannot, what is more one must not understand what happened, because to understand is almost to justify. Let me explain: 'understanding' a proposal or human behavior means to 'contain' it, contain its author, put oneself in his place, identify with him. Now, no human being will be able to identify with Hitler, Himmler, Goebbels, Eichmann, and endless others. This dismays us, and at the same time gives us a sense of relief, because perhaps it is desirable that their words (and also, unfortunately, their deeds) cannot be comprehensible to us. They are nonhuman words and deeds, really counter-human, without historical precedents . . ."

One hesitates to differ with a witness such as Levi. And yet, to assume that the *Kristallnacht* and, by extension, the Holocaust are inexplicable, "counter-human," or acts of some Antichrist lurking in our murky depths is to diminish the question of responsibility. Certainly, one cannot look into Hitler's mind. And the deepest wellsprings of human savagery are perhaps mysterious. But there were political reasons why such savagery came about. These reasons can and must be explained, especially in a German parliament. Jenninger was a politician, not a poet or a man of God.

Showing *Betroffenheit* and speaking in religious terms about the past are the easier options. Jenninger, perhaps ineptly, wanted to explain his parents, or at least people of his parents' age, the people who taught him to be a future Nazi. "Where were the professors and the writers when Hitler came to power?" he shouted in his office, stamping his feet, shod in cheap-looking, sand-colored shoes. "Why did I always hear that everybody had really been against Hitler? What was it that made them all cooperate? I think we can only reconcile ourselves with our history through the facts. To explain means telling the truth!"

Jenninger adjusted his tie, which appeared to constrict his thick neck like a noose. Tiny pearls of sweat glistened on his forehead. He told me about the 30,000 letters he received after giving his speech. He said the positive ones were from either very old people or the very young. The older people would thank him for finally saying "what it had really been like." The young were grateful for hearing the real reasons for what happened.

To strip the past of its mystery, to relate history as a series of more or less coherent events—without being subject to fixed laws—and to explain and evaluate those events critically is the historian's task. This is difficult, perhaps impossible to do when the events are within living memory, when the questions of guilt and shame are still vital. What happened in Germany and in the countries it occupied between 1933 and 1945 is not part of "normal" history. To German schoolchildren it is taught as a political morality tale. The same is true when a *Mahnmal* is unveiled, or an event, such as the *Kristallnacht*, commemorated. From the point of view of the victims it is a unique period, borne by the weight of its sheer wickedness out of the stream of time. But since the late 1960s there have been moves to treat 1933–45 more as "normal" history, not as a morality tale but as a period in history, structurally, politically, and culturally connected to what happened before and after. The German word for this process is *Historisierung*, "historicization." The paradox built into *Historisierung* is that a process aimed at a more objective view of the past leads in fact to more and more divergent subjective views. Normal history means a plurality of interpretations.

A conservative nationalist, for example, might argue that the Holocaust was a frightful but still normal form of genocide, to be understood in the context of its time, which was unfortunately rich in genocides. Or he might say that Germans in the Third Reich behaved relatively normally in the circumstances, as Hitler, after all, did restore the morale of the German people. And it was also understandable that Hitler, great master of ceremonies that he was, mesmerized a romantic people with a traditional taste for operatic spectacles. In fact, all these arguments have been made. It was Jenninger's misfortune that his audience believed he was endorsing them.

Another paradox of *Historisierung* concerns the question of identity. The object of historicizing is to take a cool distance from the past. Yet the reason why some conservative historians, such as Andreas Hillgruber, wanted to see Nazi history embedded in the continuous flow of normal German history was to identify more easily with the people who lived it—that is, with the non-Jewish German people; that is, with the point of view of the aggressors, the *Täter*. If 1933–45 is treated as sui generis, unprecedented, evil incarnate, isolated from the mainstream, identification is virtually impossible, except for a lunatic fringe. And by giving those "mere twelve years" too much attention Germans are robbed of historical pride. Now, if the Third Reich were more "normal," just another era, then Hillgruber's intention of boosting German identity and pride, by empathizing with the point of view of a German soldier defending the Fatherland against Asiatic barbarism, would be more feasible. But in the process of this willed identification, objectivity is undercut twice over: by the storyteller himself and by the imputed views of the story's main characters.

Identification, then, stands in the way of *Historisierung*. The gulf between the victims and the *Täter* is still so wide, and the contrast of memories so great, that anyone (particularly a German) seeking an objective view risks slipping into the gap. Theo Sommer wrote a blistering editorial comment in *Die Zeit* about Jenninger's speech. The headline was "About the Burden of Being German" (*"Von der Last, Deutscher zu sein"*). So Jenninger wanted to tell the truth, wrote Sommer. "Well, I agree. But please let's have the whole truth then—the truth of the victims just as cogently as the truth of the murderers. And with feeling—outrage over the fate of the hunted should be as moving as, or indeed more moving than, any empathy for the motives of the hunters."

Strong words, noble feelings, but still missing the point. For

Jenninger could not speak for the truth of the victims and would not pray for mercy through a mere expression of shame. He wanted to talk about history, to try to understand from a distance. It was not an ignoble enterprise, but he should have recognized that *Historisierung*, even forty-three years after the war, was still a highly risky business. For a "normal" society, a society not haunted by ghosts, cannot be achieved by "normalizing" history, or by waving cross and garlic. More the other way around: when society has become sufficiently open and free to look back, from the point of view neither of the victim nor of the criminal, but of the critic, only then will the ghosts be laid to rest.

Nagasaki, December 7, 1988, the forty-seventh anniversary of the attack on Pearl Harbor: The emperor was dying very, very slowly, losing large quantities of blood every day. He was dying of cancer. But in the climate of "self-restraint" this was never mentioned in the Japanese press. The atmosphere in Japan, in the dying days of the Showa era, was muted, oppressive, as though on the cusp of a storm. Traditional New Year celebrations were canceled, normally garish window displays toned down. On December 7, a Communist Party representative in the Nagasaki city assembly asked Mayor Motoshima Hitoshi a straightforward question: What about the emperor's war guilt?

Motoshima answered: "Forty-three years have passed since the end of the war, and I think we have had enough chance to reflect on the nature of that war. From reading various accounts from abroad and having been a soldier myself, involved in military education, I do believe that the emperor bore responsibility for the war . . ."

December 8, 1988: Nagasaki city legislators and the regional branch of the Liberal Democratic Party demand a retraction of the mayor's words.

December 12, 1988: Mayor Motoshima says that having come this far, he cannot "betray his own heart." But he will resign as counsel to the LDP Association. His resignation is not accepted. He is dismissed instead and refused further cooperation. Motoshima, at a press conference: "I am not saying that the emperor alone was responsible for the war. Many people were, myself included. But I do feel the present state of politics is abnormal. Any statement about the emperor becomes an emotional issue. Freedom of speech should not be limited by time or place. In a democracy we respect even those whose opinions we don't share."

December 19, 1988: Twenty-four extreme-right-wing groups ride through Nagasaki on thirty loudspeaker trucks, screaming for Motoshima's death, "as divine retribution." The LDP wants the prefectural governor to refuse political cooperation with the mayor. The governer agrees.

December 21, 1988: Sixty-two right-wing groups from all over Japan demonstrate in Nagasaki on eighty-two loudspeaker trucks, demanding the mayor's death.

December 24, 1988: 13,684 signatures in support of the mayor are presented at city hall by the newly formed Nagasaki Citizens Committee for Free Speech. They were collected in just two weeks. Representatives of various conservative associations, including the prefectural office for Shinto shrines, call for the mayor's impeachment.

January 7, 1989: The emperor dies.

January 18, 1990: Mayor Motoshima is shot in the back by a right-wing extremist. Right-wingers quoted in the Japanese press declare that Motoshima had received "divine punishment."

The mayor only barely survived. He was shot through his lungs. After coughing up blood, he waited in a car for help. He was without police protection, since conservative assemblymen had complained about the expense.

On the face of it, the Motoshima affair could not have been more different from the Jenninger debacle. Jenninger was accused of apologetics, Motoshima of laying blame; too little guilt on one side, too much on the other; glossing the truth here, exposing it there; whitewash and dirty linen. Jenninger had fallen afoul of liberals and leftists, Motoshima of the right. To his many supporters Motoshima is a hero; Jenninger left for Vienna in disgrace. Yet the two men, and indeed their two cases, have a few things in common. And these might reveal something about the state of Germany and Japan.

Motoshima is ten years older than Jenninger and has the more subtle mind, but both have the brusque, no-nonsense manners of provincial politicos. Both made their careers in post-war conservative politics: Jenninger as a Christian Democrat; Motoshima, before his troubles began, as a Liberal Democrat. Motoshima was elected mayor in 1979 with the help of the very organizations that ousted him later. And even after he had almost been shot dead, he was still ready to collaborate with the conservatives.

A controversy erupted in 1992, when builders hit upon the foundations of a former prison right next to the Nagasaki Peace Park, near the epicenter of the A-bomb. (It is a modest park compared with the one in Hiroshima, an almost apologetic stretch of land, filled with monuments donated by the various People's Republics, now mostly defunct.) Korean and Chinese prisoners had died in that prison during the war, some killed by Japanese, some by the bomb. A group of Nagasaki citizens wanted to preserve the site, to show that the Japanese were not just victims, that the bomb was dropped for a reason. Conservatives were against it: The Peace Park is a "happy place," said one. "Why should tourists want to come and see a prison?" Motoshima came down on the side of the conservatives. He needed their support to stay in office. He had good contacts in the construction industry. The remains of the prison were buried under a new parking lot. So whatever prompted his statement about the emperor, left-wing radicalism wasn't it.

Both Motoshima and Jenninger were criticized less for what they actually said (though for that, too, of course) than for their tactlessness, for picking the wrong time, for being poor judges of ceremony. Jenninger chose a memorial occasion to give a history lesson; Motoshima virtually committed lèse-majesté as the emperor lay on his deathbed. The LDP Disciplinary Committee, considering Motoshima's case, said that although private individuals were entitled to their opinions, "it was an act of extreme indiscretion for a public official to have made a public statement like that." I even heard words to this effect from people who publicly supported the mayor. One of them worked for Motoshima in Nagasaki's city hall.

I met him during the week of the emperor's funeral, on a crisp night in February 1989. We had been invited for dinner at the house of a mutual friend. The civil servant was a plump, middle-aged man with an ingratiating smile and the air of a schoolmaster used to slow learners. He removed the official badge from the lapel of his blue suit, took a sip of sake, and said: "Now I can speak to you as a private individual." Then he shook his head vigorously to express bafflement: "To be quite frank with you, I cannot understand why the mayor made that statement. I simply cannot understand."

I was with an American friend. He asked the official whether the mayor's statement was factually wrong. The man sucked his teeth, closed his eyes, as though in agony or deep thought, swiveled his short neck, and said, still with his eyes shut: "Well . . . no, not wrong exactly . . ." So he was telling the truth? "Well, yes, one could say it was correct, but I still can't understand why he said it." My friend, displaying more impatience than was polite, asked whether, in that case, he thought the mayor should have lied. The official's eyes disappeared once again behind their fleshy hoods, his face a picture not of agony so much as pained resignation. "In Japan," he said, "we all know the truth, but we remain silent. You must understand our culture . . ." He tugged at the collar of his shirt, which was damp at the edges, and sighed.

Our culture . . . I thought of the reaction of an Australian living in Japan when he heard about Motoshima's statement. "It's perfectly clear," he told me on the phone, "that Motoshima doesn't understand Japanese culture." I didn't argue with him.

What he said fitted neatly into Ruth Benedict's cultural paradigm of guilt versus shame: the Germans, riddled with guilt, feel the need to confess their sins, to unburden their guilt and be forgiven; the Japanese wish to remain silent and, above all, wish others to remain silent too, for the point is not guilt in the eyes of God, but public shame, embarrassment, "face." In sum, Jenniger had not confessed enough, and Motoshima had talked too much. This was the nature of their different forms of tactlessness. They had not played the game; they had broken the rules of their cultures.

The case for Benedict's paradigm is greatly helped by one important detail: Motoshima is a Christian. Which is precisely what some of his opponents held against him. In the words of one of his critics, Motoshima had not "behaved as a Japanese."

The mayor received a letter from a Shinto priest in which the priest pointed out that it was "un-Japanese" to demand any more moral responsibility from the emperor than he had already taken. Had the emperor not demonstrated his deep sorrow every year, on the anniversary of Japan's surrender? Besides, he wrote, it was wrong to have spoken about the emperor in such a manner, even as the entire nation was deeply worried about his health. Then he came to the main point: "It is a common error among Christians and people with Western inclinations, including so-called intellectuals, to fail to grasp that Western societies and Japanese society are based on fundamentally different religious concepts . . . Forgetting this premise, they attempt to place a Western structure on a Japanese foundation. I think this kind of mistake explains the demand for the emperor to bear full responsibility."

Motoshima Hitoshi was born on a small island off Kyushu, the only part of Japan where Catholic missionaries left their mark. Early in the seventeenth century most of Nagasaki was converted by Spanish and Portuguese priests. Later on, the Christians were tortured and massacred on orders of nervous shoguns. Rather like Communists in the 1930s, Christians were forced to apostatize, by stamping on pictures of the Virgin. But

Christians in southern Japan survived, even though persecution continued. Motoshima's grandfather had his bones crushed, by being forced to kneel with slabs of stone loaded on his lap, while police officers shouted at him: "Christ or the emperor, which is more important, Christ or the emperor?"

Motoshima himself was forced as a schoolboy in the 1930s to bow to Shinto shrines. On the emperor's birthdays his teachers would punish him for not showing enough respect. They would torment him with the same question that nearly broke his grandfather: "Christ or the emperor, which is more important, Christ or the emperor?"

Nagasaki is an odd city in Japan. It is proud of its history as a narrow window to the outside world. It has a large Chinatown. The names of some local dishes show their Chinese origins. During Japan's all but complete isolation in the seventeenth and eighteenth centuries, Dutch traders were allowed to live on a tiny island in Nagasaki Bay, visited only by officials and prostitutes. (Some people in Nagasaki still have the long-nosed features of at least one of their forebears.) "Dutch learning," culled with heroic scholarly diligence from dictionaries and medical books in Nagasaki, gave Japanese their first glimmer of European science. Nagasaki had "foreign learning" schools, a large convent, a handsome cathedral. The second A-bomb dropped on Japan (by a Roman Catholic pilot) exploded right over the cathedral and wiped out the convent. The most famous book on the bombing of Nagasaki, *The Bells of Nagasaki*, was written by a Christian doctor named Nagai Takashi. He believed that nothing was accidental. The bomb over the cathedral was planned by God, and the 73,884 people who died were martyrs, no less than Nagai's ancestors, who were crucified in the mountains a few centuries before.

For Mayor Motoshima, justice is a Christian concept. He believes—like the Australian and the Shinto priest—that this has given him a different take on life from most other Japanese. When I met him, almost a year before he was shot, he explained this view. It was important, he said, that the Japanese accept responsibility for their savage behavior during the war. And responsibility was a question of morality. And morality was a matter of religion. The problem with the Japanese was that "they worship nature. But they have no religious or philosophical moral basis."

As I pondered this, I glanced at Mayor Motoshima. He was dressed like a sports coach, in a track suit, a popular form of Japanese leisure wear, but unusual in the case of a mayor giving an interview. He returned my glance, looking me straight in the eye, not unkindly, but with a glint of toughness behind his glasses. His tight full lips lent a stubborn look to his lopsided mouth. There was none of the nervous diffidence or defensive arrogance that marks so many Japanese officials. Here was a man of conviction. He *knew* he was right.

"In Europe," he went on, "people's feelings are based upon centuries of philosophy and religion, but the Japanese only worship nature. This is what they have internalized. In a world ruled by nature, the question of individual responsibility doesn't come up."

What, I asked, was the solution in that case? Should all Japanese become Christians? "I am a Christian, so, yes, that is what I believe."

He sounded like a character in a novel by Endo Shusaku, the Catholic author, much admired by Graham Greene. Endo, like the mayor, believed that his animistic countrymen lacked a bedrock of morality, a sense of good and evil, but he also thinks they will never acquire it—that is to say, they will never be Christians. All Endo's work is marked by his despair; one famous novel, *Silence* (1966), is about the apostasy of a Jesuit missionary who has given up trying to convert the Japanese. In Endo's stories West and East never meet. But although he was perhaps the only Japanese novelist to have written about individual responsibility for war crimes from a Christian point of view, not all his Japanese characters are without conscience. They simply lack the language for it; they cannot give it a name. Dr. Toda, in *The Sea and Poison*, assists in a murderous experiment on an American POW. He is troubled by it, returns to the operating theater, the scene of the crime, but feels no "particular pain." "I have no conscience, I suppose. Not just me, though. None of them feel anything at all about what they did here."

Perhaps the Shinto priest was right. Perhaps it took a Christian to break a Japanese taboo (Motoshima's colleague in Hiroshima, Mayor Araki, not a Christian, though given to voicing noble sentiments, refused to support the Nagasaki mayor in 1988). However much right-wing nationalists and Shinto priests like to pretend that emperor worship is not a religion, but a Japanese "custom," it surely is a religion. It seems to take one faith to attack another, an alternative emperor—Buddha, Marx, Christ—to challenge the politics of Japanese emperor worship. This may be why Christians and Marxists have always been among the most trenchant critics of the emperor system and its political uses, just as certain Buddhists were centuries ago. But in fact there is more to it than that.

Because most Japanese were lapsed believers by the time the Showa emperor was dying, it was religion that nationalists wanted to revive. The fatal illness of the emperor was their chance. The imperial cult was their idea of Japanese "normality"—"normal" (*atarimae na koto*) and "natural" (*shizen*) were the terms they often used. Around the time of the emperor's death, the cultural critic Eto Jun wrote an essay in one of the leading monthly magazines arguing that the Americans had imposed a false picture of the emperor on the postwar Japanese. The Japanese, he wrote, were locked up in the "playground of postwar democracy and a merely symbolic emperor system." But when the emperor became very ill, he continued, even the liberal press, despite years of Western brainwashing, could not hide the personal grief of the Japanese people, which showed that "the sacred and solemn nature of our imperial family" had been preserved and would last forever. The right-wing LDP politician Ishihara Shintaro wrote in the same journal that the bond between the emperor and the Japanese transcended the bond between a head of state and its citizens: "It expresses the uniqueness of Japan and the Japanese . . ."

And "Tony" Kase Hideaki, the son of a former ambassador to Washington and a noted political commentator, wrote a remarkable piece for the Japanese edition of *Playboy* magazine. He described the Shinto rite called *Daijosai*, whereby the new emperor, after his father's death, would be visited by the sun goddess, enter her womb, and be reborn as a sacred ruler. "Japan's national character," he said, "was formed before history was recorded . . . When Japan was born, the emperor was already a high priest and head of state. The imperial family cannot be separated from Japanese mythology. The myths are identical to the birth of Japan. The emperor is sacred because of his blood ties with the gods that created our nation."

This is what the romantics wanted the Japanese people to believe. Like many intellectuals everywhere, indeed like many German conservatives, they worried about the spiritual vacuum caused by materialism and prosperity. Restoring the racial and imperial myths (which amounts to the same thing) was the Japanese revisionists' version of restoring Japan as a normal nation. Motoshima's statement was a challenge to their ideal of harmonious, natural bliss. It was an essentially antiliberal, antidemocratic ideal, perfect propaganda for authoritarian politics.

As in so many clashes of *mentalités*, Japanese revisionism may be partly a matter of age. The most active revisionists have been men in their fifties, educated during the war, shocked by the occupation. As in Jenninger's case, Motoshima's support, in the form of letters, often came from the very old, born before the height of the chauvinist hysteria, and the very young, who were never affected by it. Possibly, the dreaded spiritual vacuum is felt most keenly by those who were robbed by history of the religion in which they were raised. Jenninger and Motoshima said very different things, which complicates the comparison, and might even be thought to invalidate it. Jenninger, after all, was associated with the revisionists, the whitewashers, the neonationalists. And yet, I think the comparison holds. For by dealing with history in secular terms, both Jenninger and Motoshima upset the utterly disparate groups that sought to fill the spiritual void: in Bonn, the confessional pacifism of leftists and Greens; in Nagasaki, the attempted revival of the imperial cult.

This is why I think Motoshima's Christianity was less important than it might seem, and his challenge more than a clash of faiths. His personal motives were no doubt religious. Justice may well be a Christian concept to him. But his statement was secular, and so was its effect. Some of his supporters were Marxists and some were Christians, but all of them, to judge from their letters, grasped the main point, which was political, not religious.

Two weeks after his statement, Motoshima had received more than 10,000 letters supporting his case. A few months later there were more than 300,000—from housewives, old-age pensioners, army veterans, high school students, office clerks, peace activists, film directors, university professors, etc. Although liberal intellectuals, with a few exceptions, remained oddly silent in public—no Japanese Zola writing a *J'Accuse*—the letter columns in the liberal *Asahi Shimbun* were alive with debate. I shall quote just one letter, for being typical rather than the exception. It was written by a seventy-three-year-old retired mechanic:

"The emperor system led to military rule and caused the worst tragedy in Japanese history. The conservative authorities are once again turning to traditional monarchy to attack democratic rights . . . It is our responsibility to history to analyze scientifically the mechanism which has shaped popular consciousness since the Meiji period and led to war . . . only then can the question of our leaders' war responsibility be fully resolved, not by 'victors' justice,' but by the Japanese people themselves."

This was not the voice of God, Marx, or sacred ancestors. It was the voice of reason.

The question of political responsibility is, of course, a tricky one in the case of regimes that have effectively abolished politics, or indeed individual responsibility for anything, except to obey orders. As we have seen before, even the responsibility of Japanese leaders was complicated by the murky role of the emperor—part constitutional monarch, part divine priest-king. And by the time they led their country into a suicidal war, it was of course too late. Karl Jaspers, in his essay on war guilt, wrote that people should be held responsible, collectively, for the way they are governed. If their country is ruled by a criminal regime, the people cannot escape responsibility. He may have been thinking of German town squares in the 1930s filled with frenzied mobs screaming for their Führer. Yet there are problems with Jaspers's notion. For what constitutes a criminal regime? Criminal according to whose laws? And can a people be held responsible for a state of affairs in which they had no choice?

In fact, the Germans had more choice than the Japanese. Hitler and his bands of brownshirts did not bring down the Weimar Republic alone. Many Germans voted for the Nazi Party in 1932. But after the war, with Hitler safely gone, he could be blamed for everything. And the more he was blamed, the more the German people could feel absolved. It was *him*; they had only been mesmerized, understandably in the circumstances. It is a perception which Jenninger never seriously challenged. Which is why his speech was read as an apologia.

Motoshima's remark about the emperor, on the other hand, had the opposite effect. In Japan, there was no Nazi Party to vote for, and the emperor never ran for election. The emperor didn't go away, nor was he demonized—except in very few circles. By changing from his military uniform into a businessman's suit after the defeat in 1945, and by escaping blame in the Tokyo trial, he became, quite literally, a symbol of his nation. His innocence was the innocence of the Japanese people; like their emperor, they had been "deceived" by the military leaders. They had never been told what was going on. All they had ever wanted was peace. They had been tricked into going to war.

In fact, the emperor knew a great deal of what went on, even though his political influence might have been limited. And a large proportion of the Japanese people had been keener to be duped by belligerent propaganda, at various times since the turn of the century, than many would admit after the war. But the image of a deceived, innocent, peace-loving emperor had to be maintained, for it was one of the unifying factors in postwar Japan—that and pacifism; once the generals and admirals were purged, the Japanese people, with their emperor as the ever-changing, almost amoeba-like national symbol, could prosper innocently together.

Some criticized this charade. The filmmaker Itami Mansaku wrote an article in 1946 about the question of war guilt. He ridiculed the notion that everyone had been deceived or that those who were deceived were necessarily innocent. He argued that the deceived had to share the blame with the deceivers, and so "responsibility for the war—in varying degrees—lay on both sides." Those who were deceived, he wrote, were not guilty just because they let themselves be duped; no, the entire people was to blame for its lack of criticism, its slavishness, its incapacity to think. Like many leftist intellectuals, Itami was disgusted that "the Japanese hadn't been able to free themselves from feudalism and national isolation, and were not able to gain basic human rights without the help of foreign powers."

"We have been politically liberated now," Itami wrote, "but so long as the Japanese persist in slavishly passing the buck to the military, or the police, or the bureaucrats, they will never reflect seriously on their own guilt in allowing them to dominate us, and there never will be any hope for the Japanese people."

Itami, then, came to the same conclusion as Karl Jaspers. People must be held responsible for the society they live in. It is a harsh judgment, to hold the slave accountable for his condition, or worse, for the actions of his master. But it is an important idea, without which the institutions necessary to maintain open, liberal societies cannot survive. This is why Motoshima's statement was so vital, and so provocative. For by holding the emperor responsible for the war, he was not absolving the Japanese people. On the contrary, by exposing the fiction of the unresponsible high priest, he was challenging the self-image of his followers, the image of submissive victims, the image of pawns in some great impenetrable game.

Jaspers, like Motoshima, was a devout Christian. And as with the mayor, his sense of justice sprang from his faith. But Itami—like others who shared his views—was not a Christian. Christianity—like the distinction between shame cultures and guilt cultures—was never really the point. By breaking a Japanese taboo, Motoshima struck a blow for a more open, more normal political society, and very nearly lost his life. Jenninger, I like to think, wanted to strike a blow for the same, but failed, and lost his job. Perhaps he wasn't up to the task. Or perhaps even West Germany was not yet normal enough to hear his message.

TWO NORMAL TOWNS

PASSAU

PASSAU, LIKE MANY TOWNS along the great German rivers, is pretty rather than beautiful. It is too sentimental to be beautiful. It lies, like a handsome little jewelry box, at the confluence of the Danube, the Ilz, and the Inn. The landscape, so green, so picturesque, with pretty houses nestled on the woody mountain slopes, is straight out of a German fairy tale. Siegfried's widow, Kriemhilde, passed through Passau: reason for Bishop Wolfger to have the Nibelungen saga transcribed there in the twelfth century. The architecture of the town, with its baroque cathedral, its narrow cobbled streets, its low-slung arches, its corners filled with stucco saints and putti, is so freshly painted, so well tended, that it gives a faint impression of a beautifully laid-out corpse, expertly made up to resemble a living being.

As in all popular tourist sites, the prettiness of Passau tends to collapse into kitsch. Passau kitsch is an exaggerated German folksiness: souvenir shops offer wood carvings of gnarled peasants with pointed hats, bone-handled hunting knives with Gothic inscriptions, outsize beer mugs, and cut-glass saints. Tourist boats with names like *Nibelungen* and *Kriemhilde* glide along the rivers, with the sound of yodel music wafting from their decks. I had a cup of coffee with thick cream at an outside café, and read the local paper, which devoted entire pages to the meetings of shooting clubs (men in green uniforms and feathered hats). German and Austrian tourists walked by, clutching ice-cream cones and beer in plastic cups. The men wore shorts, ankle socks, and sandals, and the women flowered frocks.

Graffiti on the walls along the riverbanks showed the darker, aggressive side to the sentimentality of "Nibelungen City." Some of the texts were downright weird: "To burn of love or hate"; "Fear comes after death"; "Schönhuber, you must croak!" (a reference to the leader of the right-wing Republican Party). And oddest of all: "We won't wait for Santa Claus."

I retreated to my hotel room, which had a good view of the Inn. Just a few miles up the river was Braunau, where Hitler was born. He spent part of his childhood in Passau. I switched on the television and caught the end of a German film made in 1940. It was a romantic comedy, set in the 1870s, about Prussian officers and their Fräuleins in crinolines. I changed to another local channel. It was showing a documentary film called *Our Home*. Silent images of a village in a green Bavarian valley with red-roofed houses clustered around a creamy church, and swans swimming in the lake, as the mist came down from the hills, were accompanied by a Beethoven sonata. The narrator spoke in a tone that was meant to sound poetic: "The land behind the clouds, so wide, so strange, yet so familiar, like the land of my childhood . . ."

I had come to Passau because of a film I had seen some months before in London, entitled *Das schreckliche Mädchen*, translated, rather clumsily, as *The Nasty Girl*. It was based on the true story of a high school girl who entered a national essay contest. The theme was "everyday life in your hometown during the Third Reich." The girl, who had never misbehaved, who was her teacher's pet and got on well with her conservative Catholic parents, began to ask around. She spoke to the prelate, the newspaper editor, her grandmother, the city archivist, and so on. But when she began to stumble across evidence that people who had always been known to her as anti-Nazis, even "resistance fighters," had in fact been Nazi sympathizers, even Nazi officials, she ran into trouble. She was told to drop her project. Why not write about more important subjects, like Europe? What could she possibly understand about the past? When, some years later, she decided to turn her findings into a book, she ran into even greater trouble. Libraries and archives shut their doors. Death threats, to herself and her family, poured like poison out of the phone. Her cat was killed and nailed to her door. Bombs came through her window. All the town's dignitaries turned against her. Her respectable parents —mother, a teacher of religion, father, a headmaster—were embarrassed. Yet, encouraged by her grandmother and an old ex-Communist, she persisted. She wrote her book, became a national figure, and put her town, or at least its most prominent citizens, to shame.

It was an arresting film. The story was about repressed history, but the underlying theme was a conflict of generations. Even though the heroine was not born until 1960, the film expressed the rage of an earlier generation, the director Michael Verhoeven's generation of 1968. It is interesting how often in German accounts of Third Reich history, common cause is made between the young and their grandparents—the people who sent supportive letters to the mayor of Nagasaki and Philipp Jenninger. The Nasty Girl was too young to be Hitler's child, but her grandmother was a typical example of the pre-Nazi voice of reason. Amnesia is always the parents' disease. This point was made in another German film about memory, Edgar Reitz's *Heimat* (*Home*). There, too, the grandparents, born in the nineteenth century, represented the old virtues, uncorrupted by modern materialism and totalitarian propaganda: decency, honesty, self-reliance, family values.

In a way, Reitz's *Heimat* and Verhoeven's *The Nasty Girl* sprang from the same source, to which many German artists and scholars turned in the 1970s and 1980s: *Heimatgeschichte*, or local history. The old nostalgia for the paradise lost, the childhood village, the "land behind the clouds," under constant threat from soulless modernity, was given a new twist. The idea of history as a puppet play, moved at will by great men, was replaced by histories of everyday life, the past as a million stories, lived by common men and women. Not the great cities, but the small towns and villages were the stages upon which these little histories were played out. History of this type was partly a reaction against the often arid theorizing of those who sought to expose structures and systems, to explain history. No doubt Emmanuel Le Roy Ladurie's descriptions of French peasant life had an influence too. But there was in local German history a tone of nostalgia, as lush as nineteenth-century romantic music. This could lend an odd perspective to histories of the Third Reich.

Reitz's *Heimat* was an interesting example of this oddity. Filled with nostalgia for old-fashioned values—honest handwork, warm family life, etc.—it is also nostalgic about "normal" daily life in the 1930s. The loving creation of an imaginary village in the Rhineland, called Schabbach, celebrates simple country pleasures, as well as the popular culture of the time: nights at the movies of Zarah Leander and so on. The wealthy landowner's son becomes an SS man, there are glimpses of slave labor, and one of the dimmer, though always decent, characters joins the Nazis and becomes mayor of a local town. So the rise of the Nazis is not ignored, but it never really poisons the warm normality of local life. Nazism's peculiar modernity—Autobahns and the like—is shown to be a greater threat to the old values than, say, the *Kristallnacht*, which is not shown at all. Schabbach is a village. Perhaps nothing of consequence happened there. But people barely mention anything much happening anywhere else.

The film is a true exercise in identification, for we see the past through the eyes of the people who lived it. The film *is* a memory. And to the good people of Schabbach, the 1930s, by and large, were a time of happy memories, before the war took their sons away, in some cases to die. It is as though *Heimat* were made as a reaction to all those postwar years of denying a local, German identity. Intellectuals of the '68 generation had always mocked the kitschy taste for Heimat nostalgia. They were Europeans. Now it was their turn to look back and dig up roots. *Heimat* was a glorious—and beautifully contrived—effort to retrieve the Heimat, or, to paraphrase Reitz's comment on *Holocaust*, to take back "our narrative," which the Americans had stolen.

In the case of the much younger Nasty Girl, it was the other way around. Her subject was also Heimat history, but she had always been at home. She had never rejected her local identity; it was her opponents who tried to take the Heimat away from her, by making her feel she didn't belong, that she was a "Jewish whore," to cite one of the more common phrases in her hate mail. Yet the past she managed to retrieve from the murky swamp of willful oblivion was less benign than Reitz's re-creation of his village idyll.

The Nasty Girl was more like a book of photographs taken by a local photographer in a town not so very far from Reitz's Schabbach. Otto Weber became a photographer in Kleve in 1932 and took pictures of the town until his studio was destroyed by a bomb in 1944. The collection, published in 1987, is entitled *A Thousand Absolutely Normal Years* (the Reich was supposed to have lasted that long). It starts quite normally, with photographs of old cobbled streets after a snowfall. People greet one another in the town square as they help to clear the snow with their shovels. A procession of choirboys from the Catholic church goes by. In these early pictures, the burghers look content, harmless, respectable, a bit dull. Then, gradually, things change; a creeping brown blot stains the picture. First there is one dignitary standing in the square, hesitant but proud in his new uniform. Then there are two, three, four, and finally the whole square is filled with brown and black uniforms, swastika banners, marching boots, and thousands of shining eyes gleaming in the torchlight. This is local history too, for these were not great villains; these were the headmasters, the vergers, the town hall officials, the newspaper reporters, the dentists, the factory foremen, the printers, the butchers and the bakers. It was this page in the history of Heimat that the Nasty Girl was not allowed to see.

It was a strange sensation at first to be sitting in the living room of the Nasty Girl herself—the real person, that is, not the actress. Her name is Anja Rosmus. She has frizzy blond hair and keen blue eyes. She dressed with care in a slightly dowdy fashion. She was no longer a schoolgirl, but a divorcée with two children. Since she wrote her first essay, she had published several books on the brown history of Passau. One wall of her living room was decorated with pictures she had painted herself, of rabbis and bearded Jews, and mud-colored villages in an imaginary desert homeland. There was also a death mask hanging on the wall. It was the face of Kurt Tucholsky, the German satirist, who took his life in despair in 1935, after escaping from Nazi Germany to Sweden. It was a gift from Tucholsky's widow.

"It was pretty much all true," she said about the film. Except for a few details, like the bomb tossed through her window. That didn't really happen. But she showed me some of the hate mail. "Jewish whore" was by no means the most offensive phrase. She and her two small children were promised death by gassing, among other things. She had spent many nights awake in terror, hearing people beating on her windows and rattling her doors. She was sued for defamation by the brother of a man whose past was actually worse than she had suggested. The man in question, a pillar of the local Catholic church named Emil Janik, was known during the war as "brown Emil" for his Nazi sympathies. Rosmus was asked during a public meeting whether she thought he had really been a Nazi. She said that even though he wasn't a real Nazi, he certainly had not been a resistance fighter either. Janik's brother sued her, so she had to produce documents to support her case. These showed that Janik had not just been antisemitic but had told all Catholics to vote for Hitler. The charges against her were finally dropped. But an attempt was made during the trial to use the security service against her, for being a "threat to the state" (*staatsgefährdendes Element*).

Virtually all her hate mail was, of course, anonymous. But the most interesting letter was signed, and was not abusive. It was from a former army officer who had served during the war in Western Europe as well as on the eastern front. His application for the Waffen SS, "our elite," was turned down. And in all his war years he "never came across camps or people whose presence was in any way out of the ordinary." He was arrested by the Americans after the war and "treated like a criminal," even though he had "neither committed crimes nor seen any." He had only "done his duty."

The letter was interesting because its use of language sounded much like Jenninger's. But he actually believed the arguments that Jenninger was quoting. The old soldier painted the usual picture of Weimar Republic doom: unemployment, national humiliation, and "small businesses destroyed by Jewish capital." So, obviously, when the Nazis came to power, "the majority of the German people were happy that at last something was being done . . ."

Whiners, know-it-alls, and obstructionists were of course not wanted and "taken out of circulation." They went to so-called preventive detention camps, later known as concentration camps . . . To rescue Germany from the claws of the Versailles Treaty, one thing had to be made clear: you were either with us or against us . . .

I must say that things were moving in the right direction when I was young. We educated one another, defended ourselves against everything that was unnatural, and we were not exposed to any negative influences . . .

The Jews had not made themselves exactly loved in Germany, and it became clear they were not wanted. But no normal person condoned the hatred being stirred up and

the so-called *Kristallnacht*. After all, we had tolerated the Jews before . . .
We who lived through that time have to ask ourselves why we should keep on besmirching our own name. Surely it is not in our interest to paint things blacker than they were. I find it monstrous that the likes of Mr. Galinski [head of the Jewish community in Germany] and Mr. [Simon] Wiesenthal stoke the fires ever higher. I myself am not conscious of having done anything wrong, and I cannot tolerate that my children and grandchildren should be made to feel guilty.

Anja Rosmus, then, was besmirching her Heimat, and by extension her country. In fact, however, she found that some people had behaved more admirably than they had been given credit for. The wartime mayor, for example, had been vilified as a demonic Nazi and blamed for everything bad. In truth, he had tried to stop deportations and allowed Jews to escape. Rosmus found out about others who had taken risks to help the persecuted. Town hall clerks issued passports, her own grandmother brought food to prisoners in a local camp, housewives offered refuge. Their quiet heroism was never recognized. Nobody was much interested in them. And she found that these people themselves were reluctant to talk.

I asked her why she thought this was. She said that they had helped for purely humanitarian reasons. They were not political in any way. But there was another reason too: "Most people don't want to be criticized for breaking the law. People here feel very ambivalent about resistance. They confuse such things as patriotism and law. That is why resistance, even to the Nazis, was never really condoned. Passau is ninety-six percent Catholic. There were people who resisted for religious reasons. A priest was murdered for defending the Jews in church. Another priest refused to swear an oath of loyalty to Hitler. He was killed too. But nobody ever spoke about these men with any respect. They had broken the rules. They were disobedient. And civil disobedience is thought to be a bad thing. My own grandmother still feels guilty about breaking the laws to help people. That is why I am hated so much here. Even if what I say is the honest truth, I am thwarting the authorities."

I wondered about her own religious feelings. Did they play any part in her activities? She laughed and said: "I left the church when I was twenty-five. It was a great shock to my parents, since they lived for the church. Even now they don't understand; they refuse to see that I'm not religious." I still wondered, though. My eyes kept being drawn to the pictures on the wall, of Orthodox Jews. Anja Rosmus was too young to share the neurotic philosemitism of her parents' generation. Then again, perhaps she was not. Perhaps it transcended age. I thought of the young people I had seen in Berlin, young Germans sipping tea in newly established Jewish cafés around the husk of the damaged synagogue, young Gentiles wearing Stars of David around their necks.

As though she could read my thoughts, Anja Rosmus said: "I did get involved in the Jewish religion. I think Jesus was such a typical Jewish man. After all, you know, so many things in Christianity are not religious: Christmas, Easter—these are old German customs. At the same time, on Sundays we celebrated many Jewish rites in church. Later I read Freud. He wrote what I had always felt myself, that people invent their religious dreams out of a deep psychological need."

It would be unfair to this courageous woman to reduce her efforts to a religious impulse. I had no reason to doubt her dedication to finding the truth. And she was politically astute. The fact that she often appeared to enjoy her fame, or, indeed, her notoriety, did not bother me. Her vanity, such as it was, no doubt helped to keep her going in very trying, even dangerous circumstances. But there was, nonetheless, an element of zeal in her which was, if not perhaps religiously inspired, certainly moral. There was a glint in her eyes as she told more and more outrageous stories about her hometown. The first printed text in Passau, dated 1476, showed pictures of the destruction of the synagogue. A gasworks now stood where the Jewish community hall once was. A neighbor had been a guard at Auschwitz. He had hidden a cache of treasures there, gone back to retrieve his treasure, and shot the friend who had helped him when he learned that the friend was a Jew. This story was made into a film, called *Abraham's Gold*. I had no reason to doubt Rosmus. She was scrupulous about the truth. But there is a point beyond which the exposure of myths spawns its own legends.

The story of the swastika breads, for example. Every year members of the far-right DVU (German People's Union), followed by bands of skinheads, assorted misfits, and resentful old comrades, meet in Passau at the Nibelungen Hall. They rant, they sing songs, they drink beer, and no doubt listen to the old stories again. And possibly some Nazi souvenirs change hands. But as though this weren't sinister enough, a story went around about loaves of bread baked in the shape of the swastika, which were sold, crisp and warm, on the market square. It was picked up by reporters, who used it to add a piquancy to the image of Passau, this incorrigible town, where Hitler had lived and Eichmann was married. Anja Rosmus was not responsible for spreading this story, which turned out to be untrue. But it was typical of the kinds of myths that grow in dark places.

Rosmus told me about something else, however, which was undoubtedly true. There had been a small concentration camp outside Passau, a so-called *Aussenlager* (subsidiary camp) of Mauthausen. It was one of the things nobody had talked about in Passau when Anja Rosmus was growing up, attending the Gymnasium where Himmler's father once taught Latin. There had been the usual debates in Passau about the proper way to memorialize the war. A decision was made in 1946 to rename the town center in memory of the victims of National Socialism. And a memorial was planned for the same purpose. Neither project came off. Instead, years later, a memorial stone was placed in the Innstadt cemetery. Soldiers were buried there, as well as more direct victims of Nazism. This, said the mayor, was good enough. The site of the camp would have slipped the public memory entirely had not a local branch of the Social Democratic Party decided to sponsor a memorial stone in 1983. The place was not easy to find. There was a lake dissected by a large dam. I walked toward it, past a sign which said: "Auf die Dauer hilft nur Power" ("In the long run, only power works"). The only sounds were of birds singing and cows lowing softly in their long wooden sheds (former barracks?). An old man in a blue peaked cap was working near the dam. I asked him whether this dam had been built by prisoners "back then." He said, "*Ja*," and resumed his work. Did he happen to know where the memorial stone was? "No," he said, without looking up. I was about to give up when I spotted it, almost invisible, hidden behind bushes. A simple gray stone marker was planted in the earth. "For the victims of the subsidiary concentration camp of Mauthausen in Oberilzmühle, 1942–1945," it said. Under the text were five crosses and the date of the stone, 1983. The letters were designed to resemble runic signs, the ancient and supposedly mystical Teutonic script favored by the Nazis.

It was an insensitive choice of style, no doubt made by people of goodwill. But archaism of one kind or another is ubiquitous in Germany. The more insecure, the newer a regime or institution, the more it will fabricate tradition. Much of nineteenth-century Germany is marked by phony medievalism. The Nazis in their way continued the practice. And it persisted in the rebuilt façades of postwar German towns. After all, what were a mere twelve years compared with the glories of the Holy Roman Empire, the Teutonic Knights, or baroque and rococo?

The town hall of Passau actually contains late Gothic remnants, though most of it dates from the nineteenth century. Ferdinand Wagner (1847–1927) painted the inside with murals from the Nibelungen saga. The outside wall facing the Danube has a late Gothic style. I had made an appointment to meet one of Anja Rosmus's adversaries there. His name was Gottfried Dominik. He ran the tourist office, next door to the town hall.

Dominik was in his mid-forties. He sported a mustache, and

his pink forehead shone through a thinning fringe of blond hair. He wore a Bavarian-style suit with horn buttons. His expression was not unfriendly, but pained, as though he were suffering from indigestion. When agitated, he would turn red.

As I sat down in front of his desk, Dominik pointed to a framed motto on the wall. It was signed by a German cardinal. "That's my motto in life," said Dominik. It read: "Happy are those who dream dreams and are ready to pay the price to make them come true." I nodded and asked about Anja Rosmus. His face instantly took on a pained expression, and Dominik began to explain. There were two issues here, he said, the good name of Passau and the personality of Frau Rosmus. Passau lay in a peculiar part of Bavaria. People here were somewhat proud and conservative. And along comes this Frau Rosmus calling Passau a Nazi town, insulting people left and right, and putting on a "perfect one-woman show." This is very bad for Passau. One should really not be surprised that it caused a great deal of trouble.

Yes, I said, I could see that. But were Rosmus's allegations true? Dominik chewed his mustache and opened a brown folder on his desk. He produced a newspaper article about Rosmus and Passau published in the *Sunday Times* of London. His face flushed as he tapped the article with his index finger. "All lies," he said, "all lies!" Could he be more specific? "This story about the swastika bread. There never was a swastika bread." But is that what Rosmus had said? Dominik didn't exactly know, but he was sure she was behind the article.

Wishing to avoid the topic of the swastika bread for the moment, I asked Dominik whether he thought Rosmus's book about Passau during the war was factually true. His agitation subsided and the pained expression returned. That, he said, was difficult for him to answer. The thing is, he himself wasn't from Passau. His family was. Then he pointed at two glossy photographs on the wall. They were tourist office pictures of Bavarian landscapes. "Look at those," he said. "The truth is not merely a matter of detail, but of color, of tone." Then, turning back to the newspaper article, he said: "But these are conscious fabrications, terrible lies that blacken the image of our town. And she adores her international fame, the good girl against the bad city."

Perhaps, I ventured, the problem began with the manner in which history was suppressed for so long. No, said Dominik, this was quite untrue. "I always knew a great deal about the past. I met Albert Speer, and I knew Göring's daughter. Why, I even met Hitler's secretary. No, I always took an interest in historical things. I read Speer's memoirs and the Anne Frank book. And my own grandmother was beaten by the Nazis, and my mother had witnessed a death march. You must also realize it was more difficult for us. I am from 1946. Our teachers didn't tell us much. But for Frau Rosmus's generation it was quite different. Nothing was suppressed."

I told Dominik about my trip to the site of the concentration camp, and asked him whether 1983 had not been a bit late to officially remember the place. He made a jovial gesture with his hand and invited me to go next door for a stein of good local beer. On the way, he said that the camps had been bad, pretty bad, but a lot of nonsense was talked about them too. People are always saying that Dachau was a death camp. "Completely untrue! It was just a labor camp."

We drank our beer. The foam stuck to his mustache, making him look old beyond his years. I asked him again about the local camp and the small hidden memorial. Dominik showed signs of distress. "It was difficult," he admitted, "very difficult. I know what you mean. But let me give you my personal opinion. When you have a crippled arm, you don't really want to show it around. It was a low point in our history, back then. But it was only twelve years in thousands of years of history. And so people tend to hide it, just as a person with a crippled arm is not likely to wear a short-sleeved shirt."

I looked at Dominik's pink face and his frothy white mustache. He was not a bad man, just a singularly unimaginative one. He was from the same '68 generation as the radically antifascist intellectuals. But when others were demonstrating or uncovering fascist continuities, or judging their parents, Gottfried Dominik, like many, many others, was an obedient boy, a member of the local Catholic youth association, a conservative out of habit. He didn't judge his parents. He talked just like them.

We chatted amicably enough. He asked me what I was working on. I told him about my book. Ah, he said, he had been to Japan once, to Tokyo. But he found it impossible to talk to the people there. They had no understanding of the way the Germans had faced their history. "They saw our honesty toward the past as a weakness, as a loss of face toward former enemies. No, I didn't understand them at all. What with their emperor staying in power. No, they have a completely different idea about history, a completely different way of dealing with it."

HANAOKA

In the summer of 1945, not long before the end of the war, Yachita Tsuneo was only five years old. But he can still remember the "Hanaoka Incident." He didn't know it would be called that, of course. Nor did he know exactly what happened on the night of July 30. But he remembers seeing a crowd of men surrounding Chinese slave workers cowering on their knees in front of the village community hall. There were screams of "Death to the Chinks! Death to the Chinks!" The Chinks, it was said, had killed a Japanese and cannibalized him. Yachita remembers catching a glimpse of bamboo sticks coming down on the naked Chinese, before he was whisked away by his mother. This was not for young children.

What actually happened was this: On the night of July 30, more than 800 Chinese slave workers in a small town in the northeast of Japan had escaped into the hills. The local militia, mostly farmers and shopkeepers armed with bamboo spears and clubs, helped the police to hunt them down. Rabbit hunting they called it. The Chinese were marched into a yard in front of the village community hall and forced to sit on their knees, hands tied behind their backs, naked from the waist up, for three days and nights, without food or drink. It was the hottest time of the year. Yachita later heard that some Chinese had tried to drink their own urine. About fifty men were tortured to death inside the hall. Some were suspended from the ceiling by their thumbs and beaten. Others had water forced down their throats, after which men would stamp on their stomachs. Schoolboys were told by their teachers to spit on the Chinks. And they were handed sticks to beat them with. In one village, not far from where Yachita saw the prisoners, teenage boys of the local youth association clubbed several Chinese to death.

The slaves had been brought over from China to Hanaoka, in Akita Prefecture, in 1944. This was not unusual. The Imperial Army was paid to hand over POWs and kidnapped civilians to work as slaves for Japanese corporations. About 40,000 came to Japan during the war. About 7,000 died. A relatively small number, perhaps, compared with the casualties among the 7.8 million foreigners working in Nazi Germany, but the brutality with which the Chinese were treated was bad enough. About 2 million Koreans lived in Japan, but since Korea was formally part of the Japanese empire, and all Koreans were regarded as Japanese subjects, their position was different, if not necessarily better. Nearly half of these resident Koreans were conscript workers, pressed into service during the war, and often mal-treated. Statistically, the Hanaoka Incident was a small affair, and it was probably one of many similar "incidents," but through sheer chance it is the only one whose details are known.

The Chinese in Hanaoka were made to work for Kajima Gumi, a large construction company under contract to the Dowa Mining Company. They worked in the copper mine. And in midwinter they were ordered to build a dam in the river and redirect the stream. They wore thin rags, even in winter, when Akita is buried in thick snow. They subsisted on a diet of rotten apple skins and one bowl a day of watery rice gruel. On a visit to Hanaoka, an official from the Health Ministry decided their treatment was too soft. "They should be squeezed like a damp towel until not one drop remains," he said. Of the 986 Chinese, most of them farmers and POWs, only 568 survived the war.

There had been a vague plan behind the June 30 uprising—to reach American and Australian POWs who were in a small camp nearby. Together they would find their way to the coast, where they would grab a fishing boat to get to Hokkaido, which they thought had already been liberated. If the plan failed, they would drown themselves in the sea. In fact, they got no farther than the hills around the labor camp. A monument erected near the site of the camp long after the war describes the uprising as a blow struck to "protect the dignity of man." In September 1945, *after* the Japanese surrender, a court in the city of Akita tried the Chinese survivors and found them guilty of breaching national security by rioting in wartime. They were sentenced to prison for life.

The Hanaoka Incident would never have become an incident—that is to say, it would have slipped into the same obscurity that cloaks much of the history of slave labor in wartime Japan—if American occupation authorities had not caught employees of Kajima Gumi digging up a mass grave to hide the evidence of their treatment of the Chinese. This led to the only war crimes trial held in Japan against a private corporation. The Chinese prisoners were released from jail in Akita and appeared as witnesses in the trial of their former bosses. Eight local employees of Kajima Gumi were sentenced by the Allied tribunal in Yokohama in 1948, some of them to death by hanging. None of them was very important and all were released in 1956, as was, a few years earlier, the man formally responsible for slave labor during the war, Kishi Nobusuke, who, as we know, went on to become Prime Minister. And Kajima Gumi, now Kajima Kensetsu, is one of the largest construction companies in the world, with huge interests in China.

A few Chinese survivors of the Incident remained in Japan. One of them committed suicide when Chou Enlai signed an agreement with the Japanese government in 1972 absolving

Japan from any responsibility for what happened in the war and so of any obligation to pay compensation to the Chinese victims. And until a few years ago the Chinese government effectively prevented Chinese survivors from making a fuss about it. China needed cheap Japanese loans. Not only were the former victims cut off from Japanese compensation, but in the xenophobic logic of Mao's China, Chinese who had spent time in Japan during the war were under suspicion anyway. During the Cultural Revolution, the former slave workers were accused of having been Japanese spies. One can only imagine how they were treated by the Red Guards.

But at least the information was there, albeit mostly in American archives. Much of this information was released in the late 1980s through the Freedom of Information Act. At the same time the few remaining Chinese survivors became freer to travel to Japan and press their claims, if not against the Japanese government, then at least against Kajima Kensetsu. In 1990 a group of four survivors visited Hanaoka for the first time since the war. They could hardly recognize a thing, for all the landmarks were gone. All they had to go on were their memories. They were met in Hanaoka, now a district of the city of Odate, by a handful of Japanese, including two men who had refused, against all odds, to let the memory die. One of them was Yachita Tsuneo.

Yachita took time off from his job as a trade union organizer to show me around the town. He spoke in the thick accent of the northeast, a clipped brogue, which reflects, so one is told, the cold climate. He dressed casually in the manner of Japanese men who take pride in their independence from corporate life: colorful open-necked shirt, slacks, sports jacket. We had been out drinking the night before at a Korean restaurant, for he wanted me to meet the Korean couple who owned it and hear their stories about anti-Korean discrimination. They were among the very few Koreans in town. They were his friends.

Yachita pointed out several times in the course of the evening that Japanese had treated Koreans and Chinese as subhumans. He remembered a Korean girl in his school whom he and his Japanese classmates hadn't really regarded as a human being. And this was after the war.

The area where the Chinese camp used to be still belongs to the Dowa Mining Company. On the dirt road leading to the stone monument that marks the former camp is a sign which reads: "Danger! No Trespassing." We ignored the sign and saw a Dowa company car following us from a distance. Yachita laughed and said it was always like this. The landscape had a kind of poisonous beauty. The reddish soil was covered with flinty slate the color of green mold. There was a large lake, used by Dowa for dumping toxic materials. There was an orange film on the surface, but when you tossed a stone into the water, black bubbles emerged from the thick slime. The former Chinese camp was at the bottom of this lake.

Yachita pointed out the main landmarks from a spot at the top of a hill near the location of the old camp. Hanaoka lay in a large flat basin surrounded by snow-topped mountains, which looked from a distance like chocolate cakes dripping with cream. Not only had the towns and villages on the plain changed, but the landscape itself was no longer what it was in 1945. The lake was new. Rivers followed different courses. Hills had disappeared to make way for roads or new buildings, while other hills, of slate and sludge, had been formed. A former lake was now a field of soggy scrub. The town hall had disappeared. The old community hall had been razed in the 1960s and replaced with a dull concrete building on the other side of the yard where the Chinese prisoners had been held. There was a large supermarket where the village shops used to be, and Odate sprawled where once there had been paddy fields.

But not everything was gone. Yachita pointed to a cluster of shabby-looking barracks. This was where the American POWs had been housed. I asked him whether they had also worked in the mine. "No," he said, "we Japanese always take good care of white people." His mouth tightened in a grim little smile. I smiled back. I thought of all the stories I had heard about the Burma Railroad and the "Jap camps" in the Dutch East Indies. But, comparatively speaking, Yachita was surely right.

He also pointed out the road on which the Chinese had escaped into the hills. There remained a dense cluster of wooden houses along the road. Yachita said that older people still remember the muffled sound of bare feet passing by on the night of the escape. He mimicked the sound: pata pata, pata pata. In 1945, the Chinese workers no longer had shoes.

We visited the cemetery, where two stone memorials stood out. One commemorated the "loyal spirits" of Japanese soldiers who died in the war. The other was in memory of the "martyrdom of the Chinese heroes." It was erected in 1963, after a certain amount of agitation, by the city of Odate, the Dowa Mining Company, and Kajima Kensetsu. In 1985, the socialist mayor of Odate decided to declare June 30 a Day of Peace, and a ceremony is held at the memorial each year. But the monument looked neglected. There was a bunch of dead flowers wrapped in plastic on the ground, and a plastic container of long-decayed rice balls lay open at the base of the monument.

Near the river, where the Chinese, as well as Koreans, had worked and often, as a result of beatings, hunger, and exhaustion, died, was another, much smaller memorial stone. The words were hard to read. The stone was cracked like broken glass. Tin cans and the remains of snacks offered to the dead souls littered the ground. The inscription read: "A Buddhist memorial to the Chinese dead." The story of the monument is as sordid as the history it commemorates. When the Kajima employees had been caught digging up the bones of Chinese workers, they were asked to build a proper Buddhist crypt to store them in. They refused and instead they buried them on this little hill behind a Buddhist temple. In 1949, more bones were discovered near the old Chinese camp. The newly discovered remains were buried with the other bones and the stone memorial was hastily erected. In recent years, Kajima Kensetsu has offered to erect a new, larger memorial. But the small organization fighting for the rights of the Chinese survivors refused the offer, until proper compensation is paid and a museum built. "They are good at putting up memorial stones," said Yachita, "but when it comes to historical research and financial compensation, we have had no help at all."

Odate is about seven and a half hours by train from Tokyo, roughly the same time it takes to get from Berlin to Passau. The northeast, especially Akita, is still strikingly shabby, even poor, when compared with the central and southern parts of Japan. The town centers are dark and charmless: raw concrete buildings and dingy shopping streets with plastic roofing to keep the snow from blocking the shops in winter. Rubbish is carelessly strewn around wooden houses on the outskirts of town, houses that are often little more than shacks. The only color in Odate, apart from the ubiquitous advertising, which is the same all over Japan, is provided by small drinking establishments where the men get drunk at night.

The northeast has always been poor, in spite of being the rice bowl of Japan. Before the war, especially during the depression, farmers were so poor they often had to sell their daughters. Japanese and even Southeast Asian brothels were always well stocked with northeastern girls. And while the eldest sons would inherit the farms, their brothers would frequently join the army, where life was brutal but at least they were fed. The harsh life in the northeast bred resentment against politicians and businessmen, who were regarded, not entirely without reason, as greedy and corrupt. The Communist novelist Kobayashi Takiji was born near Hanaoka, and grew up even farther north, in Hokkaido. He was tortured to death by the police in 1933 for spreading dangerous thoughts. I felt that Yachita's leftism and his Korean friends' political identification with North Korea (even though they had been born in the south) were part of this tradition. They were not doctrinaire Marxists. They were against graft, discrimination, and greed, which they identified as "capitalism." For the same reason, radical right-wing "agriculturalism" was popular before the war.

The cold north nurtured a self-image of stoic virtues: loyalty, honesty, hard work, and so on. In front of the Odate station is a statue of one of Japan's favorite icons, the loyal dog Hachiko, who would turn up faithfully every evening to meet his master at the station. One day his master died before reaching the station, but Hachiko refused to budge from his usual place. The dog stayed at his post until the day he died. The neck of Hachiko's stone head is still decorated with fresh flowers—fresher and more copious tributes than at any of the memorials for the Chinese workers.

The villages and towns of the northeast are celebrated in folk songs. They are also a favorite territory for the Japanese version of Heimat or *furusato* stories. Filmmakers searching for roots have often used the northeast as a location. Akita and Aomori still have an air of primitive mystery. The northeast, to use a popular expression of urban intellectuals, "reeks of mud." People who were born there would often long to escape, and frequently did, but to writers, artists, and poets in Tokyo the same *furusato* (literally "old village") could be viewed through the warm haze of nostalgia, a long-lost muddy Japanese Heimat.

Oshin, the heroine of the most popular television soap opera ever made in Japan, was born in a village in the northeast. The series, entitled *Oshin*, was broadcast by NHK, the semi-national television network, in 1984 and 1985, precisely when *Heimat* was shown in Germany. The 297 fifteen-minute episodes were aired every morning (63 percent ratings) and repeated in the afternoons (20 percent ratings). In style, *Oshin* was very different from *Heimat*. The German film was a personal work of art; *Oshin* was a well-crafted melodrama. And although *Oshin* was, like *Heimat*, a celebration of traditional rural values and a lament for their loss, the Japanese heroine leaves her village early on, when her family is unable to feed her. The loss of Heimat is literal, as it has been for so many people during the industrialization of Japan (and Germany, and pretty much everywhere else). But the idea of home does not have to be regional. In *Oshin*, the whole country becomes a kind of Heimat. The war years, especially, are seen from the perspective of home, as they were in Reitz's *Heimat*. Both the German film and the Japanese TV melodrama were local answers to the Hollywood version of history. It was history as "we," the national family, remember it. Herein lay much of their appeal.

As in *Heimat*, where the bedrock of the family history is the mother, Oshin functions as a repository of supposedly traditional values. She represents the conservative Japanese ideal: long-suffering, hardworking, honest, cheerful, and polite, gentle in her manners and disciplined in her habits. She is soft-spoken and respectful, but also tough; everyone depends on her. If Edgar Reitz was part of a wave of leftist nostalgia, *Oshin* is what might be called the officially authorized memory of the past. Oshin is a peaceful woman. She is opposed to war. But she could not do anything about it. Her duty, as the narrator's voice tells us more than once, was "to take care of her family." The series loudly proclaims its pacifism, while celebrating at the same time the sincerity with which most Japanese supported the war.

All the Japanese soldiers in the story are handsome, sincere, courteous, upright men, even Oshin's brother-in-law, a militant patriot who urges her to send her son to the military academy. Oshin's husband, Ryuzo, becomes caught up in militarist propaganda, too. His opportunism is not disguised; his business prospers because he supplies the army. But he becomes increasingly authoritarian toward his wife and children, and chauvinistic in his views. In a way, the official Japanese soap opera is harder on its characters than Reitz is on his. The good people of Schabbach are neither fanatical nor chauvinistic; only the bad SS man is shown to be that way. And yet, Oshin's husband is not an unsympathetic character. He is a good man who sincerely believes in his country. (To present a good and sincere Nazi is obviously more difficult to do.) When Oshin protests that supplying the army means collaborating in the war, Ryuzo tells her that when Japan goes to war, every Japanese must do his duty.

The fall of Nanking is cause for celebration. In a beautifully contrived scene, shot in slow motion, we see the town turn out for a lantern parade. The slowly laughing faces look eerie, almost monstrous. Oshin, despite her pacifist views, is pleased too. The voice of the female narrator tells us that Oshin "felt the enormous power that was forging the future of Japan. She didn't know the nature of this power. Nanking had been conquered and the whole family turned out for the parade. Oshin, too, was one of the happy Japanese."

In the very next episode, we are told that Oshin had no idea about the cruelty of the war on the continent (nor, for that matter, does the television audience: the enemy is never shown, let alone what happened to the enemy at the hands of Japanese soldiers). Oshin is worried and depressed when her two sons become fanatical, like their father, and express a desire to die for their country (not for their emperor, note: the emperor is carefully brushed out of NHK's version of the past). We see Oshin's maternal anguish, but we are also meant to be impressed by her sons' youthful enthusiasm, their sincerity, and the purity of their feelings. Their handsome, open faces are lit up, during the patriotic speeches at the family table, in the manner of Hollywood movies showing James Stewart going to Washington. Unlike in Schabbach, there are no rotten apples here, no equivalent of the bad SS man.

This is perhaps the greatest difference between the German Heimat and the Japanese *furusato*: there were no Nazis in the Japanese village, just soldiers. There were no deportations, or concentration camps nearby. There was no *Kristallnacht*; neighbors didn't disappear during the night. People may not have liked the war, or the economic hardships it brought, or the swagger of village pedagogues and military bullies, but virtually everyone did his or her bit. And the war itself, well, that was something that happened elsewhere, far, far away from home.

There was one exception. For those who were unlucky enough to live on Okinawa, the war came home with a vengeance in 1945. Okinawans were treated as inferior Japanese and distrusted by the Imperial Army, and many civilians were sacrificed in the battle with the U.S. marines. About 160,000 civilians—more than a third of the local population—were killed in the cross fire, and hundreds died in mass suicides. The experience has left a far greater sense of bitterness on Okinawa than anywhere else in Japan, notwithstanding the bombings of Tokyo, Hiroshima, and Nagasaki.

But Hiroshima and Nagasaki were also the locations of slave labor camps, like the one in Hanaoka. There were such camps all over Japan, and Japanese civilians must have been aware of them. Every day the good people of Hanaoka saw the emaciated figures of Chinese slaves being whipped along the road to work by overseers. And it was the same good people who helped the police go "rabbit hunting" when the slaves escaped. At some point during our drinking expedition in Odate, Yachita told me about his father, who had hated the war so much that he made himself unfit to pass the medical test for military service by drinking a whole bottle of soy sauce. And he tried to stay away from war-related work at home. But when it came to the rabbit hunt, he was there, with the posse, chasing up the hills. He did his duty, just like everyone else. Which is why after the war people did not like to talk about what happened. Before 1979, local history textbooks did not even mention the Incident.

One of the schoolboys told to spit on the Chinks was Nozoe Kenji. He never forgot the experience: "When I question people about the Incident, memories flit through my mind, and I find it hard to speak. I start to shake. I become conscious of having been one of the aggressors." Yet Nozoe never stopped asking questions. For thirty years he has been piecing together precisely what happened that night. As a result, his family was threatened, his children couldn't leave the house at night, his windows were smashed, and he received death threats from anonymous telephone callers, usually after midnight. Things got even worse when he published a book about his findings in 1975. Nobody denied the facts, but he was accused of being a traitor to his people, of having besmirched the reputation of his Heimat, his *furusato*.

I visited Nozoe at his house, in a small town not far from Odate. It was the usual small northeastern town: empty streets, corrugated-iron roofs, seedy houses. The entrance to Nozoe's house was in a narrow alley behind a dry-goods store. It smelled dank inside, of old wood and blocked drains. His study was on the second floor. We sat on the tatami floor in the midst of piles of books, documents, and periodicals. Nozoe was dressed in an old kimono. His large, round head sprouted great tufts of un-combed gray hair. He has the air of a professor, but in fact he never finished high school. He survived on odd jobs. Poor all his life, he now scrapes by on his books about the Hanaoka Incident (he has written four to date). They are his lifework. It is all he wants to write about.

Talking to Nozoe, I thought of the man who introduced me to him, a Chinese resident in Japan in his fifties, living in a one-room apartment in Osaka. Chu Hakkai (a name he adopted when forced by Japanese bureaucrats to Japanize his name) drives a truck in a garbage dump and spends his earnings on gathering information on the history of Chinese slave labor during the war. Like Nozoe, he has had no institutional back-ing. I was told that not one Japanese academic historian has done work on the subject. So, like Nozoe, Chu has had to go to China himself to find documents and talk to survivors.

At first the difficulties for Nozoe were immense. There was no documentation available on the Hanaoka Incident, so all he could do was track down eyewitnesses. The first four or five times, he said, people would slam their doors in his face. Some called the police to chase him off. Then, reluctantly, peering down the street to make sure the neighbors hadn't seen, some invited him in for tea. At first they would talk only about in-consequential things. But gradually, after another four or five visits, facts would emerge, names were mentioned, stories told.

The process was so slow that it took him more than twenty years to compile enough material for his first book.

"I was never actually beaten up," he said, "but the Dowa Mining Company hired gangsters to make sure I didn't prowl around the old camp. And the gangsters were supported by the police."

He got no help from the company, of course, but the trade union didn't wish to be involved either. I asked him whether he had been in touch with others who were investigating wartime history. I knew that a network of such people existed, since its members had been helpful to me in furnishing introductions. Mori Masataka, the middle school teacher, knew Chu Hakkai, who put me onto the lawyer representing the Chinese survivors, who knew a man in Nagasaki . . . and so on. "No," said Nozoe, "until about three years ago I was alone."

This might have been a slight exaggeration. Official initiatives to commemorate the Hanaoka Incident had, after all, been taken in the town itself in the mid-1980s, and Yachita had been working on the case too, though not for as long as Nozoe. But talking to the various members of the network, one soon realized that relations were not always smooth; casual remarks revealed jealousies and prickly disputes. It is, of course, always thus in fringe groups, doggedly pursuing an unpopular cause. In any case, the situation eased a bit in the late 1980s, when Chinese, and especially Koreans who had been repatriated after the war to South Korea, were freer to travel to Japan. The Akita Broadcasting Company made a television documentary on the Hanaoka Incident, which won a prize and was shown nationally.

Still, Nozoe was a truly brave man, for he knew his lifework would lead to social ostracism, a fate few Japanese would accept for the sake of a cause. Once again I wondered what drove people like Yachita, or Nozoe, or Ienaga, or indeed Anja Rosmus. What motivated them to carry on their lonely quests? I asked Nozoe, and he answered vaguely that he wished to pass on the truth to the next generation. It was hard to get him to say much more than that. But he has written about his school days: about the schoolmaster who had ordered his pupils to spit on the Chinese. He was a bully, typical of the time, who forced the boys to beat one another with sticks to harden their spirits. But after the war was lost, this martinet, who had been so full of belligerent talk about fighting the war against the Anglo-American demons to the end, simply carried on without the slightest indication that he had done or said anything wrong. The same was true of the other teachers, who had supported the war, with the backing of the village notables. "It was for that reason," wrote Nozoe, "that I developed a visceral distrust for the type of people who call themselves teachers."

I think it is this basic distrust, this refusal to be told what to think by authorities, this cussed insistence on asking questions, on hearing the truth, that binds together Nozoe, Rosmus, and others like them. There are not many such people in Japan, or anywhere else for that matter. And I suspect they are not much liked wherever they live. If Rosmus was less isolated in Germany than Nozoe and Yachita are in Japan, it is only because the Federal Republic was and still is a more open society. There were always lawyers and newspapers and academics to champion her cause. But in Japan the individual scholar finds much less institutional support.

As far as most people are concerned, however, the difference between nations is less wide than many might imagine. When directly confronted with unpleasant truths, Japanese react pretty much like Germans. Most either turn away or beat their breasts. I was shown a questionnaire prepared for a small exhibition of the Hanaoka Incident held in 1990 in Odate. The visitors were asked to write down their ages, how they knew of the Incident, and what they felt about it. The responses were similar to the ones scribbled in visitors' books at German memorial places—the same expressions of "national" shame.

"Japanese are the most barbaric people in the world!" wrote a man in his thirties. "I feel deeply sorry as a Japanese." He had heard about the Incident from his parents. Another visitor, a woman in her sixties, who had known about it from the time it happened, wrote: "I feel shame as a person from Hanaoka, and as a Japanese. It might be a small thing compared to the Incident, but I would like people to know that my own father used Chinese workers to manufacture things for him, while hiding behind his superiors by pretending that they had issued the orders." Public confession—or, as the Chinese Communists called it, "self-criticism"—is not confined to Christian cultures.

Yachita had grown up as a Christian, but said he was "embarrassed" to say so. He regarded himself as a secular man, a socialist. Christians are not rare in northeastern towns. As they did everywhere else, the missionaries attracted the poor. Yachita's wife and children were neither Christians nor interested in his work on the Chinese. His wife nagged him about his frequent trips to China. She wanted him to take her on holiday to Europe. His daughter had helped him distribute leaflets for the trade union when she was small, but drifted away from her father's activities as soon as she grew older. His son had never shown any interest. Yachita smiled as he told me this.

Socialists from Christian backgrounds often have a religious bent, however secular they think they are. I did not detect this in Yachita. There was nothing zealous about him—or, indeed, about Nozoe. Why had Yachita become so involved in the Hanaoka Incident? Why did history have him in its grip? Like Nozoe's, his answers were vague when I asked him, but later in the conversation, after I thought my question had been forgotten, he came back to it. When he was still in his twenties, he had spent some years in Kyoto, working in a post office. He had been shocked when he was told not to drink from a particular cup, because that cup was only for *burakumin*, the descendants of former outcasts, who did polluting work, such as animal slaughter and leather tanning. Social discrimination against such people is especially strong in the central and southern regions. In the north, perhaps because it was settled more recently, the problem hardly exists. Yachita didn't stay in Kyoto, but the experience had marked him: "I decided I would always be on the side of those who are discriminated against. That is why I am interested in finding out what happened in Hanaoka. It is not just about getting financial compensation for the survivors. It is more than that. I want the Japanese to admit the truth and restore the pride of their victims."

Yachita drove me to the place where the old community hall had been, where the Chinese, tied up in the yard, had been spat on and beaten, and where some of them were tortured to death. There were some handsome trees in the yard. The ground was dark and flinty. "That pine tree," said Yachita, pointing at the oldest-looking tree, "must have witnessed the murders." Facing the new community center were three prominent sculptures: a bronze bust of a man and beside him a large stone whose polished surface was inscribed with a song. Next to the bust was a sculpture of a nude woman leading a flock of ducks to the edge of a bronze platform. Tucked behind the trees, virtually invisible if you weren't looking for it, was a tiny plaque inscribed with the history of the Hanaoka Incident.

Yachita said the nude woman leading her ducks marked the spot where the old community hall used to be. There was no text to indicate this. There was no inscription on the sculpture at all. I found out from a pamphlet, entitled *Peace City Odate*, distributed by the city of Odate, that the sculpture was called *Peace Sculpture: Pledge to the Friendship Between China and Japan*. The same pamphlet explained (in English and Japanese): "Based on the idea that PEACE is the root principle of good living, Odate became the first city in Akita to declare itself an 'Antinuclear Peace City' on December 12, 1983, and has promoted the goal of a peaceful city for each and every resident." Not everyone wanted the peace sculpture, nor was the antinuclear policy entirely to everybody's liking. But these were the products of a socialist city administration.

The bust of the man caught my attention, but not because it was in any way unusual; such busts of prominent local figures can be seen everywhere in Japan. This one, however, was particularly grandiose. Smiling across the yard, with a look of deep satisfaction over his many achievements, was Hatazawa Kyoichi. His various functions and titles were inscribed below his bust. He had been an important provincial bureaucrat, a pillar of the sumo wrestling establishment, a member of various Olympic committees, and the recipient of some of the highest honors in Japan. The song engraved on the smooth stone was composed in praise of his rich life. There was just one small gap in Hatazawa's life story as related on his monument: the years from 1941 to 1945 were missing. Yet he had not been idle then, for he was the man in charge of labor at the Hanaoka mines.

"That is how much the Japanese care about the past," said Yachita. "I couldn't bring myself to show this to our Chinese visitors. I was too ashamed." He had no need to feel that, though I could understand his embarrassment. But to me the bust of Hatazawa Kyoichi signified more than public indifference to painful truths. I looked again at the smug smile of this successful local boss and I understood what drove the likes of Nozoe and Yachita to live the lives they do.

CLEARING UP THE RUINS

IF *The Tin Drum* is the world's most famous fictional chronicle of World War II, then its main character, Oskar Matzerath, the boy who stopped growing when he was three, is the war's most famous literary witness. Oskar Matzerath, with his tin drum and his glass-shattering voice, is the ideal memorialist. He has the magical wonder of a precocious child. Nothing, however embarrassing to adults, escapes his gaze. And the beat of his drum bears witness to the horrors he has seen. At the same time, Oskar embodies adult fears and longings, above all the longing for shelter in the dark, warm, womblike world under the voluminous skirts of his grandmother, Anna Bronski, sitting at the edge of a potato field in Kashubia. There, under the "wide skirt," the child is in a world where there is nothing yet to remember, and the adult can forget that anything ever happened.

Günter Grass's magisterial novel is the most famous child's view of the past, but by no means the only one. Since few German adults who lived through the Third Reich cared to dwell on their experiences, many novels on the period were written by men and women who were children at the time. Just as in Japan, there were military accounts, written mostly by veterans. But for daily life under the Nazi dictatorship, we must turn, for the most part, to the sometimes magical, sometimes tortured perspectives of the child.

Daily life in wartime Japan has been described much less often. Even so, some of the best novels on the last stages of the war—when the war arrived, so to speak, in Japan—are about children, or written from the child's point of view. Ibuse Masuji's masterpiece about Hiroshima, *Black Rain*, is about an innocent young girl. And Oe Kenzaburo's early novel *Me-mushiri, Ko-uchi* (*Nip the Buds, Shoot the Kids*) is about a group of children evacuated to a remote village. The story is a kind of *Lord of the Flies* in reverse: the children are gentle and innocent victims in a cruel and barbarous adult world. Innocence versus evil is indeed what most books about children in war, in Japan as well as in Germany, have in common.

Such novels offer a sentimental and often moralistic view of a static universe, of an adult world that is intrinsically evil. And although most of them are political, the stories they tell are drained of politics. Because the adult world is wicked, it cannot really change, except perhaps in some distant utopia. This is not really a child's perception, but an adult's longing for childhood innocence, for a grandmother's protective skirts.

When the war is lost, Oskar decides to grow. He buries his tin drum in the sand, and grows, but he cannot grow naturally; so he grows into a humpbacked monster. And although he lives to be thirty, he never outgrows his enchanted childhood world, where demons continue to haunt him: "Always somewhere behind me, the Black Witch. Now ahead of me, too, facing me, Black . . ."

In a small town in the northeast of Japan there is a stone monument, two meters high, one meter wide, erected by members of a veterans' association in 1961, just as the Japanese Economic Miracle began. They were not just ordinary veterans, however, for they had all been purged as war criminals during the American occupation. There is an inscription on the face of the monument which reads: "Monument to the Stupid." It is not clear whom this refers to. The officers themselves? Or their judges from the victorious Allies, who purged and prosecuted at random and sometimes unfairly? Or mankind for its orgies of self-destruction? Probably all three; everyone is stupid, except, of course, the innocent child.

On the fiftieth anniversary of the attack on Pearl Harbor, the mayor of Honolulu asked President Bush to invite Japanese officials to the ceremony only on condition that they apologize for the war. Then, he said, "a new era" could begin. The Japanese government refused. Instead, the deputy chief cabinet secretary, Ishihara Nobuo, said that "the entire world is responsible for the war." The United States should apologize too, he said. "Because war could not be avoided, all those involved should reflect . . . It will take tens or hundreds of years before the correct judgment is delivered on who is responsible for the war."

The Japanese had flunked the test. They were not invited. They were still a dangerous people. Which is what the president of the Pearl Harbor Survivors' Association had thought all along. When told about the plan to invite Japanese veterans, he said: "Would you expect the Jews to invite the Nazis to an event where they were talking about the Holocaust?"

The comparison between Pearl Harbor and the Holocaust is of course absurd, and the old survivors of the Imperial Japanese Navy are far from being Nazis. But the question in American minds was understandable: could one trust a nation whose official spokesmen still refused to admit that their country had been responsible for starting a war? In these Japanese evasions there was something of the petulant child, stamping its foot, shouting that it had done nothing wrong, because everybody did it. This claim to be like everybody else was particularly odd, since one is so used to Japanese describing themselves as unique, culturally, ethnically, politically, historically.

It is tempting to see this childishness as a cultural trait, not a unique one perhaps, but nonetheless conspicuous in Japan. There is something intensely irritating about the infantilism of postwar Japanese culture: the ubiquitous chirping voices of women pretending to be girls; the Disneylandish architecture of Japanese main streets, where everything is reduced to a sugary cuteness; the screeching "television talents" rolling about and carrying on like kindergarten clowns; the armies of blue-suited salarymen straphanging on the subway trains, reading boys' comics, the maudlin love for old school songs and cuddly mama-sans.

Japan seems at times not so much a nation of twelve-year-olds, to repeat General MacArthur's phrase, as a nation of people longing to be twelve-year-olds, or even younger, to be at that golden age when everything was secure and responsibility and conformity were not yet required. There they sit, the Japanese, in their pachinko halls, in long straight rows, glassy-eyed in front of pinball machines, oblivious to both past and present, watching the cascade of little silver balls, while listening to the din of the *Battleship March* beating away in the background.

Yet I do not believe that the Japanese are congenitally a childish people, any more than I believe they are an intrinsically dangerous people. There are no dangerous peoples; there are only dangerous situations, which are the result, not of laws of nature or history, or of national character, but of political arrangements. To be sure, these arrangements are affected by cultural and historical circumstances, but they are never determined by them. If one injects politics into the enchanted Disney world of postwar Japan, things come into sharper focus. For General MacArthur was right: in 1945, the Japanese people *were* political children. Until then, they had been forced into a position of complete submission to a state run by authoritarian bureaucrats and military men, and to a religious cult whose high priest was also formally chief of the armed forces and supreme monarch of the empire.

The situation has changed since then, but not enough. Judged to be a dangerous people, the Japanese were forced, not least by MacArthur himself, to retreat from the evil world and hide under America's skirts. In effect, Japan has been subject to a generous version of the Versailles Treaty: loss of sovereignty without financial squeeze. Japanese were encouraged to get rich, while matters of war were taken out of their dangerous hands. The state was run by virtually the same bureaucracy that ran the Japanese empire, and the electoral system was rigged to help the same corrupt conservative party to stay in power for almost forty years. This arrangement suited the United States, as well as Japanese bureaucrats, LDP politicians, and the large industrial combines, for it ensured that Japan remained a rich and stable ally against Communism. But it also helped to stifle public debate and stopped the Japanese from growing up politically. As far as the history of World War II was concerned, the debate got stuck in the late 1940s, around the beginning of the Cold War: bureaucrats and conservative politicians continued to legitimize their grip on power by justifying or at least ignoring the past, while the small and largely leftist opposition tilted its spears at the ghosts of militarism and the wickedness of man.

There are many people who believe that the Japanese are incorrigible, that they are doomed to be a dangerous, inscrutable, and isolated people forever. There are Japanese who believe this too. Sakaguchi Ango wrote just after the war that the Japanese, "faced with their history, had been like children following their fate." They would develop as human beings only if they would degenerate to a level of basic human desires, stripped of false modesty, customs, traditions, and ideals. They did indeed degenerate for a short while, he said, but human beings are not strong enough to stand this kind of freedom for long. They soon build up a new system, a new set of customs, traditions, and ideals to fence them in. This new system will inevitably be built on the ruins of the old one: "Man cannot live without . . . inventing a samurai code or worshipping an emperor."

If Ango is right, if the Japanese are indeed incorrigible, it is desirable that Japan's capacity to use military power should be controlled by a pacifistic constitution and an outside force forever. Or, if they are corrigible, then the status quo should persist until the Japanese show a change of attitude, face their past more honestly, apologize to their former adversaries more profusely, and so on. But perhaps we have got the Japanese problem backward. Without political responsibility—precisely over matters of war and peace—Japan cannot develop a grown-up attitude toward the past. Political change must come first; the mentality will follow. A constitutional change is only part of this; a change of government is at least as important. For only a new government can break with the postwar order, whose roots are still tainted by the wartime regime. Willy Brandt went down on his knees in the Warsaw ghetto, after a functioning democracy had been established in the Federal Republic of Germany, not before. But Japan, shielded from the evil world, has grown into an Oskar Matzerath: opportunistic, stunted, and haunted by demons, which it tries to ignore by burying them in the sand, like Oskar's drum.

When Kim Young Sam, the first democratically elected civilian President of South Korea, was asked by Japanese journalists what the Japanese government should do to compensate the former Korean sex slaves of the Imperial Japanese Army, he answered: "It is not your money we want. It is the truth we want you to make clear. Only then will the problem be solved."

Barely a year later, in the summer of 1993, four years after the fall of the Berlin Wall, it finally happened: the monopoly of the Liberal Democratic Party was broken by a coalition of young conservatives who had left the LDP, the socialist party, and Komeito, a Buddhist party. The new Prime Minister was Hosokawa Morihiro, the grandson of Prince Konoe Fumimaro, Prime Minister at the time of the Nanking Massacre in 1937 and of the signing of the Axis Pact in 1940. Konoe committed suicide in 1945, after being charged as a Class A war criminal. One of Hosokawa's first acts, as the new Prime Minister of Japan, was to state in public that Japan's military actions in the 1930s and 1940s amounted to "an aggressive war and a wrong war." It was only a beginning, but the signs were good. And with a glimmer of new hope, I thought back to my last glimpse of the orthodoxy which had prevailed for forty-eight years. I caught it in, of all places, Disneyland.

Tokyo Disneyland is located in the bleak suburban sprawl between Tokyo and Narita Airport. It is almost an exact copy of the Disneyland in California, except for one entertainment, which is unique to Tokyo. It is called Meet the World, and is sponsored by Matsushita Electric, one of the most successful corporations in postwar Japan. Meet the World is inside a large white dome, containing a revolving cinema, which smells vaguely of plastic. On display was a potted history of Japan's relations with the outside world. The story was told by a friendly heron, with a chirpy female voice, to two small children, who were actually robots. It was a rather selective history, however: the influence of Chinese civilization was acknowledged, but only to make the point that Japan turned it into something uniquely its own. Korea, a much closer neighbor, was ignored.

But the most interesting part, the bit that I was waiting for, was the period between 1895 and 1945, when Japan's meetings with the world were marked by a succession of wars. It came right after the arrival on stage of Commodore Perry's "black ship"—which in reality appeared off the Japanese coast in 1853—like a malevolent ghost. The ship faded out and a cannon was projected on the screen, followed by a bang, and then the theater went dark. "Ooh," said the child robots, "it's sooo dark!" Yes, said the chirpy heron, and "now let's turn to the future." Which led to the grand finale: a quick succession of slide photographs of kindly Japanese explaining various instruments of high technology to grateful foreigners—Malaysians, Indians, Chinese . . . Americans. A song swelled on the soundtrack, with a refrain that went, on and on, over and over: "We meet the world with love, ah, we meet the world with love, we meet the world with love, ah . . ."

With the music still playing, the lights came on. I looked

around, and saw that my daughter and I were the only ones left in the theater.

One of the most beautiful metaphors of history is Walter Benjamin's description of Paul Klee's painting *Angelus Novus*. The Angelus Novus is the angel of history; he has a human face, but the wings and feet of a bird: "His face is turned toward the past. Where we perceive a chain of events, he sees one single catastrophe which keeps piling ruin upon ruin and hurls it in front of his feet. The angel would like to stay, awaken the dead, and make whole what has been smashed. But a storm is blowing from Paradise; it has got caught in his wings with such violence that the angel can no longer close them. The storm irresistibly propels him into the future, to which his back is turned, while the pile of debris before him grows skyward. The storm is what we call progress."

The idea of progress, as well as British bombs, turned Dresden into a city of ruins and monstrosities. Walking through the hideous streets of central Dresden, seeing the few bits and pieces of the old city, like fragments of a beautiful antique jar, produced in me precisely the irrational feeling of guilt by association that I have argued against in the cases of Auschwitz and Hiroshima. The reason had little to do with the respective death tolls (roughly 30,000 in Dresden), for mass killing is shocking, whatever the actual numbers. (As Christopher Isherwood said to the man who pointed out that more Jews were murdered than homosexuals: "What are you, in real estate?") And the feeling of special regret was not particularly noble. For what is so shocking about the bombing of Dresden is that it smashed in one night the accumulated beauty of centuries. Dresden, like Prague or Venice, was one of the architectural wonders of the world. Its destruction was an act of perversity, like putting an ax to a Chippendale chair, or knifing a Michelangelo, or burning a priceless library. It was all the more perverse since there was no compelling strategic reason for it. Which is not to say that the bombing of ugly slums is any less ghastly, in human terms, than the destruction of Dresden's baroque heart. It's just that being in the new, empty hole of Dresden, where there once was a heart, is to be constantly aware of what was lost.

Parts of the old city could have been saved after the war. Enough was left of some of the palaces and churches to make restoration feasible, as in Nuremberg or Munich. But the first Communist leader of East Germany, Walter Ulbricht, decided that the past had to be eradicated. "Dresden, More Beautiful Than Ever" ("*Dresden, schöner als je*") was his slogan, and for the second time the city fell victim to perversity: art historians were forced to draw up plans for the final destruction of Dresden's remains, and party hacks took commissions to design the frightful city that was to be the showcase of socialism. The Sophienkirche, opposite the eighteenth-century Zwinger Palace, was the finest Gothic church in Dresden. It was torn down and a squat concrete bunker, housing a workers' canteen, was built in its place. This was Ulbricht's idea of progress.

But not all the rubble was cleared. The Zwinger Palace was restored in the 1960s, as were one or two other ruins, and the remains of the eighteenth-century Frauenkirche were left as they were, because neither Ulbricht nor anybody else could agree on what to build in its place. Thus the sad pile of stones became a warning place, a memorial (to cite the official plaque) "to the tens of thousands of dead, and an inspiration to the living in their struggle against imperialist barbarism and for the peace and happiness of man."

I asked the new curator of the municipal museum, Matthias Griebel, what exactly was meant by imperialist barbarism. Griebel answered: "They meant every imperialist war: Israel in the Sinai, America in Vietnam, everything but socialist wars."

Griebel, whose shaven head and luxuriant whiskers made him resemble a great German eagle, was one of the small number of people who had tried to keep historical consciousness alive in Dresden, by organizing lectures and informal exhibitions. At first the Communist government opposed this kind of thing, for Dresden's "feudal" past belonged in the dustbin of history. It was only in the 1980s, when Communist dogma had utterly lost its popular appeal, that the regime tried to bolster its credentials by claiming a historical legitimacy: from Thomas Münzer, the peasant rebel, to Frederick of Prussia. Even Karl May, the nineteenth-century romantic, whose novels about Old Shatterhand, the German hero of the Wild West, were read avidly by Hitler and Einstein alike, was declared to be one of us. His house, "Villa Shatterhand," can be visited just down the Elbe, northwest of Dresden.

A few miles up the Elbe, on the other side of town, is Pirna, a crumbling but quaint little town with fine nineteenth-century villas and the odd bit of late Gothic architecture. I went there in search of a historical site which is not mentioned in any guidebook of the Dresden region. There was an old hospital there, once used for mental patients. I knew it was still there for I had seen photographs of it. And Griebel confirmed its existence. The mental hospital was not insignificant, for it was there that doctors first experimented on their patients with the murderous gas known as Zyklon B. More than 10,000 people died at the Sonnenstein Euthanasia Institute.

I had some trouble locating the place. An old lady cheerfully sent me up a hill, but then I got lost. "What did you say it was?" The former Euthanasia Institute. "When was this?" The Hitler period. "Sorry, I wouldn't know about that."

But I found it in the end. In a pleasant park next to Sonnenstein Castle were several turn-of-the-century buildings. I entered a villa with yellow walls which had a sign that said: "Sauna facilities for sick and old people." A young woman asked me what I wanted. I told her. She winced and said: "No, it wasn't here. We only deal with patients for specialized treatment here. You want the other building over there where they used to have a turbine factory."

The "building over there" had a rusted wire fence around it. It looked sinister enough to have been a Euthanasia Institute. And there was a plaque which commemorated one Albert Barthel, "our party comrade, murdered by the Nazis in 1942."

Yet this wasn't it either. I walked into a room and saw several young people having their lunch. They turned out to be deacons who looked after retarded children. "The former Euthanasia Institute? No, no, thank God it wasn't in this room. No, it was in the building next door."

I peered into the cellars of the building next door, a rather elegant French-style villa. There was no plaque anywhere. The grass grew wild and high around the bolted door. I listened to the birds sing in the rustling trees and I thought of the pile of teddy bears I had seen lying about in the hall of the house of deacons.

Architecture, said Mr. Griebel, is time expressed in stone. The thing about Dresden is that the stones remind its citizens of times they would like to forget. The Third Reich is but a ghostly nightmare, but the dictatorship from Ulbricht to Honecker is still visible in every jerry-built housing project and concrete workers' canteen. You cannot blame people for feeling a deep nostalgia for the old Dresden of palaces and spires. As Griebel said, "we live in the rump of a city, which we'd dearly love to restore."

I paid a last visit to the ruins of the Frauenkirche, to make a note of the memorial plaque. But I found that it had gone. Instead, there was a fence around the rubble. A man in a blue uniform was giving orders to some workmen. I climbed over the fence to get a closer look. The uniformed man, a stocky little figure, spotted me and rushed over in great strides, flushed with anger, and shouted in a thick Saxon accent that I had no business being there: it was *streng verboten*! How typically German, I thought, as every childhood prejudice flooded back in an instant. But I obeyed his orders and retreated across the fence, away from the man, who was still sputtering with rage. I took one more look at the workmen, who were piling stone upon stone. In a year or two, the Frauenkirche would be there again, fully restored in its old glory, as though nothing had happened at all.

    After the war, Oskar Matzerath and his friend Klepp start a jazz band. Their tour of West Germany takes them to Düsseldorf, or, to be exact, the stretch of the Rhine between Düsseldorf and Kaiserswerth, where they play ragtime music on the riverbank. The time is 1949, one year after the currency reform which saw the birth of the Deutsche Mark. They are asked to play at an expensive, "high-class" nightclub called the Onion Cellar. It is done up in a fake old German style, with bull's-eye windowpanes, and an enamel sign outside, hanging from wrought-iron gallows. When the club is full, the main entertainment begins. The guests are handed little chopping boards with paring knives and an onion. And what does the onion do? "It did what the world and the sorrows of the world could not do: it brought forth a round human tear. It made them cry. At last they were able to cry again. To cry properly, without restraint, to cry like mad."

    The Onion Cellar is, of course, an expensive and temporary cure for the "inability to mourn," the moral and spiritual numbness that overcame the German people after the war. Many thoughtful Germans I have met are irritated by this phrase: inability to mourn. Mourn what? they ask. Mourn whom? You mourn loved ones you have lost. But, say my liberal German friends, how can you mourn for the victims you have murdered? Reflection, yes; apology, certainly; compensation, of course; but mourning, surely not. And so, in liberal, thoughtful circles (the circles expected to welcome nosy foreigners in their midst) there has been—still is—much reflection and apology. But the mourning of the German dead—the soldiers, and the civilians killed by Allied bombs, or by vengeful Polish, Czech, or Slovak neighbors, who drove them from their homes—such mourning was an embarrassing affair, left largely to right-wing nationalists and nostalgic survivors, pining for their lost homelands.

In village squares and churchyards in the western half of Germany there are many memorials to the war dead of World War I. There are very few reminders of those who died in the second war, except in the rancid cellars of provincial beer halls, where foreigners are less than welcome. In fact, there appear to be more World War II memorials in the East, perhaps because guilt was never an issue in the Democratic Republic.

Helmut Kohl tried to redress the balance, clumsily, tactlessly, by dragging Ronald Reagan to the cemetery in Bitburg. He was rightly condemned. But traveling through Germany, I often felt that too much apology could become a form of self-abasement. Mourning, after all, has its purpose. The ritual expression of grief and loss strengthens the sense of continuity and community. Yet it was precisely these things that thoughtful, liberal Germans were wary of: the national community, the *Gemeinschaft*, had been twisted into murderous racism, and cultural continuity had become a delicate matter in a nation whose history was smeared with blood.

I also detected, during my year in Berlin, in 1991 and 1992, an interesting generational shift in German philosemitism. Guilt was at least a partial explanation for the Israeli calendars one saw on the walls of Germans who lived through the war. But what were those young German Gentiles doing in the new "Jewish" cafés that sprang up around the façade of the old synagogue in East Berlin? Why did some young Germans go so far as to adopt the Jewish family names of their grandfathers or great-uncles? Wasn't there something odd about the way almost any Central European Jewish writer was showered with literary prizes? Residual or inherited feelings of guilt might have had something to do with this, but I believe there was something else at work: nostalgia for a culture that is lost to Germany, an attempt to identify with a past that was erased: in short, a gesture of mourning.

Marlene Dietrich was not Jewish, but she belonged to the ruined world of Jewish Berlin. The mourners who filed past her grave, after her modest burial in Berlin, were almost all under forty. This stood in contrast to the small-minded refusal of the city authorities to give her an official funeral. Dietrich, whom some Germans never forgave for wearing an American uniform when German cities were bombed, represented another Germany, with which those young mourners wished to identify.

The supposed lack of identity, of community feeling, was a cause of much soul-searching in the Federal Republic—the problem, it seemed, was that there was no more soul to search. Which is why some romantics, of both the right and the left, looked toward the eastern half of Germany as the repository of German identity. But, to me, it was the suspicion of historical mythmaking and national romanticism that made the Federal Republic intellectually bracing. I like the idea of "constitutional patriotism." Maybe it isn't enough. Perhaps more is needed to transform a once dangerous nation. But I found it hard to share the playwright Arthur Miller's worries, expressed during Germany's unification, that Germans lacked "very transcendent feelings toward the Federal Republic" and that "it does not seem to have imbued them with sublime sensations, even among those who regard it as a triumph of German civic consciousness risen from the ruins of war." Surely, Germans have had enough sublime sensations during the last hundred years. Miller was anxious that Germans might not defend their democracy in a crisis, because "it came to life without one drop of blood being shed in its birth" and it was invented by foreigners.

There will always be Germans (and their counterparts elsewhere) who would wish, in the words of a long-forgotten Nazi ideologue, to "select the stones from the ruins of German mythology, to serve, after cleaning and polishing, as the building blocks of a new German shrine [and] to build a new German *Weltanschauung* from the remains of fallen walls." But I believe there have been enough German shrines already. Let the ruins be.

Günter Grass was not the only one to worry about German unification. Most liberal anxieties on this score were the exact opposite of the worry that West Germany lacked a soul. Unification, many warned, would revive German nationalism; the brakes were off, the dangerous German people would start to shift their bulk. There was no immediate evidence of this, however. I was in Frankfurt on the night of unification, and apart from the odd firecracker popping off in the cold sky, I saw no sign of nationalist rejoicing. Comedians in a fashionable nightclub cracked feeble jokes about sacred Deutsche Marks and banana democracy. But most people stayed home, in front of the television, a night like any other. I had seen more popular enthusiasm when the German soccer team won the world cup the year before.

Then came the neo-Nazis, the shaven-headed youths screaming "*Sieg Heil!*" and waving the old battle flags. They were nasty and brutal and murderous. In 1992 there were 4,587 attacks on foreigners. Seventeen people were killed. The year before, 7,780 racist attacks were reported in Britain, but the swastikas, the slogans, the *Sieg Heil*'s, made historical comparisons in Germany irresistible. There was a hint of *Schadenfreude* in European press reports of racist German youth crimes. It was Us and Them again.

I spent one day in Halle, a broken-down East German town, waiting to see a parade of neo-Nazis. It was November 9, the anniversary of the *Kristallnacht*, as well as of the fall of the Berlin Wall. The people of Halle were terrified. The police had blocked off every main street. An old man in the main square shouted at the mayor that it was just like Hitler's time all over again. The owner of a café locked his door after letting me in and proudly showed his gun. And finally, there they were, the neo-Nazis, the young men with heads shaved on back and sides and the young women in white socks, with their long blond hair in plaits, the look of the Hitler Maidens. They were spoken to by a pudgy figure with a Viennese accent and by the British historian David Irving. The old trams of prewar design screeched on their rusty rails. Fat men in undershirts leaned from their windows and the abolished couplet of the *Deutschlandlied* ("From the Maas up to the Memel, from the Etsch up to the Belt, *Deutschland, Deutschland über alles . . ."*) filled the air. It was unpleasant and utterly ludicrous—violent children dressed up in their grandparents' clothes, history repeating itself as Grand Guignol. But it wasn't all theater. The behavior of the extremists— who, a year later, went on to burn down refugee hostels in West and East Germany, killing people, as the police stood helplessly by—proved that Germans were still capable of barbarous deeds. It was a revolting spectacle to see screaming German youths smash their boots into the faces of helpless foreigners, as the neighbors cheered and jeered. But similar or worse events in the rest of Europe—not to speak of other continents—proved that nationality, race, and culture are inadequate explanations for barbarousness. People are dangerous everywhere, when leaders acquire unlimited power and followers are given license to bully others weaker than themselves. Unbridled power leads to barbarousness, in individuals and in mobs. Auschwitz and Nanking, despite the differences in scale and style, will always stand as proof of that. But such is not the situation in the German Federal Republic, or indeed in Japan, today. Human nature has not changed, but politics have. In both countries, the rascals can be voted out. Those who choose to ignore that, and look instead for national marks of Cain, have learned nothing from the past.

The most successful German film in 1993 was *Stalingrad*, directed by Joseph Vilsmaier. It was two and a half hours of recreated horror, on the German side. At least 150,000 Germans died in the actual battle, which was a crime committed by Hitler against the Soviet people, but also against the Germans themselves. The film is mainly about German suffering, not atrocities committed against Jews and Slavs. It shows German soldiers dying of hunger, exposure, or Soviet fire. There are several ways of reading the eagerness of mostly young Germans to see *Stalingrad*. Historical curiosity might be one reason. A new German assertiveness could be another: we've had enough of Auschwitz, now let's mourn our own. This is possible. But it might also be that a new generation of Germans is capable of reflection without guilt. This may be a minority. But I think it is a larger minority than the bald-headed thugs who cannot reflect at all.

In 1992, the Filmmuseum in Munich showed a film which is hard to watch without feeling sick. It was Veit Harlan's *Jew Süss* (*Jud Süss*), the antisemitic propaganda film made under Goebbels's auspices in 1940. Ferdinand Marian plays the wicked Jew who, through his evil schemes, almost succeeds in wrecking the *Gemeinschaft* of eighteenth-century Württemberg. At the end the Jews are driven out of town like rats. The showing of the film in Munich was followed by public discussions. On one occasion, two right-wing radicals took part. They tried to deny the Holocaust. But that couldn't be helped, said the professor of German literature, who led the discussion: "It is part of being a democracy that we show such a film nonetheless."

I saw *Jew Süss* that same year, at a screening for students of the film academy in Berlin. This showing, too, was followed by a discussion. The students, mostly from western Germany, but some from the east, were in their early twenties. They were dressed in the international uniform of jeans, anoraks, and work shirts. The professor was a man in his forties, a '68er named Karsten Witte. He began the discussion by saying that he wanted the students to concentrate on the aesthetics of the film more than the story. To describe the propaganda, he said, would simply be banal: "We all know the 'what,' so let's talk about the 'how.' " I thought of my fellow students at the film school in Tokyo more than fifteen years before. How many of them knew the "what" of the Japanese war in Asia? Or more to the point: how many of their professors would have thought of showing them the "how," by screening old propaganda films?

Witte made some remarks about the use of music: how Bach's choral music is gradually submerged in the sound of a cantor singing a Hebrew prayer during the opening credits. One of the students, a man of about twenty, raised his hand and said he had noticed a similar trick in the visual presentation: how the coat of arms of Württemberg dissolved into a sign in Hebrew. Another student observed that snow fell in the final scene of the wicked Jew's public execution. He attempted to paraphrase the intended message: "The snow cleanses Germany, purifies the land. Winter will then turn to spring, the season of regeneration." Someone else remarked that the wealth of the Württemberg court was always on display: fine paintings in large rooms, great palaces, and so on, whereas Jewish wealth was hidden away in secret cupboards, in cramped, fetid rooms. "This is meant to show that German wealth was the fruit of a long and glorious tradition, of history and culture, while Jewish riches were nothing but money."

Karsten Witte, whose pale skin, red lips, and short-cropped blond hair made him look curiously like the Nordic ideal in Nazi art, was clearly pleased with his students. They had analyzed the film intently, without missing a trick. The more grotesque examples of racist propaganda provoked bursts of quiet laughter, but their concentration was intense. I listened to their comments, sharp, reflective, critical without being moralistic, confident but never aggressive, above all unblocked by guilt. And I remembered something Oda Makoto, the novelist and peace activist, had said to me when I visited him in Japan during the Gulf War. I was educated from the point of view of the victim, he said, whereas he had been raised as an aggressor. Sitting in that tiny screening room in Berlin, five minutes away from the building where Goebbels had broadcast his radio speeches, I realized with a sense of relief that we had all been watching this odious film from exactly the same point of view.

NOTES

1. WAR AGAINST THE WEST

19 "Amos Oz was interviewed": Amos Oz, *Frankfurter Allgemeine Zeitung*, February 14, 1991.

20 " 'No blood for oil' ": Wolf Biermann, *Die Zeit*, February 1991.

22 " 'The heart of Pietism' ": Gordon Craig, *The Germans* (New York: Penguin Books, 1984), p. 87.

25 "He compared Saddam to Hitler": H. M. Enzensberger, *Der Spiegel*, February 1991.

35 "the most unique fusion": Albrecht Hürst von Urach, *Das Geheimnis Japanischer Kraft* (Berlin: Zentralverlag der NSDAP, 1944).

36 " 'When speaking of the New World Order' ": Nakamura Tetsuo, *Asahi Shimbun*, February 22, 1991.

37 "Hayashi's anti-Western nationalism": Hayashi Fusao, *Daitowa Senso Koteiron* (Tokyo: Yamato Bunko, 1964), p. 22.

38 "Several months after the Gulf War": Matsumoto Kenichi, *Tokyo Shimbun*, April 8, 1991.

44 " 'For the ancient Greeks' ": Aurel Kolnai, *The War Against the West* (London: Victor Gollancz, 1938), p. 24.

2. ROMANCE OF THE RUINS

49 " 'The ruin of the city' ": Stephen Spender, *European Witness* (New York: Reynal & Hitchcock, 1946), p. 15.

50 "How to purge": Lingua Tertii Imperii, or LTI, is the title of Victor Klemperer's book: *LTI* (Halle: Niemeyer Verlag, 1957).

50 " 'hearing such words as nation' ": Yoshimoto Takaaki, *Seiji Shiso* (Tokyo: Daiwa Shobo, 1956), p. 72.

52 "Salomon describes the Americans": Ernst von Salomon, *Der Fragenbogen* (Frankfurt: Rowolt, 1951), p. 648. *The Questionnaire*, trans. Constantine Fitz Gibbon (New York: Doubleday, 1954).

53 "he described the bombing raids": Sakaguchi Ango, *Darakuron* (Tokyo: Kadokawa Shoten, 1946), pp. 95, 96.

54 " 'There was a swell' ": Wolf Dietrich Schnurre, quoted in *Vaterland Muttersprache: Deutsche Schriftsteller und ihr Staat von 1945 bis heute* (Berlin: Wagenbach, 1979).

55 "Böll identified himself ": Heinrich Böll, *"Bekenntnis zur Trümmerliteratur,"* 1952.

55 " 'Consumers' ": Heinrich Böll, *Hierzulande* (1960), pp. 367, 373.

56 "The 'inability to mourn' ": Alexander and Margarethe Mitscherlich, *The Inability to Mourn* (New York: Grove Press, 1975).

62 " 'All those who were purged' ": Letter from Helmuth Wohltat to Ministerialdirigent Dr. Reinhard, June 30, 1951, at the Bundeswirtschaftsministerium.

65 "a masterpiece in the short history": Nosaka Akiyuki, *American Hijiki*, trans. J. Rubin, in *Contemporary Japanese Literature* (New York: Alfred A. Knopf, 1977).

67 "He remembers how hungry": Oshima Nagisa, *Taikenteki Sengo Eizoron* (Tokyo: Asahi Shimbunsha, 1975), p. 72.

3. AUSCHWITZ

69 "The past . . . is in our bones": Christian Meier, *Vierzig Jahre nach Auschwitz: Deutsche Geschichtserrinerung heute* (Munich: Deutschen Kunstverlag, 1987), pp. 75, 63.

71 " 'One comes to understand' ": George Steiner, *Language and Silence: Essays 1958–1966* (London: Faber & Faber, 1967; New York: Atheneum, 1967), p. 137.

71 " 'These *Sprichworter*' ": Stephen Spender, *European Witness*, p. 7.

73 " 'the remaining rudiments' ": Hans-Jürgen Syberberg, *Hitler: A Film for Germany*, trans. Joachim Neugroschel (New York: Farrar, Straus and Giroux, 1982), p. 9.

74 "Peter Weiss visited Auschwitz": The same visit is described by Amos Elon in his book *Journey Through Darkness* (London: Andre Deutsch, 1967).

82 " 'through the thousand darknesses' ": Peter Demetz, *After the Fires: Writing in the Germanies, Austria, and Switzerland* (New York: Harcourt Brace Jovanovich, 1986), p. 47.

82 "Weiss wrote a play": Ibid., p. 55.

83 " 'spiritual labor' ": Quoted in A. Söllner's *Peter Weiss und die Deutschen* (Wiesbaden: Westdeutscher Verlag, 1988), p. 184.

83 "One of Hochhuth's few": Marcel Reich-Ranicki, *Die Zeit*, March 6, 1964.

83 " 'there is not a single aspect' ": Demetz, *After the Fires*, p. 29.

84 " 'One cannot really describe it' ": Elon, *Journey Through a Haunted Land*, p. 244.

86 " 'As the teller' ": *Das Brandopfer*, by A. Goes (Frankfurt: S. Fischer Verlag, 1954). The new preface was written in 1965.

87 "He told his story": Wolfgang Koeppen, *Jacob Littner's Aufzeichnungen aus einem Erdloch* (Frankfurt: Jüdischer Verlag, 1992).

88 "An American television series": Anton Kaes, *From Hitler to Heimat: The Return of History as Film* (Cambridge: Harvard University Press, 1989), p. 31.

89 "the Americans have stolen": Ibid., p. 184.

89 " 'the last stage' ": Heiner Müller, interview in *Transatlantik* (Berlin), July 1990.

90 "After *Holocaust*": *Holocaust—Briefe an den WDR*, ed. Heiner Lichtenstein and Michael Schmid Ospach (Wuppertal: Peter Hammer, 1982).

91 " 'he doesn't have to think' ": Martin Walser, *Über Deutschland reden* (Frankfurt: Suhrkamp, 1989), p. 25.

4. HIROSHIMA

97 "Hiroshima . . . should have been left": Uno Masami, *Doru ga Kami ni Naru Hi* (Tokyo: Bungeishunju, 1987), p. 234.

98 "One of the more eccentric books": Koochi Akira, *Hiroshima no Sora ni Hiraite Rakkasa* (Tokyo: Daiwa Shobo, 1985).

99 " 'this historical amnesia' ": *Die Tageszeitung*, January 18, 1991.

100 "As late as 1949": Kyoko Hirano, *Mr. Smith Goes to Tokyo: Japanese Cinema Under the American Occupation 1945–1952* (Washington, D.C.: Smithsonian Institution Press, 1992), p. 62.

100 "In 1983, a compendium": *Nihonno Genbaku Bungakiu* (Tokyo: Horupu, 1983).

101 "films like *Hiroshima*": Donald Richie and Joseph L. Anderson, *The Japanese Film* (New York: Grove Press, 1960), p. 219.

101 " 'something that occurs' ": *From Hiroshima: Three Witnesses*, ed. and trans. Richard Minnear (Princeton: Princeton University Press, 1990).

101 "All the quasi-religious elements": Oda Makoto, *The Bomb*, trans. D. H. Whittaker (Tokyo: Kodansha International, 1990).

102 "His vision of the end": *From Hiroshima: Three Witnesses*, p. 102.

105 " 'disgusted once again' ": *Asahi Shimbun*, July 20, 1992.

105 "Only a British writer": Alan Booth, *Asahi Evening News*, July 20, 1992.

106 "One of the few literary masterpieces": Ibuse Masuji, *Black Rain*, trans. John Bester (Tokyo: Kodansha International, 1969), p. 283.

5. NANKING

115 "His video and his booklet": The video is entitled *Katararenakatta Senso* (*Invasion: The War That Could Not Be Discussed*). The booklet is called . . . *So Shite, Mina Senso ni Itta* (. . . *And So We All Went to War*).

116 "She made this distinction": Ruth Benedict, *The Chrysanthemum and the Sword: Patterns of Japanese Culture* (London: Routledge & Kegan Paul, 1967; New York: Houghton Mifflin, 1989; first published in 1946).

117 "The story made a snappy headline": *Tokyo Nichinichi Shimbun*, November 30, 1937.

117 " 'After we occupied' ": Quoted in Honda Katsuichi, "*Nankin e no Michi*" ("The Road to Nanking") (Tokyo: Asahi Bunko, 1989).

117 "He wrote it up": Honda Katsuichi, *Chugoku no Tabi* (*A Journey to China*) (Tokyo: Asahi Bunko, 1981).

117 "In 1984, an anti-Honda book": Tanaka Masaaki, "*Nankin Gyakusatsu*" *no Kyoko* (*The Fabrication of the "Nanking Massacre"*) (Tokyo: Nihon Kyobunsha, 1984).

120 "Ienaga Saburo, for example, wrote": Ienaga Saburo, *The Pacific War, 1931–1945* (New York: Pantheon, 1978), p. 187.

120 "Heiner Müller observed": Heiner Müller in *Transatlantik* (Berlin), July 1990.

132 " 'Killing enemy soldiers' ": Ishikawa Tatsuzo, *Ikiteiru Heitai* (*Living Soldiers*), quoted in Donald Keene, *Dawn to the West* (New York: Holt, Rinehart and Winston, 1984), p. 913.

6. HISTORY ON TRIAL

143 "few things have done more": Hellmut Becker, *Quantität und Qualität: Grundfragen der Bildungspolitik* (Freiburg: Rombach, 1968), p. 74.

145 "When the American chief prosecutor": Kranzbuhler, 14 DePaul L.R. 333, 1965.

145 " 'The less the Nuremberg tribunal' ": Eric Reger in *Vaterland Muttersprache* (Berlin: Wagenbach, 1979), p. 35.

145 " 'a trial never seen before' ": *Süddeutsche Zeitung*, quoted in Klaus R. Scherpe, *Erzungener Alltag*, in *Nuchkriegsliteratur in Westdeutschland 1945–49*, eds. J. Hermand, H. Peitsch, K. R. Scherpe (Berlin: Argument, 1982).

147 " 'one of the four chief prosecutors' ": Christian Geissler in *Vaterland Muttersprache*, p. 219.

149 "Stephen Spender ran into a friend": *European Witness*, p. 221.

150 " 'For us Germans' ": Karl Jaspers, *Die Schuldfrage: Für Völkermord gibt es keine Verjährung*. My translation is not meant as a criticism of E. B. Ashton's translation, published as *The Question of German Guilt* (New York: Dial, 1947).

151 "Peter Weiss, in his play": Peter Weiss, *Die Ermittlung* (Frankfurt: Suhrkamp Verlag, 1965). *The Investigation*, trans. Jon Swan and Ulm Grosbard (New York: Atheneum, 1966).

152 "Martin Walser wrote": Martin Walser, *Unser Auschwitz* (Berlin: Kursbuch, 1965).

157 "He set out his views": Joachim Gauck, *Die Stasi-Akten* (Hamburg: Rowolt, 1992).

161 "confrontation with Japan was inevitable": Hasegawa Michiko, *Chuo Koron*, April 1983, quoted in *Japan Echo*, vol. XI, 1984.

161 "In a standard history textbook": *Nihonshi* (Tokyo: Yamakawade, 1985).

161 "West German textbooks": *Grundkurs Deutsche Geschichte* (Frankfurt: Cornelsen, 1988).

163 "The story of Unit 731": *A Bruise—Terror of the 731 Corps*, prod. Yoshinaga Haruko, Tokyo Broadcasting System.

163 "But the first time": Morimura Seiichi, *Akuma no Hoshoku* (Tokyo: Banseisha, 1982).

163 "Japanese leaders should have been tried": Hata Kunihiko, *Shokun*, August 1987.

165 "In 1970": Kinoshita Junji, *Between God and Man: A Judgement on War Crimes (Kami to Hito to no Aida)*, trans. Eric J. Gangloff (Tokyo: University of Tokyo Press, 1979).

165 "The best-known Japanese book": *War Criminal: The Life and Death of Hirota Koki (Rakujitsu Moyu)*, trans. John Bester (Tokyo: Kodansha International, 1977).

165 " 'from our point of view' ": Yoshimoto Takaaki, *Bungakusha to Senso Sekinin ni tsuite*, collected in *Seiji Shiso, Zenshu 3* (Tokyo: Daiwa Shobo, 1986).

166 " 'in Japan and in the Orient' ": Mignone, quoted in Arnold C. Brackman, *The Other Nüremberg: The Untold Story of the Tokyo War Crime Trials* (London: Collins, 1989), p. 231.

166 " 'never forget the shock' ": Ishida Takeshi, *Heiwa, Jinken, Fukushi no Seijigaku* (Tokyo: Meiseki Shoten, 1990).

168 " 'These men' ": Brackman, *The Other Nuremberg*, p. 441.

169 " 'The Japanese people' ": January 8, 1953. Letter from Foreign Minister to Zentrale Rechtschutzstelle of the Ministry of Justice, II 16338/52.

170 "the trial *was* rigged": Yamashita's trial: Meiron and Susan Harries, *Soldiers of the Sun* (New York: Random House, 1991), p. 464. Becker, *Quantität and Qualität*, p. 68.

170 "system of irresponsibilities": Maruyama Masao, *Thought and Behavior in Modern Japanese Politics*, ed. Ivan Morris (Oxford: Oxford University Press, 1963).

172 "Saburo tells a story": Ienaga Saburo, *The Pacific War 1931–1945*, p. 107.

173 " 'They had a belief' ": *The Other Nuremberg*, p. 276.

173 " 'an object on which Germans depended' ": Margarethe and Alexander Mitscherlich, *The Inability to Mourn*, p. 23.

175 "the military defendants": Aristides Lazarus, letter to *The Far Eastern Economic Review*, July 6, 1989.

175 "the general agreed": *The Other Nuremberg*, p. 395.

176 " 'Early critics' ": Kyoko Hirano, *Mr. Smith Goes to Tokyo*, p. 143.

7. TEXTBOOK RESISTANCE

177 "During the war": Nosaka Akiyuki, *American Hijiki*, in *Contemporary Japanese Literature*. See p. 370.

179 " 'The non-aggression pact' ": *Geschichte: Lehrbuch für Klasse 9* (Berlin: Volk und Wissen Volkseigener Verlag, 1989).

184 "a typical history textbook": *Grundkurs Deutsche Geschichte 2: 1918 bis zur Gegenwart* (Hirschgraben: Cornelsen, 1987); written by Rudolf Berg and Rolf Selbmann of the Wilhelm gymnasium in Munich.

185 " 'constitutional patriotism' ": Jürgen Habermas, *"Apologetische Tendenzen,"* reprinted in *Eine Art Schadensabwicklung* (Frankfurt: Suhrkamp, 1987).

191 " 'education, just like the military' ": Yamazumi Masami quoted Yamagata Aritomo in *The Japan Quarterly*, 1981.

192 " 'By basing our system' ": *Japan Quarterly*, 1981.

193 " 'This tragic sight' ": *Truth in Textbooks: Freedom in Education and Peace for Children*, published by the National League for Support of the School Textbook Screening Suit.

193 "Ienaga's explanation": Ienaga Saburo, *The Pacific War 1931–1945*, p. 96.

193 "I looked at": *Nihonshi*, social studies textbook for high school students, published by Yamakawade in 1984.

197 "One notable scholar": Irie Takanori, *"Amerika ga Tsukutta Sengo Shinwa,"* in *Chuo Koron*, August 1982.

198 "The textbook goes on": *Nihonshi* (same as above).

199 " 'zeal to make people reflect' ": Morikawa Kinju, *Kyokasho to Saiban* (Tokyo: Iwanami Shoten, 1990), p. 13.

8. MEMORIALS, MUSEUMS, AND MONUMENTS

205 " 'People relate' ": Jürgen Habermas, *"Kein Normalisierung,"* reprinted in *Eine Art Schadensabwicklung*.

220 "In an essay": Eto Jun, *Yasukuni Ronshu* (Tokyo: Nihon Kyobunsha, 1986).

235 " 'the search for our lost history' ": Michael Stürmer, *Frankfurter Allgemeine Zeitung*, April 25, 1986.

235 " 'where we came from' ": Helmut Kohl, speech in the Bundestag, February 27, 1985.

236 " 'History does not belong' ": Freimut Duve, quoted in *Deutsches Historisches Museum: Ideen Kontroversen—Perspektiven*, ed. Christoph Stölzl (Frankfurt, Berlin: Propyläen Verlag, 1988).

9. A NORMAL COUNTRY

246 " 'Perhaps one cannot' ": Primo Levi, afterword to *If This Is a Man* and *The Truce* (London: Penguin, 1979), p. 395.

248 "a blistering editorial comment": Theo Sommer, *Die Zeit*, November 18, 1988.

250 "He was shot through his lungs": Motoshima's shooting is described in Norma Field, *In the Realm of a Dying Emperor: A Portrait of Japan at Century's End* (New York: Pantheon, 1991), p. 270.

252 " 'an act of extreme indiscretion' ": LDP Disciplinary Committee, *Asahi Evening News*, December 16, 1988.

253 "guilt versus shame": Ruth Benedict, *The Chrysanthemum and the Sword*, p. 156.

253 "The mayor received a letter": Shinto priest: *Nagasaki Shicho e no 7300tsu no Tegami: Tenno no Senso Sekinin* (*The 7300 Letters to the Mayor of Nagasaki: On the Question of the Emperor's War Guilt*) (Tokyo: Komichi Shobo, 1989).

255 "Dr. Toda": Endo Shusaku, *The Sea and Poison*, trans. Michael Gallagher (Rutland, Vt.: Tuttle, 1973), p. 157.

256 "Around the time": Eto Jun and Ishihara Shintaro, *Bungei Shunju*, March 1989.

257 "He described the Shinto rite": Kase Hideaki, *Pureiboi* (*Playboy*), January 1989.

258 " 'The emperor system' ": *Asahi Shimbun*, February 28, 1989.

260 "Itami Mansaku wrote an article": Quoted in Oshima Nagisa, *Taikenteki: Sengo Eizoron* (Tokyo: Asuhi Shimbunsha, 1975), p. 275.

10. Two Normal Towns

266 "*A Thousand Absolutely Normal Years*": *Tausend ganz normale Jahre: Ein Photoalbum des gewöhnlichen Faschismus von Otto Weber* (Nördlingen: Die Andere Bibliothek, 1987).

286 "a book about his findings": Nozoe Kenji, *Hanaoka Jiken no Hitotachi* (Tokyo: Shiso no Kagakusha, 1975). Nozoe wrote two more books about the Hanaoka Incident, entitled *Kikigaki Hanaoka Jiken* (1983) and *Shogen: Hanaoka Jiken* (1986), and published a revised edition of *Kikinaki Hanaoka Jiken* (1990).

288 " 'I developed a visceral distrust' ": Nozue Kenji, *Watashitachi no Showashi* (Tokyo: Shiso no Kagakusha, 1989), p. 66.

11. Clearing Up the Ruins

293 " 'Always somewhere behind me' ": Günter Grass, *The Tin Drum*, trans. Ralph Manheim (New York: Penguin, 1961), p. 580.

296 " 'faced with their history' ": Sakaguchi Ango, *Darakuron* (Tokyo: Kadokawa Shoten, 1946), pp. 90, 98.

299 " 'His face is turned' ": Walter Benjamin, *Illuminations*, ed. Hannah Arendt, trans. H. Zohn (New York: Schocken, 1969), p. 70.

303 " 'It did what the world' ": Grass, *The Tin Drum*, p. 517.

305 "Arthur Miller's worries": Arthur Miller, *The Guardian*, May 29, 1990.

305 " 'select the stones from the ruins' ": Kurt Niedlich, *Das Mythenbuch: Die Germanische Mythen und Märchenwelt als Quelle deutscher Weltanschauung* (Leipzig, 1936), quoted in Klaus Antoni, *Der himmlische Herscher und sein Staat* (Munich: Iudicium Verlag, 1991), p. 111.

ACKNOWLEDGMENTS

SO MANY PEOPLE have helped me, stimulated me, and encouraged me in the course of thinking about, researching, and finishing this book that I cannot find room to thank them all in print. But some people as well as institutions have been of such vital importance that their names must be mentioned with special thanks.

First of all, without the chance to spend nine months at the Wissenschaftskolleg in Berlin, I could not have completed the German parts of the book. I owe a great debt to the rector, Dr. Wolf Lepenies, to Dr. Jürgen Kocka, to Frau Bottomley and her splendid library staff, and to Professor Yehuda Elkana.

I am also grateful, for pointing me in the right direction and keeping me going in Germany, to Dr. Ludger Kühnhardt, Dr. Frank Schirrmacher, Dr. Karsten Witte, Dr. Bernhard Gattner, Amos Elon, and Darryl Pinckney.

In Japan, I have been helped many times with extraordinary kindness and efficiency by Kitamura Fumio, Yano Junichi, and Koizumi Kazuko of the Foreign Press Center. Other guides and mentors were Hayashi Kanako and the staff of the Japan Film Library Council, Niimi Takeshi, Mori Masataka, Chu Pa-chieh, Oyama Hiroshi, Oyama Yuko, Nishisato Fuyuko, and Minami Toru. But most important of all, insofar as one can measure such things, has been the hospitality, inspiration, and friendship of Richard Nations and Koh Siew-eng.

Finally, I am deeply grateful to Fritz Stern and William Wetherall, whose wisdom and erudition have improved the manuscript no end. It goes without saying that any errors which might have escaped the attention of Professor Stern, William Wetherall, and my excellent editors Jonathan Galassi at Farrar, Straus and Giroux, Neil Belton at Jonathan Cape, and E. Brugman at Atlas are entirely my own responsibility.

INDEX

A-bomb, 120; Bikini atoll test of, 164; *see also* Hiroshima; Nagasaki
Abraham's Gold (film), 271
Active Museum of Fascism and Resistance in Berlin, 206
Addresses to the German Nation (Fichte), 181
Adenauer, Konrad, 13–14, 20, 25, 29, 43, 44, 50, 156
Adorno, Theodor, 71, 81, 89, 91
Afghanistan, 37
After the Fires (Demetz), 82
Ainu, 12
Akita Broadcasting Company, 287
American Hijiki (Nosaka), 65–67, 177–78
Amnesty International, 237
Angelus Novus (Klee), 299
Ango, Sakaguchi, 53–55, 296
Anielewicz, Mordechai, 77
antifascists, 11, 147, 158, 181; Chinese, 126; German, 60–61, 274; Polish, 76–77
Apitz, Bruno, 212
Arabs, Japanese views on, 35
Araki Takako, 103
Argentina: escape of Nazis to, 138; in Falklands War, 163
Arlington National Cemetery, 219
Asahi Shimbun (newspaper), 36, 37, 105–6, 118, 258
Association to Honor the Special Attack Forces, 223
Atom Bomb—Hiroshima, The (Maruki and Maruki), 103
Atomic Bomb Bible (Araki), 103
August 6, 1945 (Maruki and Maruki), 100, 103
Auschwitz, 18, 21, 27, 29, 69–91, 120, 138, 154, 211, 212, 244, 245, 271, 299, 307; as argument against unification, 60; convent at, 78–79; creative works dealing with, 81–88; and German history, 182, 185, 186, 237; Hiroshima compared to, 92, 93, 97, 101, 104–5, 108–9; kitsch and, 72–73; museum at, 75–76, 79; television depiction of, 88–91; transports to, 139; and war crimes trials, 74–75, 114, 142, 148, 151, 152; war memorials and, 224
Austria, Nazi annexation of, 47
Axis Pact, 297
Azuma Shiro, 129–34

Bach, Johann Sebastian, 137
Baghdad, bombing of, 39
Baltic States, Soviet occupation of, 143
Barthel, Albert, 302
Bataan, 7
BBC, 195
Becker, Hellmut, 143, 149, 162
Beethoven, Ludwig van, 137
Bells of Nagasaki, The (Nagai), 254
Belzec concentration camp, 138
Benedict, Ruth, 10, 116, 253
Ben-Gurion, David, 156
Benjamin, Walter, 205, 299
Bergen-Belsen concentration camp, 149, 204, 217
Berlin, 179; divided, 234; film academy of, 308, 309; former Japanese embassy in, 9–10; Gestapo headquarters in, 206; during Gulf War, 22; history museum in, 236; Jewish cafés in, 270, 304; renaming of streets in, 92; ruins of, 49; 750th anniversary of, 235
Berlin Wall, 207, 297, 306
Bertolucci, Bernardo, 113–14
Berührungsangst (fear of identification), 150
Between God and Man (Kinoshita), 167–69
Biermann, Wolf, 20–21
Bierschenk, Frau, 232
Bikini nuclear bomb test, 164
Birkenau concentration camp, 70–72, 77, 182, 212
Bismarck, Otto von, 22, 209
Bitburg military cemetery, 217, 244, 304
Black Rain (Ibuse), 106, 293
Blitzkrieg, 149
Boger (SS officer), 151, 152, 168
Böll, Heinrich, 26, 54–56, 58, 83
Bolshevism, 48
Bomb, The (Makoto), 102
Bonn, 239; during Gulf War, 14–31
Booth, Alan, 106
Brahms, Johannes, 91
Brandopfer, Das (The Burnt Offering) (Goes), 86
Brandt, Willy, 9, 243, 297
Bridge on the River Kwai, The (film), 7
Britain: Battle of, 15; courts in, 140; in Gulf War, 14, 20; imperialism of, 42, 161; memorial to war dead of, 219; museums

Britain (*cont.*)
of, 209; occupation of Germany, 55; racist attacks in, 306; television in, 23; and war crimes trials, 143–46, 149; and war in China, 223; in World War I, 92; in World War II, 177, 226, 299
Buchenwald concentration camp, 72, 77, 154, 182, 209–18
Buck, Pearl, 131
Buddhism, 97, 102, 104, 128, 174, 221, 256, 280, 297
Bundestag, 28, 228; Jenninger's speech to, 239–48
burakumin (descendants of outcasts), 289
Burma, 222
Burma Railroad, 221, 280
Bush, George, 26, 35, 39, 294
Byelorussia, 179

Capesius, Viktor, 151
capitalism, 60, 89, 180, 181, 233, 282; Auschwitz as extreme expression of, 151; fascism as last defense of, 146–47
Carmelite nuns, 78–79
Catholic Church, 187, 236, 237, 253, 267–70, 275; *see also* Vatican
Celan, Paul, 81–82, 242
Cenotaph (London), 219
Charlemagne, 13
chemical weapons, 109–10, 230
Chiang Kai-shek, 126
China, 7, 9, 39, 98, 221; historical influence on Japan of, 298; Japanese invasion of, 40, 47, 112, 115, 126; Japanese investments in, 277–78; and Japanese peace treaty, 60; nineteenth-century, 106, 222; revolution in, 62; slave labor from, in Japan, 228, 275–82, 285–91; war in, 48, 63, 65, 109, 161, 171, 173, 193–96, 223; *see also* Nanking Massacre
Chou Enlai, 277
Christian Democratic Party, German, 13, 29, 217, 235, 242, 244, 251
Christianity, 104, 167, 174, 224, 261, 270; guilt culture of, 116; in Japan, 107, 221, 253–56, 258, 289; symbols of, 79
Chrysanthemum and the Sword, The (Benedict), 116
Chu Hakkai, 286, 287
City of Corpses (Ota), 101
Cold War, 10, 32, 38, 45, 56, 58, 98, 99, 296
Cologne: during Gulf War, 22; postwar, 49, 50
colonialism, 48
comfort women, 194–95, 228, 230, 297
Commemoration Day, 4
Common Market, 14
Communists, 13, 37, 77, 147, 187, 296; Chinese, 126–27, 130, 193, 289; German, 58, 59, 145, 154, 156–58, 178, 180–82, 184–86, 210–14, 216–18, 233–34, 236,

300, 301; Japanese, 54, 61–63, 98, 196, 198; Polish, 76; Soviet, 223
concentration camps: in Passau, 271–72; razing of, 203–4; warning monuments to, 204–6; *see also* Auschwitz *and other specific camps*
Confucianism, 116
constitutional patriotism, 185, 197
Council for the Preservation of Monuments to Resistance and Martyrdom, 76
Course of Our Country, The (history textbook), 191
Craig, Gordon, 22
Cultural Revolution, 278
Czechoslovakia, 154, 179, 214; Nazi annexation of, 47

Dachau concentration camp, 141, 154, 215, 274
Dafoe, Willem, 72
Daimler-Benz, 12, 58
Day the Dollar Becomes Paper, The (Uno), 97
Demetz, Peter, 82, 83
denazification, 58
Deng Xiao-ping, 126–27
Deutsche Mark (DM), 55, 59, 303, 306
Deutsche National-Zeitung, 16, 17
Deutsches Historisches Museum, 236–38
Deutschlandlied, 306–7
Deutschstunde (The German Lesson) (Lenz), 83–84
Devil's Gluttony, The (Morimura), 163
Diary of Anne Frank, The, 90, 274
Dietrich, Marlene, 304–5
Dodge, Joseph, 60
Doihara Kenji, General, 171–72
Dominik, Gottfried, 272–75
Dostoevski, Feodor, 241
Double Your Incomes policy, 60, 61
Dowa Mining Company, 276, 279, 280, 287
Dregger, Alfred, 235, 244
Dresden, bombing of, 143, 148, 149, 299–302
Dubiel, Helmut, 205
Düsseldorf, war crimes trials in, 148, 152
Dutch East Indies, 6, 280
Duve, Freimut, 236

Eckermann (friend of Goethe), 209
Ehre, Ida, 242–43
Eichmann, Adolf, 86, 148, 156, 246, 271
Einsatzgruppe (special action squad), 50
Einstein, Albert, 301
Eisenhower, Dwight D., 61
Emperor's Army Marches On, The (film), 174–75
Endo Shusaku, 255–56
Enlightenment, the, 15, 22, 89, 120, 197
Enola Gay, 95
Enzensberger, Hans Magnus, 25–27, 38, 54
Erhard, Ludwig, 55, 57, 60

Ermittlung, Die (The Investigation) (Weiss), 82
Eto Jun, 220, 256
Europa, Europa (film), 84–85
European Community, 30, 64

Fabrication of the "Nanking Massacre," The
(Tanaka), 118, 121
Falklands War, 163
Fassbinder, Rainer Werner, 59
Federal Republic of Germany, 10; in Cold
War, 56, 58; creative works on Holocaust
in, 81; democracy in, 297; *Holocaust*
broadcast in, 88–91; museums in, 235;
war crimes trials in, 74, 148, 151–53
Fest, Joachim, 19–20, 25, 150
feudalism, Japanese, 52
Fichte, Johann Gottlieb, 7, 34, 181
Fifteen-Year War, 48, 98, 230–31
Final Solution, 84, 142, 149, 172, 204
Fires on the Plain (Ooka), 51
Forum to Reflect upon the War Victims in
the Asia-Pacific Region and Engrave It in
Our Minds, 125
Fragenbogen, Der (The Questionnaire) (Salomon), 52
France, 155; deportation of Jews from, 143;
in Gulf War, 20
Frank, Anne, 90, 274
Frankfurt, 306; war crimes trials in, 146,
148, 152
Frankfurt Book Fair, 11
Frankfurter Allgemeine Zeitung (newspaper),
19, 85, 185, 216, 243
Frankfurter Rundschau (newspaper), 85, 89
Frederick the Great, 232, 301
Free Democratic Party, Germany, 242, 245
Freedom of Information Act, 278
French Revolution, 209
Freud, Sigmund, 270
Frey, Gerhard, 16
Fritzsche, General Hans, 150
Frobe, Gert, 4
Fujio Masayuki, 199
Fukoka, 96
Fundamental Law of Education, 191
Fürst, Michael, 244
Fürstenberg, 80
furusato stories, 282, 284, 286

Galinski (head of Jewish community), 269
Galtieri, General, 163
Gansel, Norbert, 28–29
García Márquez, Gabriel, 99
gas warfare, 109–10
Gauck, Joachim, 157
Gedenkstätte (places of remembrance), 80,
204
Geissler, Christian, 147
genocide, law against, 148
Genscher, Hans-Dietrich, 16
German Basic Law, 44
German Democratic Republic (GDR), 10,

81; *Holocaust* viewed in, 88–89; memorials, museums, and monuments in, 77,
202–4, 210–18, 232–35; war crimes trials
in, 155–57
German People's Union (DVU), 271
Germany: Asia and, 13–14; beginning of
war for, 47; cultural influence on Japan
of, 7–8; cultural tradition of, 50–51;
Dutch attitude toward, 3–6; east, *see* German Democratic Republic; folk tradition
in, 262; former Japanese embassy in, 9–
10; "guilt culture" of, 116, 117; during
Gulf War, 11, 14–31; Jenninger affair in,
239–49; memorials, museums, and monuments in, 202–19, 232–38, 304; Nazi, *see*
Nazis; occupation of, 52, 58, 64; postwar
literature and film in, 51–52, 54–58; racism in, 12; ruins of, 48–49; symbolism of
Auschwitz for, 69–91; textbooks in, 161–
62, 178–89; unification of, 8, 10, 11, 59–
60, 216, 305–6; war crimes trials in, 137–
42 (*see also* Nuremberg trials); west, *see*
Federal Republic of Germany; *see also specific cities and towns*
Germany in Autumn (Deutschland in Herbst)
(film), 58
Gerz, Joachim, 205
Gestapo, 6, 155, 158, 205; site of Berlin
headquarters of, 206
Glemp, Jozef Cardinal, 79
Globke, Hans, 156
Goebbels, Joseph, 48, 63, 182, 246, 308,
309; suicide of, 144
Goes, Albrecht, 86–87
Goethe, Johann Wolfgang von, 51, 91, 137,
197, 209
Good Earth, The (Buck), 131
Göring, Hermann, 63, 145, 146, 150, 182,
274
Gothic architecture, 300, 301
goyo gakusha (nationalist intellectuals), 118
Grass, Günter, 11–12, 26, 27, 54, 59, 60, 71,
86, 245, 292, 305
Greater East Asian War (*Daitowa Senso*), 48,
98, 161, 223–24
Great Wall of China, 222
Great War, *see* World War I
Greeks, ancient, 144
Green Cross, 163
Greene, Graham, 255
Green Party, 16, 241, 244, 258
Griebel, Matthias, 300–302
Grotewohl, Otto, 213
Gruppe 47, 54
Guadalcanal, Battle of, 221
Guam, Battle of, 221
guilt culture, 116, 128, 261
Guinness, Alec, 7
Gulf War, 10, 11, 99; Germany during, 14–
31; Japan during, 31–46, 228–29, 309
Gush Emunim, 79
Gypsies, 211, 217–18

Habermas, Jürgen, 185, 205
Hagi Jiro, 33–35
haisen (defeat), 49
Halle, 306
Hamburg: bombing of, 154; warning monument in, 234
Hanaoka Incident, 275–91
Hara Kazuo, 174
Hara Tamiki, 102
Harlan, Veit, 308
Hasegawa Michiko, 161
Hata Ikuhiko, 163
Hatazawa Kyoichi, 291
Hayashi Fusao, 37, 48, 170
Heimat (film), 89, 264–67, 282–83
Heimatgeschichte (local history), 264
Heimatmuseum, 209
Hemingway, Ernest, 55
Herder, Johann Gottfried von, 7, 50
Herrenvolk, 5, 9, 172
Hess, Rudolf, 208
Heydrich, Reinhard, 86, 182, 204, 206
Heym, Stefan, 59
Hillgruber, Andreas, 186
Himmler, Heinrich, 76, 150, 187, 188, 206, 241, 246, 271
Hindenburg, General Paul von, 163
Hirano Kyoko, 176
Hirohito, Emperor, 63, 221, 225, 249–61, 275, 284; birthday of, 254; cult of, 64, 99, 134, 162, 256–59; death of, 129, 228, 249–51; funeral of, 252; surrender speech of, 48, 49; and war crimes tribunal, 165, 171–76; at Yasukuni Shrine, 222
Hiroshima, 7, 10, 36, 38, 39, 52, 60, 65, 78, 92–111, 162, 167, 173, 219, 229–31, 293, 299; as American war crime, 62; creative works about, 100–103; justifications for bombing of, 105; Koreans killed in, 96–97; militarism in, 106–7; Nanking Massacre compared with, 119; 1945 films of, 49; Peace Park, 93–96, 111, 251; photographs of, in textbooks, 193; poison gas buried under, 110, 111; reconstruction of, 94, 97; slave labor camp in, 285; symbolism of, 92–93, 114
Hiroshima (film), 101
Hiroshima-Auschwitz Committee, 92
Hiroshima Peace Culture Foundation, 92
Historisierung (historicization), 247–49
Hitler, Adolf, 4, 19, 20, 29, 44, 58, 92, 105, 146, 168, 184, 232, 244, 246–48, 259, 271, 274, 301, 306; attempted assassination of, 186–87; biographies of, 150; birthplace of, 263; bunker of, 207–9; as defender against Stalinism, 217; destruction of reminders of, 203; and extermination of Jews, 70, 89, 240; Hirohito compared to, 172, 173; images of, 59; Japanese and, 9, 35, 131; last photograph of, 48–49; mourning of, 22; popular sup-

port for, 267; resistance to, 180–82, 197, 269; rise to power of, 47; Saddam Hussein compared with, 24–26, 38; suffering of Germans under, 307; suicide of, 144
Hitler: A Film from Germany (film), 73
Hitlerjunge Salomon (film), 84–85
Hitler Youth, 26, 27, 84, 154, 245
Hochhuth, Rolf, 83
Hoehne, Heinz, 88
Holden, William, 7
Holland, 155; Jews of, 4–6, 75
Holland, Agnieszka, 85
Holocaust, 20, 39, 42, 65, 79, 216, 224, 243, 244, 247, 294; creative works dealing with, 81–88; denial of, 122, 308; first stage of, 47; Hiroshima and, 101; Israel and, 17; Levi on, 246; memorials to, 217–18, 237–38; in textbooks, 182; and war crimes trials, 148, 162, 164; warning monuments to, 204
Holocaust (television series), 88–91, 148, 179, 266
Homer, 55
homosexuals, Nazi persecution of, 299
Honda Katsuichi, 118, 121, 129
Honecker, Erich, 181, 188, 302
Hosokawa Morihiro, 297
Hrdlička, 234
Human Condition, The (film), 164
Hundred-Year War, 48
Hungary, 155

"I Belong to Trümmerliteratur" (Böll), 55
Ibuse Masuji, 106, 293
Ienaga Saburo, 120, 172–73, 189–97, 199–201, 287
Ikeda Hayato, 60, 61
imperialism, 300; Japanese, 50, 54, 61, 121; Western, *see* Western imperialism
Imperial Japanese Army, 31–33, 41, 110, 231; comfort women and, 194–95, 297; documentaries about veterans of, 129, 174; founding of, 219–20; memorial to, 221; in Nanking, 112, 127, 166; on Okinawa, 285; slave labor supplied by, 276
Imperial Rescript on Education, 191, 192, 199, 200
Imphal campaign, 10
Inability to Mourn, The (Mitscherlich), 21, 56, 117
In Affirmation of the Great East Asian War (Hayashi), 37, 48
Indonesia, 223
International Military Tribunal of the Far East, *see* Tokyo War Crimes Tribunal
In the Stream of the Black River (comic book), 101
Iraq, war against, *see* Gulf War
Irie Takanori, 197
Irving, David, 306
Isherwood, Christopher, 5, 299
Ishida Takeshi, 166

Ishihara Nobuo, 294
Ishihara Shintaro, 122, 125–26, 256–57
Ishikawa Tatsuzo, 131–32
Israel, 16, 17, 85, 300; and German guilt, 90, 137; during Gulf War, 18–21, 24–26, 39, 42; invasion of Lebanon by, 15; Kohl in, 244; religious settlers in, 79
Itagaki Seishiro, General, 166
Itami Mansaku, 260

Jäckel, Eberhard, 218
Jackson, Robert H., 145, 147
Jacob Littners Aufzeichnungen aus einem Erdloch (Jacob Littner's Notes from a Hole in the Ground) (Koeppen), 87
Jahn, Friedrich, 181
Japan: army of, *see* Imperial Japanese Army; atrocities committed by, 275–82, 285–91 (*see also* Nanking Massacre); beginning of war for, 47–48; childishness in, 294–97; comeback of wartime bureaucrats in, 61–63; Dutch attitude toward, 6–7; economic growth in, 60–61; former Berlin embassy of, 9–10; during Gulf War, 11, 31–46, 228–29, 309; influence of German culture on, 7–8; Motoshima affair in, 249–61; occupation of, 50–52, 64, 176, 197, 220, 294; postwar literature in, 51–55, 65–67; racism in, 12; recent political changes in, 297–98, 307; ruins of, 49–50, 63–64; "shame culture" of, 116–17; symbolism of Hiroshima for, 92–111; textbooks in, 161–62, 178, 189–201; war crimes trials in, *see* Tokyo War Crimes Tribunal; war museums in, 219–32; wartime, daily life in, 293; *see also specific cities and towns*
Japan Association of Families of the War Dead, 220
Japanese Proletarian Party, 198
Japanese Tragedy, The (film), 176
Japan Junior Chamber of Commerce, 95
Japan Patriotic Party, 107
Japan Teachers' Union, 98, 115, 192, 193
Japan That Can Say "No," A (Ishihara and Watanabe), 122
Jaspers, Karl, 149–50, 259–61
Jenninger, Philipp, 239–51, 253, 257–59, 261, 264, 268
Jerusalem, war crimes trials in, 146, 148
Jesuits, 187
Jews, 10, 20, 74; in Berlin, 8, 304; at Buchenwald, 211, 214–16; and commemoration of *Kristallnacht*, 239–44; Dutch, 4–6, 75; during Gulf War, 25; Japan and, 34, 39, 42, 92, 97, 98, 102, 118, 197; monuments to, 77; mourning of, 21–22; Nazi persecution of, 29, 47, 141, 143, 155, 156, 180, 217–18, 268–69, 299 (*see also* Holocaust); neo-Nazis and, 138, 208; of Passau, 269–71; in postwar Germany, 17–18; symbolism of Auschwitz for, 69, 78–79;

and war crimes trials, 148; warning monuments to, 202–3, 205; Zionist, 88
Jew Süss (film), 308–9
Journey to China, A (Honda), 118
Jungvolk, 245
Just, Gustav, 156

Kabuki, 51
Kaifu Toshiki, 38–39
Kajima Gumi (*later* Kajima Kensetsu), 276–78, 280
Kaltenbrunner, Ernst, 145
Kamei Fumio, 176
Kamei Shizuka, 41–43, 45
kamikazes, 222, 231; memorial to, 223; museum for, 219, 225–28
Kapelle, Heinz, 181–82
Kara Juro, 53
Kase Hideaki, "Tony," 257
Katsube Hajime, 231
Katyn Forest massacre, 178
Kawamoto Yoshitaka, 107–8
Kazuki Yasuo, 103–4
Keenan, Joseph, 160, 165, 175
Keitel, Field Marshal Wilhelm, 145, 146
Kempeitai, 221
Kempner, Robert M., 144, 244
Kernd'l, Alfred, 207–9
Kido, Marquis, 176
Kiefer, Anselm, 103
Kiel, 29
Kimigayo (imperial hymn), 192, 200
Kimura Ihei, 63
Kinoshita Junji, 165, 167–69
Kishi Nobusuke, 61, 64
Kissinger, Henry, 42
Kitano Masaji, 163
kitsch, 72–73, 84, 85, 89, 262, 266
Klee, Paul, 299
Kleist, Heinrich von, 174
Kluge, Alexander, 84
Kobayashi Masaki, 164, 172
Kobayashi Takiji, 281
Koeppen, Wolfgang, 87
Kohl, Helmut, 9, 217, 235, 243–45, 304
Kolnai, Aurel, 44
Konoe Fumimaro, Prince, 297
Koochi Akira, 98
Korea, 39; Japanese oppression of, 161; *see also* North Korea; South Korea
Koreans, 194–95; as conscript labor, 276, 280, 287; Japanese attitude toward, 12, 102, 278–79; killed in Hiroshima and Nagasaki, 96, 107, 122, 251
Korean War, 32, 99, 102, 192
Kosmodemyanskaya, Soya, 182
Kramer, Josef, 149
Kristallnacht, 16, 47, 182, 211, 265, 269, 306; commemoration of, 239–49
Krupp, Alfred, 150
Kurosawa Akira, 99, 100
Kuwabara Sumio, 103

Kuwait, 36; Iraqi invasion of, 42; see also
Gulf War
Kwantung Army, 171
Kyoto, 107
Kyoto Museum for World Peace, 133, 228–
31

Ladurie, Emmanuel Le Roy, 265
Lafontaine, Oskar, 25
Lanzmann, Claude, 84
Last Emperor, The (film), 113–14
Lawrence, Lord Justice, 145
Lazarus, Aristides George, 175
Lebanon, Israeli invasion of, 15
Lein, Mrs., 178–82
Lenin, V. I., 234
Lenz, Siegfried, 83–84
Lersch, Heinrich, 234
Levi, Primo, 77, 245–46
Leyte, Battle of, 221
Liberal Democratic Party (LDP), Japanese,
10, 41, 196, 197, 220, 249–51, 256, 296;
Disciplinary Committee of, 252
Liberation Day, 4
Living Soldiers (Ishikawa), 131–32
Lübbe, Hermann, 151–52
Lucas, Franz, 151
Ludendorff, General Erich, 163
Ludwigsburg, 153–55, 157
Luther, Martin, 50, 51, 202

MacArthur, General Douglas, 37, 45, 60,
170, 173, 175, 295, 296
Maeda Kazuyoshi, 107
Mahnmal (warning monuments), 202–6,
218, 234, 247
Majdanek trials, 148, 152
Manchuria, 7, 171; Japanese annexation of,
47, 125, 223; medical experiments in,
162–63, 189, 194
Manga Punch (comic magazine), 101
Manila: massacre of civilians in, 64; sacking
of, 7, 169–70
Mao Zedong, 278
Marian, Ferdinand, 308
Marienkirke (Wittenberg), 202–3
Marines, U.S., 95
Marriage of Maria Braun, The (film), 59
Maruki Iri, 100, 103
Maruki Toshi, 100, 103
Maruyama Maso, 170
Marxism, 63, 82–83, 100, 119, 120, 180,
193, 197–99, 256, 258, 281
Maser, Werner, 150
Masua Rokusuke, 132
materialism, 59
Matsumoto, Mr., 227–28
Matsumoto Kenichi, 38
Matsushita Electric, 298
Mauthausen concentration camp, 271–72
May, Karl, 301
Mechtersheimer, Alfred, 17

medical experiments, Japanese, 162–63,
189, 194
Meier, Christian, 69, 91
Meiji Restoration, 106, 219–20, 258
Mein Kampf (Hitler), 131
Me-mushiri, Ko-uchi (Nip the Buds, Shoot the
Kids) (Oe), 293
Mengele, Josef, 18, 83
Menthon, François de, 148
Mignone, Frederick, 166
Miller, Arthur, 305
Minobe Tatsukichi, 198
Mishima Yukio, 73
Mitscherlich, Alexander and Margarethe, 8,
21–22, 56, 117, 158, 173
Mitsubishi, 12, 100
Molotov-Ribbentrop pact, 178–79
Mongolians, 222
Montesquieu, 201
Mori Masataka, 114–18, 121, 123, 124,
287
Morimura Seiichi, 163
Motoshima Hitoshi, 249–58, 260, 261
Müller, Gertrud, 80
Müller, Heiner, 60, 89, 120
Munich, demonstrations against violence in,
188
Munich Filmmuseum, 308
Münzer, Thomas, 301
Murakami Hatsuichi, 110–11
Murderers Are Among Us, The (Staudte), 49,
57
museums, 209, 218–19; see also specific
museums
mustard gas, 110

Nagai Takashi, 254
Nagasaki, 7, 36, 38, 52, 65, 99–100, 105,
114, 162, 164, 249–56, 258, 264; Peace
park, 251; slave labor camp in, 285
Nagasaki Citizens Committee for Free
Speech, 250
Nakamura Tetsu, 36–37
Nakasone Yasuhiro, 9, 221
Naked Among Wolves (Apitz), 212
Nanking Massacre, 64, 109, 112–35, 164,
166, 169, 189, 197, 230, 297, 307; confer-
ence on, 123–26; documentary about,
114–16; Japanese veteran's account of,
129–34; museum commemorating, 127–
28; playfulness of extreme violence in,
117–18; revisionist view of, 118–22
Napoleon, Emperor, 209
Nass, Mrs., 178–82
nationalism: German, 8, 186, 306; Japanese,
7, 36, 41, 98, 99, 107, 113, 118, 121, 129,
161, 172, 193, 197, 199, 220, 225
National Police Reserve, Japanese, 32
National-Zeitung, 74
Native Americans, 78, 102
NATO, 24, 25, 30, 64
Nature Protection Act, 209

Natzweiler-Struthof, 141
Nazis, 6, 8, 16, 23, 50–52, 58, 63, 65, 88,
90, 214, 218, 235, 241, 302; apology for
acts of, 243; Auschwitz as symbol of, 77;
daily life under, 292; education as, 245,
246; films about, 264–67, 283; foreigners
as slave labor for, 276; former, as Communists, 156; and German cultural legacy,
91, 209; images of, 15, 58; Japanese and,
9, 35, 115, 162; judiciary under, 29, 144;
kitsch and, 73, 84; literature dealing with,
83; nonaggression pact with Soviet Union,
179; Nuremberg rallies of, 159; in Passau,
267, 268, 272–74; popular support for,
259; preservation of sites associated with,
80; prewar Dutch sympathy for, 5; proletarian support for, 146; propaganda of,
153; race theories of, 218; resistance to,
26, 180–82, 186–88, 190, 269; self-
glorification of, 21; Soviet Union compared with, 216, 217; Spender on, 71;
teaching of history of, 182–88; trials of,
137–58, 168 (see also Nuremberg trials);
unification and, 59; warning monuments
and, 204, 207, 210–11, 234
neo-Nazis, 138, 188, 208, 271, 306–7
Neues Deutschland (newspaper), 156
New Deal, 60
Ne Win, General, 222
New Left, 165
New World Order, 36
NHK television network, 282, 284
Nicaragua, 37
Nichidai Matsue High School, 200
Nietzsche, Friedrich, 241
Nippon Times, 166
Nixon, Richard, 32
NKVD, 216
Nolte, Ernst, 185–86, 217, 244
Nomohan, battle of, 10
Normandy landing, 10
North Korea, 60, 281
Nosaka Akiyuki, 50, 65–67, 177–78
Nozoe Kenji, 285–89, 291
Nuremberg laws, 47, 156, 241
Nuremberg trials, 17, 114, 142–50;
Tokyo tribunal and, 159–61, 162, 164–
66, 168
Nussbaum (Holocaust survivor), 138–40

Oda Makoto, 39–43, 45, 73, 102, 229, 309
Odate, 278–82, 285, 286, 288
Oe Kenzaburo, 11–12, 293
Okazaki Isao, 200
Okinawa, 285
Okunojima Toxic Gas Museum, 109–11
Okuzaki Kenzo, 174–75
Omura Masujiro, 219–20
"On Degradation" (Sakaguchi), 53–54
Ooka Shohei, 51, 54
Osaka, 107
Osaka International Peace Center, 228–31

Oshima Nagisa, 67
Oshin (television program), 282–84
Ota Yoko, 97, 101
Our Home (film), 263
Oyama Hiroshi, 196–97, 201
Oz, Amos, 19, 20

Pacific War, The (Ienaga), 194
Palestinians, 16, 19, 26
Pan-Asian nationalism, 36, 41
Panorama (television show), 79
Passau, 262–75
"Past Must Not Be Normalized, The" (Ha-
bermas), 205
Past That Will Not Go Away, The (Nolte), 185
Patton, General George S., 212
Peace Education, 98, 104, 115
Peace Link, 107
Peace Museum for Kamikaze Pilots, 225–28,
231
Peace Sculpture: Pledge to the Friendship Be-
tween China and Japan, 290
Pearl Harbor, 7, 38, 47, 65, 101, 169, 170,
193, 223, 225, 249; fiftieth anniversary of,
294
Pearl Harbor Survivors' Association, 294
Percival, General, 177
Perel, Salomon, 84–85
Perry, Commodore Matthew Calbraith, 36,
48, 298
Philippines, 7, 51, 222; atrocities committed
in, 169–70
Pietism, 22, 104
Pink Floyd, 207–8
PKO Bill, 229, 231
Playboy magazine, 122, 257
Plötzensee prison, 186
Poland, 155, 179; Christianity in, 79; exter-
mination of Jews of, 70; German invasion
of, 47, 59; Molotov-Ribbentrop pact on,
179; Soviet occupation of, 143; and sym-
bolism of Auschwitz, 69, 76–77
Poles, German attitude toward, 12
Potsdam, history museum in, 232
Przemysl ghetto, 138, 139

Rapoport, Natan, 70, 77
Rathenau, Walther, 52
Ravensbrück concentration camp, 80, 204,
214
Reagan, Ronald, 217, 304
Red Army Faction, 58, 188
Red Cross, 75
Red Guards, 278
Red Hawk, 78
Reger, Erik, 145
Reich-Ranicki, Marcel, 83
Reitz, Edgar, 89, 264–66, 283
Republican Party, German, 263
Rhapsody in August (film), 99
Rhineland, Nazi advance on, 47
Ritsumeikan University, 133, 229

Röhm, Ernst, 146
Role of Japan, The (Katsube), 231
Roman Empire, 13
romantic nationalism, 7–8
Rommel, General Erwin, 58
Rosch, Augustin, 187
Rosmus, Anja, 267–74, 287, 288
Russo-Japanese War, 106, 222

SA, 233
Saarbrücken, 205
Sachsenhausen concentration camp, 214
Saddam Hussein, 14, 24–26, 38, 39, 43
Saeki Yuko, 171–72
Saika Tadayoshi, 93
Saipan, 95
Salomon, Ernst von, 52
Sankei (newspaper), 126
Schacht, Hjalmar H. G., 146, 150
Scheel, Walter, 185
Schiller, Johann Christoph Friedrich von, 137, 153
Schleyer, Hans-Martin, 58–59
Schlöndorff, Volker, 85
Schmitt, Carl, 184
Schneider, Peter, 18
Schneider, Rolf, 146, 167–68
Schnurre, Wolf Dietrich, 54, 58
Schönhuber (right-wing political leader), 263
Schrecklich Mädchen, Das (The Nasty Girl) (film), 263–67
Schuldfrage, Die (The Question of German Guilt) (Jaspers), 149–50
Schulte, Dieter, 232–33
Schwammberger, Josef, 137–42, 153, 182
Schwarzkopf, General Norman, 35
Scott, Francis P., 173
Sea and Poison, The (Endo), 255–56
Seidel, Irmgard, 215–16
Sekigawa Hideo, 101
Self-Defense Forces, Japanese, 32, 33, 38
shame culture, 116, 128, 261
Shanghai, Battle of, 120
Shidehara Kijuro, 37
Shinto, 10, 31, 51, 64, 99, 162, 174, 219, 223, 224, 250, 257; Christianity and, 253, 254, 256; State, 220, 230
Shiroyama Saburo, 165
Shoah (film), 84
Shochiku Fuji, 113–14
Showa Restoration, 221, 249, 256
shusen (termination of war), 49
Siberia, Japanese POWs in, 103–4
Silence (Endo), 255
Singapore: massacres in, 7; surrender of British in, 177
Six-Day War, 19
6-8-1945 (Ueno), 103
Social Democratic Party, German, 25, 28, 29, 156, 214, 236, 241–43, 272
Socialist Party, Japanese, 43

Society of Kyoto Citizens Who Will Not Tolerate the Ishihara Statement, 122
Sommer, Theo, 248
Sonderbehandlung (special treatment), 50
Sonderweg theory, 50, 51, 184
Sonnenstein Euthanasia Institute, 301–2
South Korea, 194–95, 199, 221, 228, 287, 297
Soviet Union, 3, 155, 211, 223; and atom bomb, 98; atrocities committed by, 148; Buchenwald and, 214–18; in Cold War, 56; declaration of war on Japan by, 167; East Germany and, 48, 51, 64, 80, 178; and Japanese peace treaty, 60; Japanese prisoners of, 222; nonaggression pact with Nazis, 178–79; and war crimes trials, 143, 155, 163; war memorials in, 224
Spandau prison, 208
Special Attack Forces, *see* kamikazes
Speer, Albert, 9, 61, 159, 204, 274
Spender, Stephen, 49, 50, 54, 71, 149
Spener, Philipp Jakob, 22
Spengler, Oswald, 7, 34
Spiegel, Der, 25, 26, 38, 85, 88
SS, 16, 29, 58, 71, 75, 80, 86, 91, 138, 184, 208, 209, 221, 241, 265, 283; at Buchenwald, 210, 212, 215; headquarters of, 206; photographs of, in textbooks, 182; playfulness of violence of, 117; trials of former officers of, 148
Stalin, Josef, 143, 217, 244
Stalingrad (film), 307
Stalingrad, Battle of, 9
Stasi, 155, 157, 158, 183, 232, 233
Stasi Documents, The (Gauck), 157
Staudte, Wolfgang, 49, 57–58
Stauffenberg, Count Schenck von, 186–87
Steiner, George, 50, 71, 86
Stellvertreter, Der (The Deputy) (Hochhuth), 83
Stölzl, Christoph, 236–38
Strasser, Gregor, 146
Strauss, Franz Josef, 89
Streim, Alfred, 154–55
Stunde Null (Zero Hour), 49, 62
Stürmer, Michael, 185, 235
Stuttgart, 137–42, 153, 158; unofficial war crimes tribunal in, 17
Süddeutschen Zeitung (newspaper), 145
Sudetenland, Nazi annexation of, 47
Sugamo prison (Tokyo), 160, 165, 171, 173
Sugimoto Ryokichi, 196, 197
Sukarno, 223
"Summer Flowers" (Hara), 102
Sunshine City (Tokyo), 160
Süskind, Patrick, 28
Süskind, W. E., 145
Suzuki Mosaburo, 198
Syberberg, Hans-Jürgen, 73–74, 89

Taiheyo no Washi (Eagle of the Pacific) (film), 169
Taisho period, 106

Taiwan, 127
Taiwanese, 122
Takeda Tsuneyoshi, 223–24
Takeshita Noburo, 196
Tanaka Kakuei, 199
Tanaka Masaaki, 118–21
Tavenner, Frank, 168
tenko (recanting of political views), 63
terrorists, German, 58
textbooks, 177–201; German, 161–62, 178–89; Japanese, 161–62, 178, 189–201
Tezuka Osamu, 229
Thälmann, Ernst, 188, 211, 212, 218
Thälmann, Frau, 213
Theresienstadt concentration camp, 183, 214
Thousand Absolutely Normal Years, A (Weber), 266
Times of London, *The*, 242, 273
Tin Drum, The (Grass), 245, 292, 303
Tinian, 95
"Todesfuge" ("Death Fugue") (Celan), 81–82, 242–43
Tojo Hideki, General, 175–76
Tokugawa shogunate, 219
Tokyo, 308; bombing of, 285; demonstrations in, 61; Disneyland in, 298; during Gulf War, 31–46; ruins in, 49, 53
Tokyo Shimbun, 38
Tokyo Trial (film), 164, 172
Tokyo University, 119
Tokyo War Crimes Tribunal, 114, 119, 121–22, 129, 134, 159–76, 199, 219, 259
Topf, J. A., & Sons, 77–78
Topography of Terror, 207
toxic gas, 109–10; *see also* Zyklon B gas
Treblinka death camp, 211
Trial in Nuremberg (Prozess in Nürnberg) (Schneider), 146
Trojan War, 55
Trümmerliteratur (literature of the ruins), 51, 55, 65
Tucholsky, Kurt, 267
tu quoque principle, 143, 147, 148, 164
Turks, German attitude toward, 12

Ueno Yaso, 103
Ukraine, 179
Ulbricht, Walter, 213, 300, 302
United Nations, 98, 155; Conference on Disarmament Issues, 105; and Gulf War, 229
United States: Adenauer and, 29; China and, 127; Germany and, 55, 56, 64, 178; in Gulf War, 20–21, 35–36, 39, 42; imperialism of, 161; Japan and, 43–46, 52, 54, 60–66, 97–102, 105, 223, 256; memorials to war dead of, 219, 224; in Vietnam War, 41, 230, 300; and war crimes trials, 145–47, 268; in World War II, 116, 189, 285
U.S. Air Force, 48
U.S. Army, 32, 231; occupation of Japan by, 50–52, 64, 176, 197, 220, 294

U.S.–Japan Security Treaty, 231
U.S. Marines, 95, 285
Uno Masami, 97, 98
Urach, Albrecht Fürst von, 35

Vati (Schneider), 18
Vatican, 83, 142
Veidt, Conrad, 4
Verhoeven, Michael, 264
Versailles Treaty, 268
Vietnam War, 11, 19, 37, 78, 147, 230, 300; images from, 15; Japanese and, 39–40, 61, 99, 193
Vilsmaier, Joseph, 307
Volk, 10

Waffen SS, 16, 183, 268
Wagner, Ferdinand, 272
Wagner, Richard, 7, 50–51
Wajda, Andrzej, 69
Wake Island, Battle of, 221
Waldheimer trials, 155
Walser, Martin, 91, 152–53
Wannsee Villa, 204, 237–38
War Against the West (Kolnai), 44
war crimes trials, 137–58; East German, 155–57; *see also* Nuremberg trials; Tokyo War Crimes Tribunal
War Criminal: The Life and Death of Hirota Koki (Shiroyama), 165
Warsaw ghetto, 9, 70, 75, 77, 94, 204, 243, 297
Watanabe Shoichi, 121–22
Webb, Sir William, 168
Weber, Otto, 266
Wehrmacht, 16
Weimar Republic, 51, 197, 233, 240, 259, 268
Weiss, Avraham, 78–79
Weiss, Peter, 74, 82–83, 151, 167–68
Weizsäcker, Ernst von, 142–44
Weizsäcker, Richard von, 142, 157–58, 228, 235, 243
Western imperialism, 40, 42; war against, 38, 48, 161
Wetzka, Bernd, 140, 141, 144, 182–84
White Rose, 186
Wiegenstein, Roland, 28
Wiesenthal, Simon, 141, 269
Willoughby, General Charles, 176
Wirtschaftswunder (economic boom), 156
Witte, Karsten, 308–9
Wittenberg, 202–3
Wolf, Christa, 86
Wolfer, Bishop, 262
World War I, 5, 15, 92, 183, 233; monuments to, 203, 224, 304; war crimes trials after, 144, 163
World War II, 3, 6, 9, 33, 196, 223, 292; Auschwitz as key event of, 149; debate about history of, 296; East German histo-

World War II (*cont.*)
  ries of, 180; German suffering during, 24;
  images from, 15; memorials to, 224, 225,
  304; museum exhibits on, 232 (*see also specific museums*); Soviet myth of, 211
Württemberg, dukes of, 153

Yachita Tsuneo, 275, 276, 278–81, 285,
  287–91
yakeato seidai (burnt-out generation), 51
Yamagata Aritomo, 191
Yamamoto Isoroku, Admiral, 169
Yamamoto Shichihei, 118
Yamashita Tomoyuki, General, 169–70, 177
Yasukuni Shrine, 63–64, 163, 219–24, 231
Yoshida Shigeru, 176
Yoshimi Yoshiaki, 110, 195

Yoshimoto Takaaki, 50, 165
Yoshimura Hisato, 162–63
Yukoki Ishinkai (Society for Lament and
  National Restoration), 107

Zeiler, Robert, 214–15
Zeit, Die (newspaper), 20, 248
Zentrale Stelle der Landesjustizverwaltungen
  zur Aufklärung von NS Verbrechen (Central Office of the State Judicial Administrations for the Clearing-up of National
  Socialist Crimes), 153–55
Zeppelin Field (Nuremberg), 159, 160
Zhukov, General, 10
Zionism, 88
Zusammenbruch (the collapse), 49, 55, 56
Zyklon B gas, 78, 151, 301